# THE BIRTH OF ULSTER

SIR ROBERT CECIL, FIRST EARL OF SALISBURY

*From the portrait by Marc Gheeraedts the Younger*

# THE
# BIRTH OF ULSTER

*by*

## CYRIL FALLS

*WITH EIGHT PLATES
AND AN ENDPAPER MAP*

CONSTABLE · LONDON

First published in Great Britain 1936
by Methuen & Co Ltd, London
This edition published in Great Britain 1996
by Constable and Company Ltd
3 The Lanchesters, 162 Fulham Palace Road
London W6 9ER
ISBN 0 09 476610 X
Printed in Great Britain by
St Edmundsbury Press Ltd
Bury St Edmunds, Suffolk

A CIP catalogue record for this book
is available from the British Library

TO

MY LONDON-BORN DAUGHTER ANNE,

WHO HAS LEARNT TO LOVE FERMANAGH

# PREFACE

SOME may hold that if the plan of a book requires a preliminary explanation then that plan must be faulty or at least over-complicated. I must risk that possible reproach, as it seems to me necessary to outline the method on which I have here worked.

The Birth of Ulster of my title is what is known to historians as the Plantation : the colonization of the northern province of Ireland with English and Scots, from which has sprung a clearly-defined race, differing markedly from its parent stocks and to a far greater extent from its neighbours. Any account of the Plantation appears to need a fairly long and detailed introduction, especially as the history of Ireland, as a whole, in the sixteenth and seventeenth centuries is little known outside Ireland. The colonization carried out in the reign of James I had its predecessors in the reigns of Mary and Elizabeth, but these did not take root, for the very good reason that they had no roots. That is to say, the Marian and Elizabethan plantations in the midlands and south amounted to not much more than the transfer of forfeited lands from Irish to English landlords. The tenantry under those landlords did not change. The consequence was that in the great rebellion of the last years of Elizabeth's reign, which is associated with the name of Hugh O'Neill, Earl of Tyrone, the tenants drove the landlords out and the settlements were almost completely obliterated in a period to be measured by weeks. It was with the fate of these earlier plantations before their eyes that James and his political adviser Salisbury in England, Chichester and his legal adviser Davies in Ireland, set to work on the new one. In order to understand the conditions which made the Plantation possible it is also necessary to have a rough knowledge of Irish laws and customs and the attitude of the Government towards them; of social and economic life, at all events in Ulster; and of the main steps leading to the rebellion of Tyrone, and subsequently to his flight from Ireland.

I have taken the most dramatic episode in the whole chain of events, the submission of Tyrone to Elizabeth at a moment when she was actually dead, as a prologue. Next I have given a sketch of Ulster, of its leading clan of O'Neill, of religious, political, economic, artistic, and social existence, and of the Scottish settlements in Antrim at the time in question. In the second section I have outlined the problems and the main events concerning Ulster up to the departure from Ireland of the Earl of Essex in 1599. The third section covers the viceroyalty of Lord Mountjoy, in which the rebellion was put down.

Book Two is concerned with the events leading more directly to the Plantation: Tyrone's visit to England and rehabilitation, the bickering and suspicion between him and the Irish Government, his final flight and his adventures on the Continent, and the revolt of Sir Cahir O'Dogherty.

It is only in Book Three that I reach the Plantation itself. I might, perhaps, have cut down the two earlier books somewhat by elimination of personalities, but I hope that they, as they stand, will conduct the reader better prepared to the Third, and that in themselves they will not be found dull. I have concluded with a very brief sketch of the colony's career from that day to the present.

With regard to personalities I have tried to confine the figures brought on to the stage to those who really have some part to play. There are perhaps fifty men bearing the name of O'Neill who might make an appearance in this volume; but the introduction of all of them would probably bore readers who have never heard of any except Shane and Tyrone himself. I have therefore often left out names when they are no more than names. Short skeleton genealogies of the ruling families of the O'Neills, O'Donnells and Maguires are included as an appendix, and may make clear any obscurities of which I have been guilty.

I have adopted English versions of Irish proper names, as I fear that, except possibly in the Irish Free State, personages such as Aodh O Néill, Prince of Tír Eoghain, Aodh O Domhnaill, Prince of Tír Chonaill, and Cuchonnacht Maguidhir, Prince of Fir Manach, might not always be recognizable as Hugh O'Neill, Hugh O'Donnell, and Cuconnaught Maguire, Princes respectively of Tyrone, Tyrconnell (Donegal), and Fermanagh.

The authorities given represent only those actually used. I have examined some others, such as the Calendar of the Salisbury MSS., without finding in them anything of particular value for my purpose. My deepest regret is that we have so few personal pictures of the colonists. There is hardly even legend where they are concerned. It is, in fact, curious that their descendants in Ulster to-day are almost as ignorant of them as is the outside world. The reason is, I fancy, that the great events at the opening of the reign of William III have obscured in the popular mind those which went before, the Plantation as much as the Rebellion of 1641. If you talk to my fellow-countrymen of Ulster's great past, they think at once of the men of "Derry, Aughrim, Enniskillen, and the Boyne." Of them, indeed, they will tell you many a tale not in the history books, all ending with praise of William of Orange. Their ancestors of the first years of the seventeenth century, who laid their pikes and muskets in the last furrow turned with the plough; those, too, of the fifth decade, who fought against odds greater than any King William had to meet, are overshadowed. All I can say in this regard is that I have done my best to discover what manner of men were the colonists and what manner of life they led; that I have not invented when I have found myself in difficulties, and that where I have speculated I have said so.

My authorities are chiefly the State Papers and contemporary chronicles, English and Irish. I have, however, found some guidance in modern works, and especially in those of two writers, which form a pleasant contrast to the generally sketchy and often inaccurate accounts of this period: Bagwell's *Ireland under the Tudors* and *Ireland under the Stuarts*, and Lord Ernest Hamilton's *Elizabethan Ulster* and *The Irish Rebellion of 1641*. Acknowledgement of two minor unpublished sources will be found in the bibliography.

As regards the illustrations, the plans of the three

Plantation townships in County Londonderry are from the Carew MSS. at Lambeth Palace, and are reproduced by kind permission of his Grace the Archbishop of Canterbury. I am indebted to the Marquess of Salisbury for the use of the portrait of Sir Robert Cecil, first Earl of Salisbury; to Viscount Bangor for that of Sir James Hamilton, first Lord Claneboye; and to Viscount Charlemont for that of Sir Toby Caulfeild, first Lord Charlemont. James Hamilton's portrait has previously appeared, I believe, once only, in Mr. John Stevenson's *Two Centuries of Life in Down*, published by his firm, Messrs. M'Caw, Stevenson & Orr, who were good enough, with Lord Bangor's permission, to lend me the block. Toby Caulfeild's portrait has, so far as I am aware, never before been published, and Lord Charlemont was so good as to have it photographed specially for me. The picture of Monea Castle I owe to the kindness of Miss Constance Reade, whose family has long owned it, and that of Dogh Castle to the courtesy of the Irish Tourist Association.[1] The sketch-map of Ulster was drawn by Mr. J. S. Fenton.

If I have failed to make my record interesting, the fault lies wholly in the telling, not in the tale. I know none more dramatic or absorbing in the history of any land. The Plantation of Ulster is not only that; its interest belongs to present and future as well as to past, and it represents a problem of extreme importance and difficulty at this very moment. As for " human interest ", it were

[1] Speaking in the text of the good state of preservation of Monea, I should perhaps have added that its present dilapidations are due rather to warfare than time, though time has doubtless carried on the work begun by the destructive hand of man. Had time been its only foe, it might be now almost in its original state, as it was far better constructed than most Plantation castles.

hard to find a collection of men better worthy of observation and study, both as individuals and as fellow-actors in a great drama, than, say, Shane and Tirlagh Luineach O'Neill, Hugh Roe and Neill Garve O'Donnell, and Phelim Reagh MacDavitt, on the Irish side; and, on the Anglo-Scottish, Essex, Mountjoy, Chichester, Docwra, Davies, and James Hamilton. So at least it seems to me; but perhaps, coming from those parts, I am over enthusiastic about those figures. That fact may also have sometimes warped my judgment, though I have striven to preserve the historical attitude which many years of devotion to military history ought to have ensured. But I may as well admit now—for my critics will probably find it out in any case—that I was brought up to admire the Ulster colonists, and that I, too, was taught from tenderest youth, standing up in the carriage as the train crossed the Boyne at Drogheda, to praise " the Glorious, Pious, and Immortal Memory of the Great and Good King William, who saved us from—" well, among others, some things that in the tolerant cool of approaching middle age and with a growing tenderness for the House of Stuart, I still think we are better without.

C. F.

BLACKHEATH—MUNDESLEY—ENNISKILLEN

# CONTENTS

## BOOK ONE

## ULSTER IN 1603

## BOOK TWO

## THE FLIGHT OF THE EARLS

## BOOK THREE

## THE PLANTATION

xiii

# ILLUSTRATIONS

(*The Portrait of Sir Robert Cecil and the three town plans are from
photographs by Donald Macbeth*)

# Book One

## ULSTER IN 1603

---

### PROLOGUE

## THE SUBMISSION OF TYRONE

IN the last week of March 1603, Hugh O'Neill, Earl of
Tyrone, was riding in to Mellifont Abbey in the County
Louth, the former Cistercian Monastery, which was now
the house of Sir Garret Moore. There the man who called
himself the Queen's Lord Deputy in Ireland, Charles Blount,
Lord Mountjoy, was waiting to receive his surrender.
Mountjoy was, in fact, not the Queen's Lord Deputy; for
the Queen was dead. The official message from Sir Robert
Cecil, directed to Dublin Castle and delayed by an unfavourable wind, had not reached Mountjoy, but a private
courier had brought the news to one of his officers. After
consultation with his discreet Chief Secretary, Fynes
Moryson, Mountjoy determined on a bold stroke. Tyrone
was coming in to make his submission to Queen Elizabeth;
then to Queen Elizabeth, alive or dead, he should submit.
If he heard the news the great rebel might change his mind,
and God alone knew what would happen then. Mountjoy
had been at it hammer-and-tongs these three years and was
weary of war. He ordered that complete secrecy should be
maintained; sent a message to Sir William Godolphin, the
envoy who had brought about Tyrone's surrender, bidding
him hasten Tyrone's coming; and sat down to await it with
what patience he might.

I

Strange must have been Mountjoy's reflections during those anxious hours. Gloriana dead! His thoughts must have fled back to those days when he, a youth of singular personal beauty, with dark curly hair, rosy cheeks, and eyes " great, black, and lovely ", a champion in the tiltyard, had been looked upon with marked favour by the amorous Queen. She had sent him a golden queen from her set of chessmen; he had worn it on his arm; and the jealous Essex had exclaimed that " every fool must have a favour." There had been a duel in Marylebone Fields; Essex had been wounded and taken down a peg or two. Those golden days were gone now, the last link snapped with the passing of the poor old painted harridan who, though thirty years his senior, had been the Golden Queen of his youth.

Yet there were more comfortable considerations, too. Young Blount had been reconciled to Essex and had become his devoted follower. After the failure of Essex in Ireland he had been appointed his successor. Before setting out he had been ill enough advised to plot with the Earl and to suggest to James VI of Scotland that he himself should cross from Ireland with an Army to secure the release of Essex, then in confinement for his misdeeds and short-comings in Ireland, and to secure for James the succession to the English throne. Nothing, indeed, had come of that mad scheme. Mountjoy, absorbed in the Irish war and discovering, perhaps to his own surprise, that he was a soldier of genius, had concentrated on the business in hand. He had had nothing to do with the later stages of the plot, and had turned a deaf ear to all the suggestions of the plotters. When all had come out and Essex had laid his comely head on the block, Elizabeth and Cecil had decided that Scotland must be kept out of the affair—and Mountjoy. He was indispensable, because he was succeeding where so many had failed, seeing clearly where so many had become

2

confused, keeping clean hands where so many had plundered. Yet he could not easily forget the fright he had had on hearing of the trial of Essex. He knew that Elizabeth and Cecil had equally good memories. Perhaps one day they would have called for a reckoning. Perhaps it was just as well that Gloriana was dead.

They had, at least, trusted him so fully that they had given him leave to come to any arrangements he chose with Tyrone. That in itself was remarkable, seeing that they were both by nature suspicious, and that the dealings of Essex with Tyrone were believed to have been treasonable. Tyrone had been in Glenconkeine, a wild and densely wooded area north-west of Lough Neagh in what is now the County Londonderry, reduced to five hundred followers, living the life of a hunted outlaw, but still dangerous, defiant, and inaccessible. In a letter of the 17th February the terms of the Queen's pardon had been sketched, but the Deputy had been instructed to make practically any, " rather then hee shoullde nott coom in att all." Mountjoy had sent with Godolphin for the business of the parley Sir Garret Moore, the owner of Mellifont, an old friend of Tyrone's, and a somewhat dubious character ; but straight tools were not the best for every kind of work. If only Sir Garret would bring him in, what converse they had on the way would not greatly matter. It would be for other hands to keep the rebel Earl in the straight path.

The submission would be a pleasing first offering to the new king as he mounted the throne. In any case, Mountjoy, as a strong partisan of the Stuart succession, had every right to expect favour from James. He would wind up this affair of the rebellion ; then he would ask to be relieved. In his own words, he had done the rough work, and some other must polish it. He would return to England to enjoy the honours that must surely come, and to rejoin his love, Penelope, the sister of Essex, the Stella of Philip Sidney, and alas! the wife of a disagreeable husband, Lord Rich. So much he could see, but not that the lady was to involve him in an ugly scandal, to be divorced, and to be married to him by his chaplain in circumstances of doubtful legality; still less what was to be the future of that chaplain, whose name was William Laud. Meanwhile, solacing himself, as we may well suppose, with the tobacco to which he was so much addicted, he was waiting for Tyrone, who might spoil all yet.

But Tyrone came. He arrived on the afternoon of the 30th. He, the " great rebel ", grovelled on the threshold of the room where Mountjoy sat in state to receive him. So abjectly humbled and abased was the Irishman that Mountjoy was taken aback and at a loss for words. " One of the deplorablest sights that ever I saw," says an English eyewitness, distressed at the complete humiliation of so mighty a lord, though he had been a more troublesome rebel than even Silken Thomas. Recovering himself, Mountjoy required the penitent to draw near, and on his knees for a full hour Tyrone—who was not a young man—expressed contrition for his offences, and made submission to the Queen who had been dead six days. The terms, indeed, were so mild that they were worth some humiliation. He had only to pledge his loyalty to the Queen, to renounce the title of " the O'Neill "—renounced at least twice before—and to promise that his treasonable correspondence with the King of Spain should cease. In return, he was to be restored to his earldom and all his lands, but for some grants already made to loyalists and a few hundred acres for the maintenance of two royal forts on the Blackwater.

On the morrow he put his submission into writing and presented it, again on his knees, to Mountjoy, who embraced him. On the 3rd April they rode together to Drogheda.

On the 4th they reached Dublin. On the 5th Sir Henry Danvers, the official messenger, arrived at last with news of the death of Elizabeth and of the proclamation of James I as King of England, Scotland, France, and Ireland. The Privy Council of Ireland nominated Mountjoy "Lord Justice", the title of temporary governor when there was no holder of the office of Lord Deputy. Tyrone repeated the submission of Mellifont, this time to James. He wept when he heard of Elizabeth's death. Was it sorrow? He may, indeed, have felt sorrow for the passing of so great a figure, but sharp-eyed Fynes Moryson did not see his grief in that light. "There needed no Œdipus to find out the true cause of his tears; for, no doubt, the most humble submission he had made to the Queen he had so highly and proudly offended much eclipsed the vainglory his actions might have carried if he had held out till her death."

The Earl then returned to his ravaged and depopulated country, while the Lord Deputy—reappointed to that office by the King—had, to his disgust, to take the field once more and march south to deal with a revolt in Cork, Waterford, and other towns. This affair does not greatly concern us here. It was not political, but part religious and part financial: religious, in that there had been rumours that James was half Catholic, and the towns were celebrating his accession by public demonstrations of Catholic worship; financial, in that the merchants had been infuriated by Elizabeth's debasement of the Irish currency, and were riotously protesting against it. Mountjoy was successful as usual, this time employing tact as his chief weapon. We may leave him and Tyrone for the time being, to take a general survey of the northern province of Ireland, where the latest rebellion has just been quenched.

5

# I

## THE STATE OF THE COUNTRY

THE dominion of the invading Norman lords of the Strongbow period, which had left strong roots in Leinster and Munster and traces in Connaught, had disappeared in Ulster. The de Courcy settlement in the north-east had swiftly decayed or been ruined by the Bruce invasion. The de Burghs, once Earls of Ulster, had receded over the frontier into Connaught, become Burkes, and split up into clans, much on the native Irish pattern. By the beginning of the seventeenth century the Savages of the Ards in Down represented almost the last Norman name. They were quite small men now, but at least they had kept their heads up when the big men went under, and their toughness is shown by the fact that they endure to this day. On the other side of Strangford Lough, in Lecale, there was another handful of Anglo-Normans, but even more reduced in estate.

There was thus in Ulster none of that Anglo-Irish influence which the Crown could on occasion turn to its advantage. True, these Norman noblemen had in most cases become as Irish as the Irish themselves. Irish wives, mistresses, and mothers, and still more Irish foster-mothers and foster-brothers, had taught them Irish ways. They sucked in the spirit of the country as infants with their milk, and as they grew up they found that life in Ireland was easy and pleasant if one belonged to a great family. The respect and affection of the young for the son of "the big house" was heady wine, to be drunk until within the last twenty years. Many

6

an Irish gentleman recalls as the sweetest days of his life those when some gossoon a few years his senior taught him to run wild, to back his first pony, to throw his first fly, and worshipped him the while. He may perhaps recall that twenty years later that same gossoon's brother shot at him from behind a hedge or set fire to his house.

Often enough the Anglo-Irish nobility had been the leaders of rebellion. The Geraldines, for example, both Desmond and Kildare branches, led sensational and dangerous revolts. Yet the Anglo-Irish were on occasion reclaimable by means of generous treatment and honours; never, for example, did king make a better bargain than Henry VIII when he bestowed the earldom of Clanrickard upon Ulick Burke. The older Butler peerage of Ormonde had been consistently loyal while there was a Lancastrian on the English throne.

They could be Anglicized again, and quickly. To take another example from the house of Geraldine, we chance to know that Brigid Fitzgerald, daughter of the Earl of Kildare, married in the early part of the reign of James I to a native Irish peer, Tyrconnell, could not speak a word of Irish.

The spasmodic efforts of English kings to subdue Ireland had also affected Ulster less than the remainder of the country. In any case they had virtually ceased with the reign of Richard II. The French wars and still more the Wars of the Roses had diverted energies elsewhere. The policy of Henry VII was, in brief, to rule Ireland through the Irish, and especially the Anglo-Irish, themselves. It miscarried. The Yorkist party had, in fact, established a stronghold in the country. Lambert Simnel was crowned in Dublin in 1487; Perkin Warbeck, a still more formidable pretender, was welcomed with royal honours in Cork. Henry VIII began his reign with the idea of subduing Ireland, but being almost as close-fisted and averse to war-

7

like expenditure as his father, he fell back upon the latter's policy, and had a like lack of success. When, in 1534, he summoned the Anglo-Irish Lord Deputy, the Earl of Kildare, to London to give an account of his stewardship, the latter's son, that Lord Offaly known to history as Silken Thomas, rose in revolt. The Earl died in the Tower; Silken Thomas, after great initial successes, had finally to surrender to the Marshal, Lord Leonard Grey, and was hanged at Tyburn in 1536. Yet still English rule was limited to the Pale, then consisting of the counties of Dublin, Kildare, Meath and Louth, and to a few fortresses outside it, whereof Carrickfergus and Newry were the only ones in Ulster; though it extended a little farther when there happened to be an exceptionally strong Lord Deputy. Even the Pale was continually subject to raids from the Wicklow mountains or from Ulster.

Henry then altered his tactics and embarked upon the policy known as " Surrender and Regrant ". The great lords were to surrender their lands to the Crown and to receive them again as feudatories. This, it appeared, would give some sort of guarantee for their loyalty, as it would put their possessions absolutely at the disposal of the King should they prove disloyal. They were in general willing enough, especially when they found they were to have a share of those Church lands which Henry had, actually in some cases, nominally in all, already confiscated. It is to be noted that families which afterwards posed as champions of the Church of Rome did not refuse their share. At the same time the King bestowed honours with a liberal hand. The earldom given to Ulick Burke has already been mentioned. A native Irishman, Murrough O'Brien, became Earl of Thomond. Lesser men were knighted. But a still more interesting experiment was made some months earlier, in September 1542, when the greatest of

8

the Ulster chieftains, Con Bacach O'Neill, was created Earl of Tyrone. For the first time in the history of that house—which stretched back into the legendary ages of the past—its head crossed the Irish Sea. In the Queen's parlour at Greenwich, newly decorated for the occasion, Con was girt with his sword by the King's own hands. That he understood what it was all about is not certain; for he had not a word of English. At any rate he accepted his patent and his regal entertainment with pleasure. The earldom was bestowed with remainder to his son Ferdoragh, or Mathew, who was created Baron of Dungannon. It was this latter creation that prepared so much trouble for the future.

Whatever internal wars there had been, whatever conflicting claims, there had never been any doubt that the O'Neills were the leading clan of Ulster. Over all the present county of Tyrone, which formerly included a large proportion of what is now the County of Londonderry, and over most of Armagh the O'Neill was absolute lord. The Clandeboye O'Neill of South Antrim and Down, MacQuillan of North Antrim, Magennis of Down, O'Hanlon of Armagh, O'Reilly of Cavan, Maguire of Fermanagh, MacMahon of Monaghan, O'Dogherty of Inishowen, O'Cahan of Coleraine, even O'Donnell of Tyrconnell—later known as Donegal—had all from time to time been in fact his vassals, or formally acknowledged his paramountcy. True, he was often enough at war with one or other of them, especially with O'Donnell; but then war was a normal state of affairs. Even within their own clans, within the immediate family of the ruling chiefs, O'Neills and O'Donnells were constantly fighting.

Though with far greater natural resources than Connaught, Ulster was the most backward of the four provinces. That, at least, is seldom disputed. When, however, we come to

9

study the social condition of the country, to estimate the standard of its civilization, we plunge into a very thorny thicket. Perhaps two-thirds of the evidence is English, and the English have always been inclined to look down upon the lesser breeds without the law. Sympathetic observations of foreign customs and manners has never been a national virtue, and in this case there was no impulsion to sympathy. It is curious to turn from an English picture of an Irish chieftain at home, in dirt and squalor, the house full of cattle, dogs, and equally shaggy human dependants, his daughters crouched naked round the hearth, to an Irish bard's account of a visit to the Maguire at Enniskillen. Beauteous maidens clad in silks and velvets work at their embroidery, or walk hand in hand on the green lawns, or listen to the harps of minstrels; noble youths are trying the paces of their steeds or burnishing their weapons; oars flash upon the waters of Lough Erne; gay and happy bands ride out a-hunting. At night the young prince presides over a groaning board, and the wines of Spain and France flow from beakers of gold and silver. It seems that Enniskillen must have been the most fortunate of the Fortunate Isles.

Well, any lay civilization in Ulster might be expected to appear at Enniskillen and one or two other castles. But what sort of civilization was this in truth? Not all those parties were going out to hunt the beasts of the chase. Some went to harry and to raid. They returned with rich spoil, with gold, with cattle driven before them. Women bereft of sons and husbands, children left fatherless, sings the bard complacently, were left to rue their passing. And that is surely most significant. Here, in this idyllic scene, we find pillage and murder exalted as virtues. Nor is it the Sassenach who is to be pillaged and murdered. If the raid were a very special and big one, it might be pressed as far as the Pale, at the expense of the Anglo-Irish there dwelling; but local sport was at that of men and women of the same blood and religion, nay, often of the same clan and name, as those of the raiders. The gracious young lord of Fermanagh is a robber baron, such as had not been seen in England for five hundred years. Over and over again we find the same note sounded on the Irish side, sounded with triumph and with pride. If this be the peak of Ulster civilization, what may we expect to find at the base, say, among the wild MacSwineys of Donegal?

Castles such as that of Maguire at Enniskillen, or O'Neill at Dungannon, or O'Dogherty at Buncrana were not numerous. The lesser chief might have a stone keep for defence, but it did not follow that he lived in it; possibly his ordinary dwelling, at any rate in the cold of winter, was a little " Irish house " beside it. These Irish houses seem to have been, either circular huts, shaped like a bell-tent, made of turf laid against a framework of rods supported by a central pole, or square-shaped and roughly constructed of wattle-and-daub. Towns there were none, but for what was practically an English settlement at Newry, a handful of houses lying beneath the ruined Cathedral of Armagh or the walls of the English fortress of Carrickfergus, the O'Donnell fortress of Ballyshannon, and one or two other such places. Belfast was scarcely a village. The Irish were not by nature town-dwellers, though they took to town life readily enough when settlers like the Danes gave them a start. There does not appear to have been much tillage, and it had, of course, declined during Tyrone's rebellion. What ploughing there was was " by the tail ", six horses without a scrap of harness on them being tied by their tails abreast to a cross-bar on a little plough. Then, as now, more shocked by cruelty to animals than if it were inflicted upon men, the English made many attempts to stop this practice, with little success.

Cattle and horses were numerous, though their quality did not appear good to English eyes. Large numbers of families lived by *creaghting*; that is, ranching, accompanying herds of cattle from one pasture to another, with never more than a temporary shelter of sods for their own habitation, " a very idle life and a fit nursery for a thief," in the view of Edmund Spenser.

Dress was rough and practical. The men wore short woollen jackets, tight trousers, and the inevitable rug or mantle in which they were always prepared to sleep in the open. This mantle in the case of the women expanded into the traditional big Irish cloak. Food was plentiful in Ulster, except when war made an artificial famine, but the Irish were not given to the pleasures of the table, except in liquid form. They were prepared to eat their meat raw if at all pressed for time, and made small account of bread, their corn being frequently reserved for their horses. Their meals were washed down with great draughts of *usquebagh*, or whisky, though all but the poorest drank also wine imported from Spain.

The country was thickly wooded and almost roadless, even as roads were in the England of Elizabeth. There were a few main tracks by which wheeled vehicles could move in good weather, but they were impassable after rain. Yet Ulster had a foreign trade, largely with Spain and in lesser degree with the Spanish Netherlands. Both her inland lakes and rivers and the great inlets, Donegal Bay, Loughs Swilly and Foyle, Belfast, Strangford, and Carlingford Loughs, teemed with fish, which were exported in salt. Flax was grown, and a little linen was sold abroad long before the day of Strafford. Hides, furs, tallow, timber, and even some corn were the other chief exports. But fish was by far the biggest, and what it brought in return was mainly Spanish wine. The authorities looked with some disfavour upon this trade, but only because it tended to link Ireland to Spain. They did not interfere with it, and there were no trade restrictions except a few minor ones imposed by the Irish Parliament. In that respect Ireland was favourably treated then by comparison with later times. Between Antrim and Scotland there was a busy commerce, of which mention will be made when we come to deal with the Scots in Ulster.

The coarse Irish friezes, so stout and cheap that they were used to clothe the royal troops in Ireland, were woven everywhere. Iron was mined at Toome on the Bann, and the smiths there were accounted clever. At any rate there was never any shortage of swords, skeans, or pikes.

The state of religion was strange and unhappy. By an Act passed by the Irish Parliament in 1536, appeals to Rome had been forbidden and the jurisdiction of the Pope had been abolished. At about the same time the dissolution of the monasteries and the scramble for their lands by English, Anglo-Irish, and Irish alike began. The Papacy in reply flooded the country with travelling friars, men superior in their zeal, virtue, and disinterestedness to, at any rate, a large proportion of the monks whom they replaced. The official Anglican Church, after a momentary progress, during which a number of chiefs had renounced that of Rome, was soon represented by little more than a handful of bishops and clergy who seldom spoke the language of their flocks. In a word, the Reformation was a complete failure in Ireland; as for Ulster, confusion was the only evidence that it had ever taken place. Under Elizabeth, Catholics were nowhere in Ireland subject to economic disabilities, while in Ulster, owing to the wars, the question had for some time not arisen. No Protestant bishop was in possession of a see; in some, Papal bishops were actually officiating; in others, there were nominal Papal bishops who were not resident. There was a Papal Archbishop of Armagh and Primate of All Ireland, the celebrated Peter Lombard, but he lived in Rome, just as the Papal Archbishop of Dublin lived in Spain. On the other hand, Redmond O'Gallagher, Papal Bishop of Derry, rode about the province "with pomp and company from place to place as it was accustomed in Queen Mary's days". A score of monasteries still existed. Yet, if she still had a strong hold upon the masses of the people, the Catholic Church in Ulster was sadly decayed, in quality as well as in power, by comparison with the days of Molaisse.

It is almost needless to add that art, which in Ireland had always been the Church's handmaiden, had shared in her decay. That, again, is a prickly subject, which cannot here be discussed at any great length. There had been in Ireland at least two forms of art, both of high perfection and taste, both characteristically Celtic, prior to the Norman invasion, and Ulster had had her share of them. They were metal-work and illumination. It may almost be said that among the few treasures which have been preserved, three of the loveliest belong to Ulster: the shrine, or covering, of St. Molaisse's Gospel; the *Cathach*, which was the shrine of St. Columba's Psalter and was carried before the O'Donnells into battle; and the Clogher Cross, which was discovered quite recently in a cottage at Garrison, County Fermanagh. Yet it is an absurd exaggeration to state that the "people of Ulster" had been an artistic race. It was noted as a curiosity that Molaisse dwelt "in a house of hard stone" on the island of Devenish in Lough Erne, and was a curiosity because nearly everyone lived in hovels of wicker-work. Folk who dwell thus are not a race of artists or lovers of art. They may, however, produce here and there men skilled with their hands, who, under the influence of learned and artistic monks, create noble works of art for those monks' uses. That is what had happened in Ulster.

A third art, that of architecture, had been respectable and comely, but not particularly notable. At its best, again, it had been at the service mainly of the Church. To pretend that it was widespread is demonstrably false. Those who argue that vast numbers of architectural masterpieces had been destroyed as a result of the Norman invasion must be at a loss to account for the survival of so many in districts of France, Belgium, and Italy, often ravaged by the fiercest of wars. Moreover, for what destruction had taken place it is only fair that, above all in Ulster, the quarrelsome native chiefs should bear some of the blame.

The clan system, and English dealings with it, is another question which has aroused much controversy. On the one hand, the chief is represented as the father of his people, their protector from the English; on the other, he is pictured as a selfish tyrant, battening upon them and regardless of their safety, and it is the English who are their protectors. This much at least is certain: just as in the Great War an "artillery duel" frequently meant that the artillery of either side bombarded the luckless infantry of the other, so, a tribal war in Ireland meant the slaughter and despoiling by one chief of the clansmen of another, the latter having as often as not shut himself up in his keep with his personal followers till the marauding tide should recede. Tyrone, himself, who had by comparison with most of his contemporaries a reputation for humanity, ruthlessly wasted the lands and slew the clansmen, not only of those who opposed him, but of those who refused to join him in rebellion. In Monaghan he killed and burnt at the expense of Irish tenants of an English grantee, simply and solely to annoy the Englishman, who was far from the scene.

Though the chief had most of the attributes of an absolute lord, theoretically his territory belonged not to himself personally but to the whole sept. The sept had one method of asserting its authority and securing its own safety in the custom of tanistry.

The object of this custom was to assure strong leadership in the ruler. The chieftaincy did not necessarily descend by primogeniture or even from father to son. If the eldest son, or any of the sons, of the ruling chief were too young or weakly in character to rule the sept and lead it in battle they were passed over. Occasionally the eldest son was rejected on the ground of illegitimacy, as we shall see happened to Ferdoragh, Lord Dungannon, son of the first Earl of Tyrone. In such a case a successor was chosen from the immediate family of the chief, generally a nephew or cousin.

A similar custom is to be found among many primitive peoples. Those well acquainted with the history of the Great War as it concerned Egypt will recall that Sayed Ahmed, the Grand Senussi, was nominated to that position because his nephew Mohammed Idris, the son of his predecessor, was a youth at the time of his predecessor's death. It is true that the Senussists were not a tribe but a religious sect. Their head had, none the less, great temporal power. He was the temporal ruler and commander of the tribes which opposed the Italians in the Turco-Italian War of 1911, and which attempted to invade Egypt in 1915. The principle, therefore, is almost exactly the same.

In theory, the custom of tanistry, which was, as might be expected, more vigorous in Ulster than elsewhere, suited the province and the age. The chiefry, while it was kept within the chief's family, was handed on by popular favour—naught, it would appear, could be more satisfactory. In practice, however, the tanist or successor was chosen by the chief, if he were a strong man. That, again, was perhaps not objectionable. But suppose that the chief were growing old and feeble without having nominated a tanist, or that the one he had nominated seemed to have a weak side, or that some section of the clan was dissatisfied with the choice. Then every potential candidate kept in his train the largest possible band of adherents, to fight for his nomination when the moment came, and meanwhile, as often happened, to assassinate other candidates. Queen Mary's Catholic Lord Deputy, Lord Fitzwalter, had gone so far as to declare that tanistry, which he described as "the election to the captaincy of the country", was the real curse of Ireland. The fighting men retained for such an emergency, he declared, "being brought up and fed with idleness, cannot be restrained in time of peace from stealing and a number of other enormities. To maintain them in their life, they have finding and expenses upon the country, whereby be brought in coyne, livery, bonaght, and all other Irish exactions, which be the only ground and causes of all the uncivil and detestable disorders of this realm."

Of these three Irish exactions, *coyne* was the right of the chief to draw rations for his followers, and *livery* the right to draw forage for his cavalry horses, from the peasantry on whom he saw fit to quarter them; *bonaght* was the right to draw military pay from the same unfortunates, and *bonaghts* were troops thus maintained. How evil a system was this can be fully realized only when it is also realized that over and over again Irish chiefs proved unable to restrain, and were afraid to punish the excesses of their followers. Beside these, *coshering*, the custom of the chief

17

and his retinue living on his tenants as he made his progress through his country, was mild and natural.

The other important custom to be considered is the Irish version of gavelkind. This gave the chief the right, on the death of a holder of land, not merely to divide the inheritance among his sons, but to make a fresh division of the lands of the whole sept. It had more than one unfortunate effect. In the first place, it led to a minute subdivision of property, which, in a country where power was founded on property, tended to deprive the majority of political rights. In the second, by denying fixity of tenure to the clansman, it deprived him of interest in his land, and so was a check to progress in agriculture. The best that its apologists can say for this custom is that it was frequently not put into force.

The reader may now feel that he understands the rough outline of the system. He must be disillusioned. Nothing in Irish history, still less in the history of Irish land tenure, is as simple as that. Tenure and succession were, in fact, the main preoccupations of the native Irish judges and lawyers, the Brehons. To begin with, the chief had generally a large demesne which was his absolute property. Then, certain chiefs, in Ulster as elsewhere, had already themselves established what amounted to absolute property in their lands as a whole. Moreover, the belief that all land was clan land has been shattered by the discovery that, prior to the introduction by the Crown of " Surrender and Re-grant ", conveyance of land as personal property was practised by the Irish, and that such land normally descended from father to son. There were thus three modes of inheritance : tanistry, gavelkind, and descent. And finally, when the chief, under the system of " Surrender and Re-grant " received his land as a feudatory of the Crown, he thereby renounced the clan system of tenure. He could not reasonably expect to have it both ways: remain the chief of a clan with all the powers and privileges of that office, and become a feudal grantee holding his lands directly from the Crown as personal property. Yet that is what the Ulster lords did expect.

The attitude of the English to Irish Brehon law and custom had been unduly hostile and contemptuous. It is only in the reign of James I that we find a lawyer like Sir John Davies making a serious attempt to master them. Yet the dealings of the English with the clan system had been less malevolent than is generally believed. Their methods were, and still are in some historical writing, attacked even when diametrically opposite. They are accused of injustice to the clansmen when they handed over the lands to the chief as a feudal grantee; and they are accused of meddling without justification in the chief's concerns when they strove to establish at any rate the leading clansmen as freeholders. They had done this in more than one case. We may mention here that of Monaghan, a county which did not come into the Plantation scheme. It is possibly not creditable to the Viceroy concerned, though the evidence is doubtful, but at least it well illustrates the second method.

Monaghan, like Armagh, Tyrone, Fermanagh, Cavan, Coleraine, and Tyrconnell, had only just become a county, having been formally reduced to shire-ground by the then Lord Deputy, Sir John Perrot, in 1584. In 1589 Sir Ross MacMahon died without leaving a son. He was feudal grantee of the whole county with the exception of the barony of Farney. This had been granted to the Queen's former favourite, Walter Devereux, Earl of Essex, and was now the property of his youthful son, Robert. Sir Ross was also "the MacMahon" to his clansmen. Two claimants came forward: his brother, Hugh Roe MacMahon, as feudal heir, and a kinsman named Bryan MacHugh Oge MacMahon as tanist. Very good, thought the Lord Deputy, Sir William Fitzwilliam; here was an opportunity to split up this great chiefry. He suggested a division of the spoils between the two candidates. Finding, however, that neither would agree to this, he acknowledged the claim of Hugh Roe, as he was bound to do. Bryan MacHugh fled the county, and though he returned with a band of adherents from Leitrim and Fermanagh and made a nuisance of himself, he was unable to eject Hugh Roe, who had been lent a garrison by the Deputy.

Unfortunately for himself, having been installed in virtue of English laws of succession and kept in his seat by the aid of English arms, the high-spirited Hugh Roe then proceeded to have his fling in the good old style. At the head of the very troops lent him by the Deputy, he set off to "destrain for rent", as he was pleased to call it. In other words, he killed men, women, and children on the lands of the offending tenant, and kept the latter locked up till he had paid the sum claimed. This did not gravely shock either Elizabeth or Burghley, but Fitzwilliam took another view of the case. Some months later he made an expedition into Monaghan, laid hands upon Hugh Roe, and hanged him in front of his own house. It was afterwards alleged that Fitzwilliam had grown tired of waiting for the payment of a bribe of six hundred beeves, the price of his support of the rightful heir. The Deputy was no angel, but there is no proof of his corruption in this case. He was acquitted of this and other charges brought against him after his return to England.

What is of chief interest to us here is the Deputy's treatment of the forfeited lands, when he wound up the affair in 1591. He put one or two MacMahons into each of the five baronies of the county, the one in Farney holding the barony under young Essex. Below them he created three hundred freeholders, paying a rent of 12s. 6d. for every sixty acres. The Church lands he disposed of largely to Englishmen. Here again he is accused of corruption, it being alleged that he sold these lands and put the money in his own pocket. It is not impossible, but it was not proved. The important aspect of the case is the creation of this large body of native Irish freeholders, which he might well anticipate would form a stable element. Tyrone afterwards declared that what happened in Monaghan was the cause of his own rebellion. If so, it is a matter of doubt whether it was the hanging of Hugh Roe or the creation of the free-holders which seemed to him the more serious interference with Irish rights and customs.

Opinions vary regarding the quality of the sixteenth-century Ulstermen as warriors. One English observer considered that for "light scourers", that is, for what would be called in modern military parlance duties of protection and foraging, there were no better troops than the native horsemen. As cavalry in the English sense they suffered from the fact that they rode without stirrups, and so were quite unsuited to shock action. Their chief weapon was a spear, which was not held beneath the arm like a lance but was given a back-handed thrust from above the shoulder, and sometimes hurled at the enemy. The footmen were divided into two types: *gallowglasses*, or heavy infantry, and *kernes*, or light infantry. The former wore a shirt of mail and a headpiece, and were armed with a six-foot halberd. The kerne had nothing but a sword and a bow and arrows; or, if he did not carry the bow, bore a wooden targe on his left arm and a javelin in his right hand. He was therefore suited only to guerrilla or light-infantry tactics, in which he often showed skill. When the royal troops caught a body of kernes at close quarters the affair

21

developed into a slaughter. But during the last twenty years or so of the century the Irish had used the musket and caliver more and more, and had become fairly expert in their handling. Tyrone had been modelling his infantry to a great extent on the Spanish pattern, substituting musket for bow, and pike for halberd, till at the Battle of Kinsale, at the end of 1601, it differed little in outward appearance from the Royal Army.

The Ulster chiefs cannot have been content with the fighting qualities of the native troops, to judge by their eagerness to hire Scottish mercenaries. The power of Shane O'Neill and that of his successor Tirlagh Luineach was largely based upon these troops. The O'Donnell employed them constantly, as did Tyrone himself so long as he could obtain them. The Scots could confront the Irish with their own tactics; no country was too wild for them, no hardships wearied them, no exposure to wet sickened them, as it did the English. But, when it came to hand-to-hand fighting, their dash was tempered with a dour resolution which the gallowglass could not match, and which was far too much for the peasant-kerne. Probably their greater freedom and independence in their own country reinforced their spirits, as compared with the Irish peasant. The mercenaries would, besides, be more or less picked men. At all events, English witnesses agree with Irish as to their quality in battle. One Englishman declared that in his estimation three hundred Scots were the equivalent of six hundred Irish in a fight.

This leads us to the curious history of the Scots in Ulster. It may easily be imagined that a warlike people dwelling in a harsh land, such as the western isles and the west coast of Scotland, with a thinly inhabited and fertile country never out of their sight in clear weather, would be eager to try their fortune in it. In the thirteenth century the Bissetts, whose (probably fabulous) history connected them with Greece, had established themselves on Rathlin Island. Towards the end of the fourteenth century the heiress of this house married a MacDonald of the Isles, to whom Rathlin passed, his bride. Soon hungry MacDonalds were settled all along the Antrim coast from the Bann to the very walls of the royal fortress of Carrickfergus. They sold their swords to the highest bidder, though by no means all the mercenaries who came to Ireland were of their clan ; they waged their own private wars ; and they intermarried with the great Ulster houses. They did not disdain trade. With a reaching wind for the passage out and back, they could leave the Mull of Cantyre at dawn, hire horses on the Irish side to bring their goods to market, and be back on Scottish soil by night. They also engaged in agriculture, and plainly meant to stay. The native Irish may not have loved them, but they did not hate them. Indeed, at the Reformation they were drawn closer to them by the bond of religion, the Macdonnells—we may in future give them the Irish version of their name—being Catholics like themselves.

Nor were the Scottish settlers particularly hostile to the English Government. They wanted only land to live on— and there was enough and to spare in Ulster—a chance to turn a more or less honest penny by their courage and skill in war, and an opportunity to trade across the narrow straits between their new colony and their home. They were, nevertheless, a nuisance and a danger : a nuisance because their mercenaries stirred up trouble in Ireland and made the Ulster chiefs more formidable ; a danger because they might at any time be used to further Scottish designs against England. So close at hand were their kinsmen that on more than one occasion when they were engaged in a battle in the morning their beacons brought them reinforcements by the afternoon. This was the cause of the suspicion or open hostility of successive Deputies towards them, and that of Elizabeth's unnatural and ill-advised alliance with Shane O'Neill to uproot them from Antrim. They had their ups and downs, but they were a tough breed and were not finally expelled. We shall find that they had their part in the Plantation; but that was after the Thrones of England and Scotland had been united.

In the course of Elizabeth's reign the Royal Army had assumed a regular organization. The basis of the infantry was the company, nominally as a rule in time of war of 200 men, and in time of peace half that number, commanded by a captain. A number of companies were formed into a regiment, commanded by a colonel, when large-scale operations were in hand. The proportion of muskets to pikes was about two to one, a figure at which it was to remain in all the infantry of the civilized world until the introduction of the bayonet. In some cases a company had also on its strength about half a dozen " targets ", probably Irish kerne employed as skirmishers in front of the line of battle. For the Army always consisted as to at least one-third, and occasionally one-half, of Irish troops. In some degree this was a matter of necessity, owing to the heavy demands made upon England by the Irish wars at a period when she was also carrying on considerable operations on the Continent, and to the great losses from sickness, to which the English were more liable than the natives. It was, however, also due to the custom of rewarding the loyalty of Irish gentlemen or minor nobility by giving them companies, with the attendant perquisites. The Irish soldiers made no great matter of fighting their own countrymen, and pluckily they fought. Yet they were apt to desert to the enemy after a reverse, and generally required more support than did the English troops. If, for example, they formed a rear guard, the wise commander saw to it that a body of

English cavalry was at hand to extricate them in case of need.

The English infantryman was very like his descendant of to-day, and Atkins through the ages. He took long to grow accustomed to the Irish methods of ambush and surprise, of drawing the adversary into impassable bogs, through which the kernes hopped like goats, from tussock to tussock, and he suffered heavy and humiliating defeats in the process of learning the lessons of this warfare. He growled and cursed at the lack of shelter, the wet weather, the dysentery and fever, the deep roads, the rancid butter, the shortage of beer—not a native drink and specially imported for him— the fashion in which his pay fell into arrears. He loathed being needlessly marched about as he was by Essex, and lost his self-confidence under such leadership. But with a Mountjoy or a Carew to lead him, and a reasonably good meal in his stomach, he feared no foe, Irishman or Spaniard or both combined, at what odds soever. Though utterly outmarched by the enemy, he learnt to surprise him by subtlety, to beat off his surprise attacks, and brush him aside if he dared to stand in the open.

The cavalry were few by comparison with the infantry, as the opportunities of the mounted arm in guerrilla warfare and generally close country were limited. When, however, once in a while it had a red-letter day and caught a body of the enemy on firm and open ground, its ascendancy was greater even than that of the infantry. Each cavalry trooper was accompanied in the field by a boy on a hackney, and out of his pay of 12d. a day had to maintain himself, the boy, and the two horses. The troop-horses were generally imported, the Irish garran not being up to the weight of an armoured man. The artillery consisted of a few pieces only—not more than half a dozen with the largest of armies—and was of little value except in siege warfare.

There its effects were decisive. It was with artillery that Carew reduced Munster, battering down fortress after fortress. And it was the dread of artillery that induced Tyrone and his Ulster associates to demolish their own castles when definitely committed to revolt.

## II

## QUEEN ELIZABETH'S IRISH QUESTION

THE problem which confronted Elizabeth in Ireland differed markedly from that of her grandfather, father, and brother, and still more from that of her sister. It is true that Ireland had played a greater part in the European system than was supposed until within recent years, during which fresh light has been thrown upon the country's relations with the Continent by archives, newly published or calendared, at home and abroad. There had been threats of a French invasion of Ireland in the reign of Edward VI, and France had kept a close eye on the country throughout the first half of the sixteenth century. But French flattery of Irish hopes had never gone beyond flattery; nor can it be said that danger from France had ever become for England a pressing one.

The Reformation, and the accession of a Protestant queen to the English throne changed the situation entirely. Spain, the champion of the Papacy, confronted England, who had officially abjured the Catholic Church. Philip II of Spain, widower of Mary of England, was a pious bigot—the bitterest sort. His religious hatred of English Protestantism was increased by the remembrance that this rank weed was growing in a soil of which he had been until the other day the gardener; from which he had drawn hard-bitten troops to help fight his battles. England, in fact, had been, under Mary, the faithful ally of Spain, aiding her to win Emmanuel-Philibert of Savoy's great victory at Saint-Quentin in 1557, and losing Calais in her cause the following year. The commercial and colonial rivalry which developed between the two countries still further exacerbated their relations. And where could Philip find a weaker spot in England's armour than in Ireland, the persecuted but ever-faithful daughter of the Church, ground down by an heretical oppressor? Irish soldiers in his armies, Irish priests in his cathedrals and colleges, chanted with ardour, as though it were a canticle: " Strike for the Church! Strike through Ireland! " It was a religious war to a great extent, even in the years of the semi-piratical raids on Spanish fleets and colonies, ere it was formally recognized as warfare; it became that in the fullest sense after the death of Mary Queen of Scots.

Elizabeth picked up the glove because she had to. She did not at once break the Spanish alliance, though she made peace with France in 1564. She even allowed Philip to hope for a moment that she would become his wife, in succession to her sister. That was partly because she was sparring for time to consolidate her own uncertain position at home, and partly because she was pacific from dislike of the wastefulness of war. But from the first she saw Ireland from Philip's point of view. The danger was that Ireland would become a hostile base for an attack on England, the same danger that threatened in the wars with Republican France two hundred years later—a danger that is not utterly remote to-day. To meet it, it was necessary to assert English rule in the country, to adopt a more forward policy than that of her predecessors. She did so. Yet the policy of the great Queen and of Burghley, everywhere hand-to-mouth, an ingenious makeshift—necessarily so, in many cases—shows at its most variable, uncertain, and unfortunate in Ireland. She was not only parsimonious but genuinely short of funds, and she was suspicious. If we contrast unfavourably her Irish policy with the steady conduct of affairs by James,

CORRUPTION OF THE GOVERNMENT

we must not forget that he had not only no Spanish problem but no Scottish problem. Especially before the execution of Mary Queen of Scots, Elizabeth did not care to see her viceroys too powerful, lest their power should lead them into intrigues with Edinburgh.

It is outside the scope and purpose of this book to give even a brief general sketch of Irish history during her reign. We have only to survey the rickety scaffolding of her Irish policy, to glance a little longer at affairs in Ulster, and finally to study in rather more detail the main events of the Viceroyalty of Mountjoy, which lead us to the Plantation. It was a long reign; there were many viceroys; and their terms of office often ended in sudden recall and disgrace. A few of them, like Sir Henry Sidney and Sir John Perrot—reputed to be the son of Henry VIII—were not only men of great ability, but actually popular with the Irish, having a good name even with those in rebellion. Yet the whole system was a bad one, crippling to honest men of all but the highest genius, and an invitation to dishonest courses to the less upright.

Funds were always lacking, and it seems to have been expected that the Deputies should augment them as best they could, so long as they did not plunge their arms too deeply into tainted sources and caused no scandal. Many of the Irish chiefs were very rich, in cattle if not in money. They were quite willing to pay for comfort and freedom from restraint. So many hundred beeves to ensure that a sheriff should not be put in, when a county had been made shire-ground, or to support a claim against a rival; so many score to compound for an offence or to cause eyes to be averted when one was being planned. Who took bribes and who refused them it is difficult to judge; there are accusations in plenty, but proof is hard to come by. The historian of to-day cannot, if he wants to achieve the unusual feat of

29

writing about Ireland without bias, do better than imitate the method of the seventeenth-century historian, Fynes Moryson, who, in recording such stories of the period before he came to Ireland, puts in brackets, " as the Irish say ". Fitzwilliam (as the Irish say) practised the art of " double-crossing ", taking a bribe not to put in a sheriff and then putting a most unpleasant sheriff in. Others, even the able and popular Perrot (as the Irish say), ran him close. But it seems possible that on the whole the Irish chiefs benefited from the system. Certainly the inactivity and half-heartedness of some of the senior officials and soldiers, such as Sir John Norris, reputed to be the foremost Elizabethan military commander, are hard to explain.

In no respect, however, did Elizabeth fail so completely as in her dealings with the O'Neills. It has already been mentioned that when Con Bacach was created Earl of Tyrone by Henry VIII his young son Ferdoragh, or Mathew, was given the title of Baron Dungannon. It was a most unfortunate start for English laws of inheritance. Ferdoragh's mother was the wife of a blacksmith, and Con Bacach was, in the words of Shane O'Neill, so much a gentleman that he acknowledged as his own any child whose mother imputed the paternity to him. The worthy and gallant Earl was indeed the father of his people. Nevertheless, there were those ungracious enough to allege not merely that Ferdoragh was illegitimate—of that there could be no doubt—but that he was not even Con's son. It is curious to reflect that, if this was so, two of the most remarkable men who ever bore the name of O'Neill, Hugh, the second Earl of Tyrone, and his nephew Owen Roe, the defender of Arras and the victor of Benburb, were not O'Neills at all.

Unfortunately for Ferdoragh, Lord Dungannon, Con had another son who was legitimate, and also a man of very considerable parts. Shane's personal character was repulsive.

He was savagely cruel, meanly vindictive, treacherous beyond the ordinary, and, according to some evidence, cowardly. He was a drunkard, even by contemporary standards, being wont to drink himself into a stupor wherein he lay for days at a time. Yet he had a keen intelligence, an eye for guerrilla warfare, and a personality which enabled him to hold his people together with the aid of the Scots mercenaries whom he constantly employed. Above all, he was an organizer; and one of the fruits of his organizing power was a perfect system of intelligence. Within the shortest possible time he knew not only what his neighbours were doing, but what was being projected in Dublin. Many of his victorious *coups* were very easily achieved because he did not strike until he knew that the opposition was weak or off its guard. This was the man who was accepted by the O'Neills and formally elected their chief.

Shane began promisingly. While Mary's viceroys were using their energies against the Scots in the north-east—the whole population of Rathlin was exterminated in 1553—he and Calvagh O'Donnell of Tyrconnell engaged in a struggle for the mastery. He also had Dungannon put out of the way by assassination in 1558. Calvagh thrashed Shane when they met in the open field, but in 1561 the O'Neill managed to lay hands upon his rival, whom he kept in close confinement. He then proclaimed himself Lord of Tyrconnell.

Elizabeth decided that something would have to be done to curb his power and his still greater pretensions. She sent Fitzwalter, now Earl of Sussex, back to Ireland, giving him the full title of Lord Lieutenant, as though to show that she meant business. The new Viceroy's first invasion of Shane's territory was an ignominious failure, but in his second he so thoroughly laid waste the country that the Ulsterman came to terms, and agreed to cross the Irish Sea to visit the Queen.

Shane duly went, arriving in London in January 1562; but the manner of his arrival was typical of his pride. He wore no rich English clothes as his father had when he made his submission to Elizabeth's. He and his escort of gallowglasses, their battle-axes on their shoulders, were clad in the saffron tunics which even in Ireland were old-fashioned and about to disappear, coats of mail, and fur cloaks of the shaggiest, though not more shaggy than their hair. He was well received by the Queen, who seems to have been taken with him. She allowed him to retain the title of " the O'Neill ", hinting that she would presently add to it an English title of honour. Evidently she had not made up her mind which branch of the family was the better suited to hold the predominance in Ulster. Keeping Shane by her, she sent for Dungannon's eldest boy, Bryan, then in his twenties, to see what promise there was in him.

That she was never to know. Quite possibly a messenger from Shane crossed by the same boat as hers. At all events, Bryan, riding down to the coast to take ship to England, was waylaid by Tirlagh Luineach O'Neill, and murdered.

Tirlagh Luineach, so-called because he had been fostered by the O'Looneys, was also in some ways a notable character. The son of Shane's first cousin and thus grand-nephew of old Con, he had just been appointed Shane's tanist, or official successor. As Lord Ernest Hamilton has pointed out in his *Elizabethan Ulster*, a false impression of him has been handed down by a single phrase in a letter, describing him as " a savage but timorous man ". He was far from savage by comparison with Shane; in fact, few cruelties and no barbarities are recorded against him. The murder of Bryan was a perfectly normal precaution where a rival candidate to the chiefry was concerned, and was into the bargain probably ordered by Shane. Nor was Tirlagh timorous, being a good fighting man and Shane's military commander.

32

Lord Ernest suggests " uneducated and unenterprising " as a translation into modern English. Unenterprising or not, Tirlagh was not wholly without ambition or guile, and was a force to be reckoned with. A confirmed drunkard in later life and something of a buffoon, he is yet one of the most likeable figures on either side in this grim period. It appears that at a later date Elizabeth toyed with the project of giving him her full support and making him Earl of Omagh. It would probably have paid her well; for Tirlagh had some conception of the meaning of an oath.

Shane himself had still five years of power in front of him. He broke all the many promises of good behaviour he had made to Elizabeth, beginning the process immediately after his return to Ireland. He slew and raided and tortured his prisoners to his heart's content. Egged on by officials in Dublin, he caught the Scottish colony on the Antrim coast at a moment when it was at its weakest, and exterminated it, saving from death only the famous Sorley Boy Macdonnell and some score of the leading members of the clan. These, to Elizabeth's fury, he then ransomed, letting them return to the Route, which they at once repeopled. He also seized the castle of Newry, on the edge of the Pale, burned the cathedral of Armagh, and mockingly defied the Queen.

There he overreached himself. Elizabeth ordered that he should be called to an account, and sent the formidable Sir Henry Sidney to Ireland for the purpose. Sidney invaded his realms, and though Shane kept out of the way in the inaccessible Sperrin Mountains, the Viceroy marched into Tyrconnell and replaced Calvagh O'Donnell as chief. The Queen even, for the first time, accepted the aid of the Scots against Shane, and they systematically harried him. Worse still, on the death of Calvagh, his half-brother and successor, Hugh MacManus, Shane's former ally against Calvagh, turned against the O'Neill and signally defeated him.

Shane managed to escape, as he always did on such occasions, but his nerve was broken. It does not appear that he was at his last gasp, but he probably felt that he could no longer escape the Royal Army now that all the old allies and vassals whom he had bullied and oppressed were one by one turning against him. Even Tirlagh Luineach had withdrawn from his side, becoming the ally of Calvagh O'Donnell and, when that honest and worthy man died, of his son Cormac. In desperation Shane fled to the Scots, and among them met his doom, on the 2nd June 1567. The Macdonnells received him with their customary hospitality at Cushendun, but there was too much blood between him and them. Hospitality led to a drunken orgy; that led to loss of temper and high words on both sides; and Shane was hewn in pieces. Hearing the news, the English governor of Carrickfergus rode north in haste, secured his head, and despatched it, " pickled in a pipkin ", to Dublin.

It was the Act of Attainder of Shane O'Neill, passed by the Irish Parliament in 1569, that famous " Act of the 11th of Elizabeth ", which placed the Crown in possession of the territories of the O'Neills and their adherents, including " the country and lordships of the Glynns, usurped by the Scots ", and formed one of the chief weapons for the enforcement and justification of the Plantation of Ulster, forty years later.

Meanwhile Elizabeth had taken good care that the fate of Bryan O'Neill should not befall his next brother Hugh. This young man passed the greater part of his early life at Sir Henry Sidney's seat of Penshurst, where he was expected to learn English ways and " civility ". On the death of Con, who had twice fled from his son Shane and had finally died in the Pale about 1559, Hugh had become a still more important and significant figure. The English Government had, however, determined to follow a waiting policy and to watch his development. Even after the death of Shane they pursued this plan. Tirlagh Luineach became "the O'Neill", and Hugh for the time being remained in England.

However, Shane being dead and a more cautious and less ambitious chief installed in his stead, Elizabeth decided to take stronger measures for the pacification of Ulster. Her project was a revival of one which she had previously considered: the planting of Antrim and Down with English settlers. For that purpose it was necessary to get rid of the Scots, and this was actually achieved by negotiation. Sorley Boy agreed to withdraw from the Glynns and the Route to give the scheme a chance; and in fact the Macdonnells, absorbed in their own tumultuous affairs in Cantyre, left Ulster alone between 1568 and 1571. However, the Plantation hung fire, with the natural result that the native Irish, the O'Neills of North Clandeboye and the MacQuillans, secured the old Scottish colonies on the coast, and that Sorley Boy returned and ejected them.

When the scheme was at last got under way it was a fiasco. In 1572 one, Sir Thomas Smith, was given a grant, not in Antrim, to which the Scots had returned, but of the rich district of the Ards in east Down. He sent over his son to prepare the way, and that youth had an unhappy time of it. He was promptly chased to the walls of Carrickfergus by Sir Brian MacPhelim O'Neill of Clandeboye, who laid waste the Ards and murdered Henry Savage, the chief representative in that district of the Norman settlers. In 1573 Elizabeth, in disgust, virtually withdrew Smith's grant and handed it on to Walter Devereux, Earl of Essex, but on a much grander scale. The grant of Essex comprised the greater part of the two counties, plus the island of Rathlin. Elizabeth also gave him a commission as Governor of Ulster and strong financial backing. He sailed with a great expedition, 800 troops as well as hundreds of labourers and would-be settlers.

The hopeless failure of Essex need not detain us. Eventually he resigned his claim in exchange for that barony of Farney in Monaghan, of which mention has been made. He died in 1576, leaving behind him as wretched a record of cruelty, treachery, and inefficiency as any Englishman of that time in Ireland. In inefficiency, at least, his son was to match him.

The coming of Essex was marked by the reappearance of Hugh O'Neill, then aged between twenty-five and twenty-eight.[1] Since the death of Bryan eleven years before, Hugh had been known as the Baron of Dungannon, though, as we have seen, their grandfather Con, first Earl of Tyrone, had been dead even longer. It was, in fact, not until 1585 that Hugh was to be recognized as second Earl of Tyrone. His English upbringing being completed, he had been living for two or three years under English protection at Newry, on the edge of the Pale. He was now attached to the Staff of Essex, with every reason to hope that good behaviour would eventually bring him his grandfather's inheritance.

There were, however, difficulties in his path. His kinsman Tirlagh had four years earlier made a most profitable excursion into the marriage-market, obtaining the hand of Lady Agnes Macdonnell, widow of James Macdonnell of the Isles, and daughter of the Earl of Argyll. Her dowry, in addition to her very considerable brains, consisted for the most part of as many Scottish mercenaries as Tirlagh could maintain. They proved, indeed, more numerous than he could afford, but they made him the chief power of Ulster. In any case, Hugh had for the time being no great following among his own people, to whom his upbringing made him

---

[1] The *Dictionary of National Biography* gives the date of Hugh's birth as " 1540 ? ". There is reason to suppose that he was born not earlier than 1545.

an alien. It was part of his genius that he lived down this reproach, and in a comparatively short time.

The nature of this genius is hard to define. Hugh O'Neill is an illusive and much disputed character. The heroic glamour which surrounds him like an aura will doubtless follow him through the pages of history down to the end of time, but it is the duty of the historian to seek for the real man beneath trappings such as these. What was there, in truth, beneath them? To many old Irish writers, and even to some modern ones, he is a paladin, a great warrior, a beneficent ruler, a repository of the profoundest wisdom and statecraft. Nor were the Irish alone in their admiration. His fame spread to Italy and to France, where Henri Quatre declared that he and Fuentes, the celebrated Spanish commander, were the second and third generals of the age. The King in his modesty did not say who was the first, but his hearers must have been able to make a shrewd guess.

That O'Neill had a remarkable personality and a charm recognized by the English who had to do with him, great political ability, and some military flair is beyond doubt; yet Henry of Navarre must have known very little of him when he ranked so highly a soldier so little after his own heart. Tyrone had an eye for a defensive position in close country. If he managed to entangle the opposing forces in it he was capable of beating them on occasion; and it was this method which gained him the most important victory hitherto won by Irish over English arms. Even in such circumstances he left the leadership on the field of battle to subordinates. Against his fellow-Irish he was not at all successful; for example, old Tirlagh, with the aid of a handful of English troops, utterly routed him at Strabane, though the numerical odds were at least two to one in Hugh's favour. He never displayed the slightest initiative.

If he gained a victory he did not follow it up; if he lost a battle he himself led the flight.

Fynes Moryson, who not only knew more than most men of his doings but was well acquainted with him personally, describes him thus:

> "He was of mean stature, but a sturdy body, able to endure labour, watchings, and hard fare, being withal industrious and active, valiant, affable, and able to manage great affairs, and of a high, dissembling, subtle, and profound wit."

What strikes the modern observer is that his Fabian strategy and tactics in war were so faithfully reflected in his political methods. Though personally a proud man, he treated the Queen's Viceroys with the deepest respect, even in the days of his rebellion. He moved always with extreme caution, and was ready to profess repentance if it were demanded with enough force or seemed to be profitable. During the early part of his career in Ireland he seems to have been perfectly content to accept English overlordship, provided that its machinery did not approach him too closely or interfere with his private concerns. Of a patriot zeal to free his country there was then no trace in his words or actions. It was only when the Spaniards landed at Kinsale during the viceroyalty of Mountjoy that he had a vision of an Ireland Catholic and independent, purged of the English.

Tirlagh Luineach had no great love for his kinsman, telling the English, with prophetic instinct, that they had reared a whelp who would bite their hands. However, observing that the English were enthusiastic regarding their protégé, Tirlagh thought it best to come to terms. Possibly coached by the prudent Lady Agnes, he met Hugh early in 1579 and persuaded him to put away his wife Joan, daughter of

Hugh MacManus O'Donnell, in order to marry one of his, Tirlagh's, daughters. Then Tirlagh, well warmed with draughts of sack, nominated his future son-in-law to be his tanist. It was a clever stroke of policy, as it at once bought Dungannon's friendship and ensured the hostility of Tirlagh's enemy, O'Donnell, towards him. The lady was doubtless not consulted. Like others of Dungannon's many wives, she was turned out when the marriage had ceased to be a profitable transaction to the bridegroom, and shortly afterwards died.[1]

Later in that year Dungannon was given an opportunity to prove his loyalty and the value of his English upbringing. On the outbreak of the Desmond Rebellion of 1579–83, he was given command of a troop of horse. The authorities seem to have been fully satisfied with him, though how long he was actually in the field is uncertain. It was in the course of this revolt that the Spaniard made his first intervention in Ireland. A body of troops, chiefly Italian as to nationality and under the orders of the Papacy, less than a thousand strong, landed at Smerwick on the coast of Kerry, where they occupied a half-built fort. Desmond making no move to aid them, they were forced to surrender to the Deputy, Lord Grey de Wilton, and then slaughtered almost to a man. There is no proof of the allegation that they had surrendered on promise that their lives should be spared, but it cannot be called a pretty incident. It was witnessed by both Edmund Spenser and Walter Raleigh.

Dungannon's reward was not long in coming. First of all, in 1585, he received the title of Earl of Tyrone. Then, in 1587, after Perrot's shiring of the seven Ulster counties,

---

[1] That Tyrone actually married this girl has been disputed, but there is good evidence that he did. He had had two previous wives and was, as we shall see, to have two more.

Tirlagh Luineach was persuaded to lease to him for seven years the south-eastern half of the County Tyrone. By the end of that period it was expected that Tirlagh would be dead and that the new earl would succeed to the whole. It was a typical example of the hand-to-mouth policy of the Government, and scarcely fair to Tirlagh, who never seems to have received any rent for what was in fact the richer half of his county.

In England, and certainly no less in Ireland, men were awaiting with bated breath the coming of the Invincible Armada. The rumour went that 20,000 Spanish troops were destined for Ireland. Had a well-found force of less than half that strength landed, there is small doubt that, joined as it would have been by all the elements hostile to the Government, it would have had the country at its mercy for some time to come. The English Army was inadequate in numbers and in quality; some of the maritime fortresses were unmanned; guns were rusting or tumbling off rotten carriages; reserves of powder were lacking. The connection between the disaffected Irish and Spain had never been closer. This was especially true of the south, where many an Irishman spoke Spanish who had no English, and where the fondest hopes were centred upon the great Catholic Power.

It was only a miserable fleeing remnant of the Spanish fleet that was ever seen by Ireland. Ship after ship, damaged by weather and English gunfire, reeled in to crash upon those terrible north-western and western shores, and to be broken up by the rocks and the rollers of the Atlantic. Thousands of men were drowned. Some two thousand more got ashore, half-drowned, half-starved, half-dead of thirst. In a few cases they were succoured by the natives; in most they were slain. Between the hangings ordered by Fitzwilliam and the slaughterings of the Irish, only a handful made their way to Scotland, whence they were for the most part eventually shipped back to Spain. Philip's blow had failed utterly. The very elements had fought for the Queen and discomfited her enemies. Awed by the magnitude of her triumph and of the Spanish disaster, Ireland remained quiet.

Yet the yeast was beginning to work in Ulster. First, in Monaghan, where those events following the death of Sir Ross MacMahon, which have already been mentioned, now came to pass. Secondly, in Fermanagh, where Sir Cuconnaught Maguire died about the same time, leaving several sons, of whom the eldest, Connor Roe—destined to be known as the "Queen's Maguire"—was supported by the Deputy as successor to the chiefry, and his young half-brother Hugh was preferred by the majority of the clan. Thirdly, in Tyrconnell, where the tangle was still more complicated. Here the reigning chief, Sir Hugh (MacManus), was a nonentity, whose one outstanding action was the defeat of Shane O'Neill already recorded. The real ruler of the country was his wife, the black-haired and beautiful, or once beautiful, virago, Ineenduv. This lady, daughter of James Macdonnell of the Isles and of that Lady Agnes who was married to Tirlagh Luineach O'Neill, had her mother's brains and a ferocity all her own. She had several young sons, the eldest of whom, Hugh Roe, was a particularly promising boy according to the standards of the clan. Hugh Roe (Red Hugh) was the apple of her eye and, as her usual method of argument was a knife-thrust in the dark, he was powerfully supported. Her husband had also an older, possibly illegitimate son named Donnell. A third candidate was her son-in-law Neill Garve ("the Rough"), grandson of that Calvagh who had been the friend and ally of Tirlagh Luineach, a fierce, high-tempered young man, whose lands lay in the Finn valley. Hugh Roe had been kidnapped and lodged in Dublin Castle to be held as a " pledge," after a common custom of the time; but he escaped in 1592 with the aid of Tyrone. His father at once abdicated in favour of this nineteen-year-old son, Donnell having meanwhile been put out of the way by the fair Ineen. Lastly, in Tyrone, where there was the Earl himself, old Tirlagh Luineach, still alive but besotted with drink and diminished in power, and the sons of Shane, whom we may lump together as the MacShanes; for they are shadowy personages, and their imprisonment and mal-treatment by Tyrone was to knock all the spirit out of them. Nothing could have united all these people or kept them from each other's throats. Had there never been an Englishman in Ireland, there would have been fighting in their counties. One thing, however, and one alone, could unite the greater number of them—a rebellion against England.

Another woman was to play a part. " The Helen of the Irish Wars ", as the historian of *Ireland under the Tudors* has called her, was the beautiful Mabel Bagenal, sister of Sir Henry, the Deputy's Marshal, whose family held the castle of Newry permanently, and had a grant of land in its neighbourhood.[1] Tyrone was temporarily without a wife, having got rid of three in one way or another. He approached Bagenal with a demand for his sister's hand, but met with an indignant and scornful refusal. The Earl was about forty-six; the lady twenty. Nevertheless, he had such a way with him that he induced Mabel to elope. She rode away on a pillion from the house of Sir Patrick Barnewall and was married to Tyrone by no lesser cleric than the Protestant Bishop of Meath, who explained his part in the transaction by the plea that he had performed

[1] An interesting survival of this grant is the Lordship of Newry, which exists to this day. It takes rank as a barony and will be found under that title on any baronial map of County Down.

the ceremony in order to save the bride's honour. Bagenal was infuriated. He cursed himself that his blood should be "mingled with so traitorous a stock and kindred". His rage was later on to be whipped to deadly hatred by Tyrone's treatment of his new Countess. Unwilling to share her husband's favours with two mistresses, she eventually fled from Dungannon to her brother at Newry, to die there in 1596.

Early in 1593 troubles began. Young Hugh Maguire suddenly turned upon the sheriff put into his new-shired County of Fermanagh, who appears to have behaved very brutally, and drove him out. A series of parleys, with Tyrone acting as go-between, were as unsuccessful as might have been expected with such a negotiator. Finally Fitzwilliam despatched a small expedition against Maguire under Sir Henry Bagenal. Tyrone, still professedly loyal, joined him, and their combined forces utterly routed Maguire's at a ford over the Erne near Belleek, on the 10th October 1593. A farcical incident of the battle was that both the brothers-in-law, neither of whom had the reputation of being a thruster, were wounded, and that both made a hubbub over their hurts, each alleging that he alone had won the fight. The real victor was the gallant hothead Sir Thomas Lee, who was to be involved in the fall of the younger Essex and to die by the headsman's axe. In February of the following year Maguire's stronghold, Enniskillen Castle, was captured and garrisoned. It appeared in England that the spark of rebellion had been snuffed out and that all would be quiet as before.

Never was there a graver mistake. That spark was indeed quenched, but it had but been blown into the open from a subterranean fire, now smouldering but ready at any moment to burst into a great conflagration. It might, indeed, have broken out there and then, had the fight at Belleek gone the other way; for Hugh Roe O'Donnell had been hovering in the neighbourhood with a strong force awaiting the result. His mother was bringing Scots, it was said by the thousand, to Tyrconnell.

Tyrone himself was maintaining quite a small force, and using it in the service of the Crown; but actually he had established a sort of short-service system, with a view to training gradually all his clansmen. Why he did not take his golden opportunity that year it is hard to say. Perhaps he was waiting for Spanish troops; perhaps his habitual indecision had him in grip; perhaps, after all, he thought he might make terms for himself, remain an independent prince, free of sheriffs, free of English law, and would have been satisfied with that.

Meanwhile Hugh Maguire and his adherents were besieging Enniskillen Castle. A weak relief force moving to its succour was caught by Maguire and Tyrone's brother, Cormac MacBaron, at the ford of Drumane, where the western of the two roads from Cavan to Enniskillen crosses the Arney River. It is an ideal spot for a surprise attack. The road tops a slight hill and runs towards a taller and steeper one, at the foot of which it swerves right-handed, crosses the Arney—the present bridge being obviously on the exact site of the old ford—and passes round the hill, which overlooks it as seats in a theatre gallery overlook the stage. The hill is wooded still and was doubtless more so then. So far as one can reconstruct the action, the mounted advanced guard was allowed to pass the ford and ride round the hill, where it was engaged by the Irish horse. Then the " gentlemen in trousers " on the hillside had only to let off their ear-splitting yell, followed by a cloud of arrows, and come charging down the slope. The whole supply column fell into the hands of the Irish. The river-bed was so littered with stores from wagons that the place was thereafter known as " the Ford of the Biscuits ".

That was the last event of Fitzwilliam's generally unfortunate administration. He had himself begged that he should be recalled, and his wish was now granted, not before it was time. He was nearly seventy; so fat that he could scarcely walk, afflicted by the stone and the gout, and fast losing both his sight and his memory. His successor, Sir William Russell, reached Dublin on the 1st August 1594, to be met by Tyrone, who fell on his knees before him and handed him a written submission. Tyrone laid all the blame for the Ulster troubles upon the departed Deputy and the Marshal, vowing that he himself was and had always been loyal to the Queen.

The new Deputy was puzzled. His predecessor had no very high reputation, and Russell perhaps thought that there might be something in Tyrone's accusations. It is a curious picture. On the one hand there is the Deputy, intelligent but a newcomer; on the other his Council, every man of whom must have known that Tyrone was behind the recent victory on the Arney, in which a prominent part had been played by his brother Cormac. How much gold passed into Dublin pockets on that occasion we shall never know. At all events, Russell was persuaded to let the Earl go, while his charges and the counter-charges of Bagenal were thrashed out. Elizabeth was annoyed. She had treated Tyrone tenderly, but it was the Tudor instinct to clap under lock and key any troublesome or suspicious person; and now Tyrone, who had not even asked for a safe-conduct, had been allowed to ride home in peace. It is scarcely necessary to say that he fulfilled neither of his two promises to the Deputy; to send his son to the new University of Dublin, and to dismiss his and O'Donnell's Scots.

Russell showed his energy by at once marching to the relief of Enniskillen, withdrawing the starving garrison, putting in a fresh one, and provisioning the place. He was then, however, forced to give his attention to unrest in Leinster.

Directly he had had time to look round him, he had reported that the forces were hopelessly inadequate for their task, and had asked that strong reinforcements should be sent, together with a good commander to conduct the operations in Ulster. The Queen and Burghley decided to send the best-known Elizabethan soldier, Sir John Norris, with 2000 veterans who had been serving in Brittany. Unfortunately Norris was appointed Lord General, with independent command in Ulster. As Russell was also a soldier with a distinguished record, this was a slight upon the Deputy, the more so as the two men were not friends. Though Russell supported Norris to the best of his power, their policies clashed, the Deputy being all for a resolute attack upon the rebels, while the Lord General was remarkably—one may say, suspiciously—complaisant towards them.

Tyrone now came into the open at last. In February 1595 his brother, Art MacBaron, suddenly attacked the fort on the Blackwater which constituted the gateway into Tyrone, captured it, and levelled it with the ground. The Earl himself had taken no part in this affair, but he celebrated it by sweeping into Cavan, burning the county town, and then into Monaghan, where he laid waste the barony of Farney. In May, Cormac MacBaron and Hugh Maguire regained possession of Enniskillen Castle. Now, indeed, it did seem that a fight to a finish was inevitable.

But no. Norris cleared Monaghan and appeared on the Blackwater; Tyrone burned his own strongholds in affright; he was solemnly proclaimed a traitor on the 23rd June 1595; but nothing happened beyond some skirmishing. In Tyrconnell, Red Hugh O'Donnell raised the siege of Ballyshannon and forced Sir Conyers Clifford to retreat at top speed into Connaught.

Tyrone was still further increased in prestige when, in September, Tirlagh Luineach O'Neill died at his castle of Strabane. The old man had lost a great deal of his importance, and had actually resigned the title of " the O'Neill " to his kinsman a short time before. Yet while Tirlagh lived he had never ceased to count, and it was not until he was dead that Tyrone had himself formally elected chief at the traditional site of Tullahogue. Now the latter was supreme in the sentiment of Ulster as he was in fact. There are few men on either side for whom one feels affection or respect, but Tirlagh is one of them. Beside the shifty Tyrone and the bloodthirsty O'Donnell, yes, and beside the savage mountain of ailing flesh that was Fitzwilliam, and the Fentons and Gardiners of Dublin with their ceaselessly itching palms, old sherry-swilling Tirlagh, simple but with a measure of sturdy mother-wit, reasonably honest, at least to his friends, is a gentleman, if not a hero.

Tyrone's gain by the death of Tirlagh was balanced by a loss due to a political slip, very unlike him. He had for some years now depended on the Macdonnells when in need of Scottish aid, as he had mortally offended the Macleans and Campbells by hanging Shane's son, Hugh MacShane, who was allied through his mother to both these great clans. Now he put himself into the black books of the Macdonnells also. It will be recalled that Mabel Bagenal had left him because of his infidelities, because, in his own words, he " affected two other gentlewomen ". These mistresses were Catherine Magennis, daughter of the Lord of Iveagh, and a daughter of Angus Macdonnell. On the death of Mabel the Magennis alliance appeared the more profitable of the two, so he married Catherine and sent the Scots girl, somewhat damaged goods, back to her father. In face of this affront the great majority of the Macdonnells refused to recruit his armies, and left him to his own resources. He

47

now set himself, with the aid of Spanish drill-sergeants, to drill his native gallowglasses and kernes to the Spanish standard; so much to their disgust that they vowed that the worst Englishman was preferable to the best Spaniard. He did succeed, however, thanks to the Spanish instructors, to Spanish gold, and Spanish arms, in finally putting into the field a large and well-found army that was almost purely Irish.

Camden declared that it was difficult to follow Tyrone through " all his shifts and devices ". We may be pardoned for hurrying over those of the next two years. Truce, pardon, new rebellion, fresh truce succeeded one another, Tyrone playing, in general, a waiting game and urgently demanding troops from Spain, while his more vigorous ally, Hugh O'Donnell, raged up and down Connaught, burning and slaying on the lands of the loyalists, Lords Clanrickard and Thomond. Disappointed in Russell, the Queen despatched Lord Burgh to Ireland in early 1597. The new Deputy arrived in the midst of a financial scandal, to find all the corrupt functionaries shaking in their shoes regarding the discoveries due to a recent audit of their accounts. Early in July, with 3000 somewhat indifferent troops, he marched north, forced the passage of the Blackwater, being himself the first man to plunge into the stream, and rebuilt the fort. Tyrone's counter-attacks were defeated largely through the personal courage of Burgh, which shamed his men into standing their ground or re-forming after they had fled. In September Burgh was back again in Dublin; in October on the road to the north again, with provisions for a long campaign in Ulster. But there was to be no campaign; the Deputy was taken suddenly ill, and after eleven days of great suffering he died at Newry.

The autopsy revealed symptoms of poisoning. There is evidence at least to suggest that this able, honest man was murdered, at the instigation of Tyrone, by one of his own Anglo-Irish officers.[1]

Sir John Norris, now President of Munster, died of old wounds soon after the Deputy. In accordance with the usual custom pending the appointment of a new viceroy, the civil government was placed in the hands of two Lords Justices : Archbishop Loftus and the Chief Justice, Sir Robert Gardiner, being appointed. The military command was entrusted to the Earl of Ormonde, with the title of Lieutenant-General. Loftus and Gardiner were, to put it in the most delicate manner, very friendly to Tyrone. Ormonde was not unfriendly. There is no reason to believe the hints of his disloyalty, but " Black Thomas " was Irishman enough to feel a certain sympathy with the rebel. After a conference between the two in December 1597, Tyrone was granted a two months' truce, which was subsequently extended, on very easy terms. In the following April he was accorded a free pardon by the Queen.

No treaty with Tyrone could be counted on unless the Blackwater fort was held by an English garrison, and, on the other hand, no terms would content him while that vital door into his dominions was open. The fort was the Government's Gibraltar in Ireland ; for without it the passage of the river had to be forced in face of strong permanent entrenchments on the left, or west bank. In the words of Fynes Moryson, it was " a great eyesore to him (Tyrone), lying on the chief passage into his country ". In June 1598 he once again surrounded it, vowing that he would not depart until it had fallen.

[1] This evidence comes from both English and Irish sources, and is discussed fully by Lord Ernest Hamilton in *Elizabethan Ulster*, p. 223 *et seq*. There is no definite proof of the crime, which would not, however, have been beyond the Ireland of that moment. Nor can it be said that Tyrone would be open to heavy reproach if, in fact, he instigated the murder. Poison was a weapon of the day, and at a later date Hugh Roe O'Donnell was almost certainly poisoned by English instrumentality. In any case, Burgh had put a price on Tyrone's head.

The fort had a garrison of 300 men, commanded by a resolute veteran soldier of fortune, Captain Thomas Williams, whose gallantry inspired his men to a defence seldom excelled. They routed an attempted escalade, and then fought a far grimmer battle against hunger. They were without provisions and half-starved even when the siege began, having been for some time subjected to a virtual blockade which prevented them from foraging. When they had eaten the last of their horses they subsisted on roots and grasses. The attempt to relieve them was to bring about the greatest victory ever won by Irish over English arms, and to set alight the flame of revolt—a revolt more serious than those of Silken Thomas, of Shane O'Neill, or of Desmond—from Malin Head to Mizzen Head.

On the 12th August a relief force marched out from Newry. Ormonde, who was experienced in Irish warfare and had taken the chief part in the overthrow of Desmond, had been urged to lead it himself. The Lieutenant-General was, however, now an oldish man and had much other business on his hands. He entrusted the expedition to Sir Henry Bagenal, who was burning to be revenged on his brother-in-law. It was not a good choice, Bagenal being an indifferent soldier and lacking the confidence of his officers. The force was, however, stronger and better found than that with which Burgh had been successful the previous year. It consisted of between three and four thousand foot and three to five hundred horse, with four guns. About half were Irish, but they were well trained and equipped, and of the English a number were veterans with continental experience.

Armagh was reached without opposition, but the enemy's forces were seen to be drawn up astride the main highway to Dungannon. Bagenal decided to avoid this, and to march by a track a mile or so to the right of it, which must have followed roughly the course of the present Armagh-Loughall road. Early on the 14th he put his army in motion, in six divisions, marching at 600 yards' distance. These dispositions proved fatal. The leading regiment, harassed on either flank by the kernes and galled by musketeers firing from the cover of woodland, pushed on across the Callan brook, which it passed at a point known, from the colour of the banks and the bed of the stream, as the Yellow Ford. Soon afterwards, struggling out of the boggy ground on to better, it found itself confronted by a trench a mile long. It fought its way across, but was then assailed from all sides. It was almost overwhelmed by the time Bagenal arrived to support it with the second regiment. The unfortunate Marshal had been accused of lack of spirit in action. He was now given no opportunity to show his mettle upon a stricken field; for he was instantly shot dead.

The wildest confusion followed. The guns were stuck fast in the bog, and their teams were picked off by Irish sharpshooters. A great explosion among the powder-wagons increased the chaos. The Irish charged in on all hands, and the three leading regiments were destroyed within a few minutes. Covered by the cavalry, the rear half of the army fell back in disorder to Armagh, while the kernes set about the congenial task of beheading the wounded and plundering the dead.

It was nothing short of a disaster. Twenty-four officers fell upon the field, including one of the few northern Irish loyalists, young Mulmore O'Reilly of Cavan, who was killed while trying to rally the flying mob. Hundreds of Irish soldiers deserted to Tyrone; the rest threw away their arms in the flight. The stores intended for the fort, nearly all the equipment, the colours and the guns were captured. The losses in killed, wounded, and missing were nearly 2000. The army was left a sorry, half-armed remnant, shivering with fear and starving within the walls of Armagh Cathedral.

Ormonde being absent from Dublin when the news arrived, Loftus and Gardiner addressed to Tyrone a craven letter, begging that he would not attack the unhappy rabble at Armagh. The Queen had put up with some humiliation in this Irish business, but never such as this. She declared in anger and contempt that the Council had framed " such a letter to the Traitor after the defeat as never was read the like, either in form or substance, for baseness ". The letter did not reach Tyrone, but, typically, he held his hand. He announced that he would allow the wretched force in Armagh to go free if the Blackwater fort were handed over to him. This was done. Captain Williams, vowing that he would never have abandoned his post but to save the lives of his comrades, handed over the fort, and the remnant of Bagenal's army marched out from Armagh to Newry.

Then the rebellion became general. In every province the Irish hurled themselves upon the castles and minor garrison towns. The two chief leaders of the revolt did not, it is true, themselves move. Their view was not broad enough to reveal to them the scope of their unique opportunity. Tyrone, far the abler of the two, did not see Ireland as a whole, and probably felt that where he himself was concerned he could still patch up a favourable peace, as it was afterwards proved he could. Meanwhile he was lord of all Ulster but Carrickfergus and Newry. O'Donnell, in essence a freebooter, " a warlike, predatory, aggressive plunderer of other's territories ", as his biographer remarks with pride, had harried Connaught till the spoil remaining did not seem worth the taking.

However, both sent troops southward. O'Donnell despatched an expedition to the aid of the rebellious Burkes in Connaught, with the result that Sir Conyers Clifford, the

President of the province, was penned in Athlone. Tyrone's force of 1500, under an Anglo-Irish soldier of fortune named Tyrrell and Owen (" Owney ") MacRory O'More, went down into Munster. The whole of that province rose also, and one James Fitzthomas Fitzgerald, proclaiming himself Earl of Desmond, set himself at the head of the rebels, whose other leaders included Ormonde's kinsmen, Lords Cahir and Mountgarret. The English colonists on the escheated Desmond estates fled in panic for the coast towns, but were in great part intercepted on the road and murdered or horribly mutilated. Those who escaped included the poet, Edmund Spenser, but according to tradition one of his children was burned to death in the flames of his castle.

In Leix and Offaly (named Queen's County and King's County in honour of Mary and Philip) the Marian settlement met with the same fate, though a few castles held out here. Did anyone mark the irony of the fact that the county peopled with English when Philip of Spain was Consort of the Queen of England and renamed in his honour, was ravaged by his allies in the very month of his own death? In the other midland counties, in the Pale itself, affairs were little better. Old Ormonde did his best, but the rebels, well coached by Tyrone, would not meet him in the field. He could do little but hurry to relieve and revictual one town after another, and directly he left any district the flood flowed back in his wake. The Queen let him know that so long as he maintained the more important towns no more would be expected of him. Meanwhile there was some hesitation in England as to the next step.

Robert Devereux, Earl of Essex, had, as we have seen, a hereditary interest in Ireland. To us, who look back upon his whole career, he appears only a brilliant adventurer, who soared up rocket-like to erupt in a shower of golden stars and then disappeared like a rocket-stick in the dark. It is hard for us to realize the magnitude of his position in 1598. Burghley had been spared the news of the Yellow Ford which had comforted his rival Philip of Spain on his deathbed, having died a few days before that battle was fought. He left Essex not merely the chief Court gallant, as he had long been, but the most prominent figure on the Council, the greatest power in the State. Essex had begun to see the finger of fate pointing to him, bidding him go to Ireland. The rebellion there had grown so vast that only a man of his stature could affront it. His honour and glory were engaged. The Queen and Council were not so sure. As more than once before, Elizabeth seemed to dread risking the reputation of the man she loved so well, and whose weaknesses she divined intuitively. For months she blew hot and cold upon the venture. But at last she agreed.

Did he relish the task? His boastings of what he would do with "Tyr-Owen" make it appear so, but there is evidence to the contrary. He was not a fool; he must have heard from many who had fought in Ireland what the difficulties were; and he knew that his own position was not too strong. A failure would be awkward. But then, would not shirking the crisis be awkward too? And how could he fail? He felt boiling within him the splendid vitality that was his one real asset, and vowed he would succeed. "Into Ireland I go," was his brave resolution.

He was to be better furnished than any of his predecessors. Sixteen thousand foot—2000 of them veterans from the Continent under a young captain named Docwra, of whom Ireland was to hear a great deal—and 1400 horse were to constitute his army. Some of the best blood in England eagerly followed him. He was to go as Lord Lieutenant, the first to bear that title since Sussex, nearly forty years before, when the Queen was a young woman and he was unborn. All London turned out to cheer its great man and bless his venture. He reached Dublin on the 15th April 1599.

Then the Council began to talk. It would be unwise to move north against Tyrone till Leinster was pacified. Why, a day's march from the walls of Dublin the O'Byrnes were out in the Wicklow Mountains! (He did not, it would appear, ask whether the O'Byrnes were normally in any other state.) Put Leinster in order first.

There was something in the advice, but there was not the slightest need for the force with which Essex marched out, which was the greater part of all he had available. Also, he changed his mind almost at once. He would drop a detachment to rout out the O'Byrnes and then go down into Munster. All went well at first. There was plenty of skirmishing, but the army was well handled and brushed the Irish aside. At Athy he was met by Ormonde with my Lords Cahir and Mountgarret who had decided that the Queen's was now the safer service. However, Cahir Castle on the Suir was held for the rebels by another Butler, and there was a very pretty little siege and storm. Then he marched on to Waterford, where he was excellently received. There he got news that those infernal O'Byrnes had cut up his detachment—all as Irish as themselves—and chased the remnant at top speed back into Wicklow town. He marched back, beat off the O'Byrnes after quite heavy fighting, and reached Dublin again. Nothing had been done in two months. The Lord Lieutenant was sick in mind and body; the Army was discouraged and much depleted by disease and fatigue; the Queen was angry and ironical by turns. He demanded reinforcements for the north, and got them.

Then came news of a reverse beside which the Wicklow affair was a flea-bite. O'Connor Sligo, who had been with him in Munster, had returned to his castle of Collooney, where he was besieged by O'Donnell. The Lord President of Connaught was ordered to relieve him and to occupy Sligo. Clifford set out for the north in early August. Marching across the Curlieu Mountains by the pass-road from Boyle to Ballinafad he was heavily attacked by the Irish. A panic followed; Clifford himself was shot dead; and the force, after losing heavily, fled headlong back to Boyle. Clifford's head was cut off and sent as a trophy to O'Donnell. The men of Connaught mourned the honest, even-handed Clifford, who had always kept his word to them, whereas O'Donnell had always harried them.[1] But O'Connor Sligo at once submitted to Tyrone, and it may be said that the poor man had small choice in the matter.

Affairs were now at a pretty pass. English prestige had sunk to its nadir. Defeat had followed defeat, and the fame of the victorious Tyrone was ringing all over the Continent. What with casualties, desertions, and the demands of garrison towns, Essex could no longer muster above 4000 troops for open warfare. It was therefore quite out of the question to put a force into Lough Foyle, as he had been ordered to do; he had no more than enough for a direct invasion of Ulster. Moreover, there were ominous mutterings among the troops, whose spirit was thoroughly shaken. The season was far advanced. However, he decided at least to make a demonstration on the Ulster border, and set off for that purpose with his whole force on the 28th August.

After the army had reached Ardee in Louth, Tyrone appeared in greatly superior strength, but did not attack, marching parallel with the English. Presently his henchman, Henry O'Hagan, came in with a flag of truce to propose a parley. This took place on the 8th September at the ford of

---

[1] Clifford was long remembered. When forced to abandon the siege of Ballyshannon Castle in 1595 and almost surrounded, he had led his men out across the Erne by the scattered rocks above the Salmon Leap, losing many who slipped in and were drowned. The Irish generously named the crossing " The Ford of the Heroes ".

Anaghclint, or Bellaclint, on the Lagan.[1]  All that was then
decided was that the two commanders should meet alone
at the same place next day.  And there for half an hour
they conversed in private, Tyrone in the water up to his
horse's belly, Essex a few yards away on dry land.

It was the act either of a madman or of a traitor; there
is no third interpretation.  If Essex had no evil motive in
talking with Tyrone without witness, then he was crazed;
for he opened himself to the gravest suspicions.  If he had
an evil motive, it can only have been treason to the Queen.
And, indeed, evidence was afterwards produced pointing to
treason.  Tyrone, so the story ran, was to take certain action
in Ireland, while Essex prepared the way of James VI of
Scotland to the throne of England.  For us it does not
matter; Essex was on the point of burning his boats.
Another meeting, this time with several followers on each
side, took place next day.  That led to a formal conference.
The upshot was that a truce was signed, to last six weeks,
and renewable by six-weekly periods, but terminable by
fourteen days' notice on either side.  It was as great a
disaster as the Battle of the Yellow Ford.

We may finish quickly with Essex.  Stung beyond what
he could bear by the bitter reproaches of the Queen, eager
to lose sight of the accursed country which had brought
him to shame, he decided to stake all on his personal
magnetism, which had so often won Elizabeth over.
Handing over the government to Archbishop Loftus and
Sir George Carey, the Treasurer, he sailed for England on
the 24th September, reached London on the 28th, hurried
on to Nonsuch, and flung himself into the Queen's presence
before she was dressed or had had her face painted for the

---

[1] Readers who do not know Ireland may perhaps need to be reminded that
this is the Louth Lagan, not the much-better-known river of the same name
which divides Antrim from Down.

day. The end is one of the most famous of stories, but not ours. Trial followed confinement; he was acquitted of the graver charges but deprived of his offices. Then the mad outbreak; apprehension; the second trial, during which his guard was broken down by that matchless legal swordsman, Francis Bacon; the block.

His failure in Ireland could not have been more abject, yet the magic of his name and personality was such that he was long remembered there with something like respect. When the third Earl, afterwards the Roundhead Commander-in-Chief, visited Dublin in 1633, the streets were so thronged that it was difficult to make a way for the carriages, and an old woman cried out as he passed: "Blessed be the time that I live to see a son of thy father!"

## III

## THE VICEROYALTY OF MOUNTJOY

AFTER the departure of Essex the Irish Government, with only the remains of an army and scarce the shadow of authority, lived from hand to mouth. Their chief object was to maintain the truce with Tyrone. Sir William Warren, representing the Council, had several interviews with the Earl, who demanded " a general liberty of religion throughout the kingdom." To us this may appear reasonable; but it was not practically possible in an age when liberty of religion was almost unknown outside France, least of all when the Papacy was leagued with the power which was seeking to destroy the rule of Elizabeth. However, we know from Tyrone's own intercepted letters that it was the last thing he really aimed at. What he did put forward to his Spanish allies as the goal was the " extirpation of heresy "; a little later we find him alluding to Protestants as " pagan beasts ". To Warren he complained that some of his men and his Geraldine friends in the south had been killed by Ormonde in time of cessation. Finally, he broke off negotiations, and in January 1600 marched south, personally to light the torch of rebellion in Munster once more.

Picking up a detachment of rebels in Cavan, he set his course so as to be able on his route to deal with those who had not come out during the earlier stages of his revolt. Westmeath suffered particularly, there being naught left on the lands of the O'Carrolls but " ashes instead of corn and embers in place of mansions ". His main object was to ensure that the Munster chieftains should not only come out but remain out, for which purpose he would take hostages from them, to be executed on the spot if they made terms with the English. On entering County Cork he was met by James Fitzthomas, the *Sugane* ("Straw-rope") Earl of Desmond. The two camped on the Lee above Cork city and sent out parties to ravage the lands of the few who hesitated, while from all parts of Munster the chiefs sent in vows of fidelity and put hostages in the hands of Tyrone. Ormonde watched without being able to interfere.

In this hour of his triumph Tyrone suffered, by the death of a single adherent, an irreparable loss. His son-in-law, Hugh Maguire, had accompanied him to Munster. At the end of February Hugh was out with a small party near the walls of Cork, when there appeared a handful of English horsemen. It was Sir Warham St. Leger and Sir Henry Power, the commissioners for Munster—the newly-appointed Lord President of the province not having yet arrived—with an escort, but out merely for air and exercise. The two parties seem to have been on the top of one another before either saw its enemy. St. Leger fired at Maguire with his pistol and wounded him to death; but with his last force the Irishman drove his half-pike into the body of his foe, who likewise died soon afterwards.

Hugh Maguire was by far the ablest and stoutest warrior of the chieftains in rebellion, neither Tyrone nor O'Donnell being prominent on the field of battle. He was, it may be said, little more than an attractive brigand, but his bravery, good looks, and generosity had impressed themselves upon the minds of his people, and he was really popular in Fermanagh. The shock of his death seems to have caused Tyrone to lose his head; in fact, the statement of the Annalists that he was overcome by " giddiness of spirits " is another phrase for the same symptoms. He had also news of the arrival in Dublin of a new Lord Deputy, together with a new Lord President of Munster; and though the former was an unknown quantity, the reputation of the latter was intimidating. To some extent also the work he had come down to do might be said to be done. At all events, leaving 2000 mercenaries in Munster, he suddenly fled north with 600 picked troops, eluding by forced marches the attempt of Ormonde to intercept him, and reached home in safety.

The new Deputy was Lord Mountjoy; the new President was Sir George Carew. Mountjoy had been proposed for the viceroyalty the year before, but had been objected to by Essex on the ground that he had no military experience except in a subordinate rôle, and that he was rather bookman than soldier. As a fact, Mountjoy had had his share of the smell of powder, and if it was afloat rather than ashore, that was common with the fighting men of Elizabeth's amphibious age. Not yet thirty-seven, he had fought at Zutphen, had built and commanded his own ship against the Armada, and had sailed with Essex to the Azores. His health was poor, but by taking as much care of it as the fussiest of women—extra pairs of stockings, extra waistcoats, an afternoon sleep in his tent directly the day's march was over—he managed to display an activity never equalled by any predecessor and to keep well when everyone about him was going down with fever. If he was a dandy, a gourmet, a bookworm, and an eccentric, many a great captain has been one or the other, though the combination of all four with high military qualities is possibly rare.

He was fortunate in some of the chief subordinates whom he either brought with him or found but recently arrived in the country. Sir George Carew, who crossed to Ireland with him, was a man of forty-five, a typical Devonian of that day, resolute, adventurous but crafty and hindered by few scruples, a master of tactics as Mountjoy was to prove himself a master of strategy, a gunner who chose his own battery positions and laid his own pieces. Unlike Mountjoy he had some previous experience of Ireland. He was one of the closest friends of Sir Robert Cecil, Burghley's son and successor as the Queen's adviser. These two carried on petty intrigues over the head of Mountjoy, but it is only fair to add that neither one nor the other ever failed the Deputy.

Sir Arthur Chichester, born in the same year as Mountjoy and the son-in-law of Perrot, had seen more fighting than any of them. He had commanded a ship against the Armada, accompanied Drake on his last voyage, been a volunteer in the Cadiz Expedition of 1596, and served in more than one campaign on the Continent. As energetic as Carew and, like him, a Devonian, he was marked, at least before the days of his own viceroyalty, by a cold savagery very different from the other's ebullient brutality. While to uninstructed Irish Nationalists Cromwell is the English villain of Irish history, the better read reserve that place for Chichester. But we shall have ample occasion to note the qualities and the extraordinary development of this man, the greatest of Irish viceroys, not excepting Strafford or Mountjoy himself. Chichester had been at Carrickfergus for a year now, with one short interval, and was to stay there until the end of the war, though speedily promoted Major-General of the Army.

The youngest of the party was Sir Henry Docwra, who had hitherto served in Connaught, but was destined for a more serious task. He was perhaps not of the calibre of the other three men, but his personal character was far more attractive, and his is the most likeable figure in Ireland at this moment. His enemies, the Donegal Masters, who are singularly fair historians, call him " an illustrious knight, of wisdom and prudence, a pillar of battle and conflict."

Before sailing, Mountjoy had worked out with the Privy Council the broad lines of the policy he was to pursue. There were to be no more useless progresses up and down the country by the bulk of the army. In the first place Ulster was to be bridled by the occupation of Lough Foyle, to which a force of no less than 4000, chiefly fresh troops from England, was to be despatched by sea under the orders of Sir Henry Docwra. The plan was to establish a strong base in the estuary and thence work southward up the valley of the Foyle and Mourne until the province was almost cut in half by a line of fortresses ; to reduce to submission the peninsula of Inishowen to the west and if possible also O'Cahan's Country, or Coleraine, to the east ; and in general to take every opportunity of weakening both Tyrone and O'Donnell. Either from Docwra's force or elsewhere, a small garrison was subsequently to be placed at Ballyshannon. For the pacification of Munster Carew was to have 3000 foot and 250 horse. There were 1400 foot allotted to Sir Richard Savage in Connaught, and 700 to Chichester at Carrickfergus.

This left about 5000 men at the Deputy's immediate disposal; but after deducting the Leinster garrisons and the usual " dead pays "—non-existent men for whom pay was drawn by the company commanders—he would be unable to take the field with above 2000 foot and 800 horse. Given a force established in Lough Foyle; given ready co-operation by the local commanders when he campaigned in their areas; given that the field army was competently handled, this was about the ideal strength for Ireland, neither too weak for safety nor too unwieldy for rapid movement and easy supply. Should there be a Spanish landing the case would, of course, be different.

Fynes Moryson, who became Chief Secretary to the Lord Deputy after his predecessor had been killed in action, carefully enumerates the measures which made Mountjoy so successful. He restored discipline and, anticipating Cromwell in this, encouraged the practice of religious worship. He made a valuable asset of his personal charm, inspiring by his affability and familiarity those of his subordinates whose hearts seemed to be really in the business. A smile and a kindly word from such a master were in themselves worth striving for. In the earlier actions he deliberately exposed himself time after time to hearten his men, and perhaps to mark the contrast between himself on the one hand and Tyrone and O'Donnell, who did not lead from in front, on the other. He blooded the troops with carefully prepared easy successes on a small scale, so that the army should forget the defeats of the past and regain its confidence. His strategical dispositions, in part, it is true, laid down for him by the English Privy Council, were admirable. They left no quarter unthreatened, and allowed no chieftain to march abroad from his own country without the risk of its being overrun in his absence. Instead of making two or three annual expeditions, and those in good weather, he kept the field virtually the whole year round, harassing the rebels and wearing out their cattle by driving them to and fro, cutting down their corn before it ripened, and burning their granaries. Every difficult pass where he might be surprised he cleared of woodland once he had possession of it. These passes and the fords where the main routes crossed deep rivers he protected by forts wherever possible. He forbade all parleys, gave pardons with a grudging hand, but faithfully kept his word to all whom he did admit to mercy. Lastly, and not least important, he was sparing in his speech, so that his designs and views were not easily to be gathered. In short, he realized from the first, with an insight amounting to genius, the true counters to the Irish methods of war.

While Carew set out for his province of Munster, Docwra sailed with a considerable fleet from Carrickfergus for the Foyle. He took with him equipment not merely for a garrison but for a settlement, including beds for a hospital, and a number of masons and carpenters to build houses. On the 13th May 1600 he entered the lough. His landing-party met with little or no opposition, and he quickly made defensible and garrisoned the ruined fort of Culmore, covering the mouth of the river. While this work was in progress he seized Elagh Castle, which the owner, Sir John O'Dogherty, had begun to dismantle; dropped a smaller garrison to repair and hold it, and went on to Derry.

Once, years before, in the days of Sidney, the English had occupied this place; but they had been forced to evacuate it, and there was now no trace of their stay. Nor was there anything but ruins to mark a little town that had in still more distant times stood upon this easily defensible site— forty acres of ground, high and dry, but virtually an island, with the Foyle on one side and a bog on the other. With stones from the ruins, with timber cut from O'Cahan's country to the east, no stick of which was brought in " that was not well fought for ", Docwra consolidated his position.

At this risky moment he was not forgotten by his chief. Mountjoy marched up to the Blackwater, drew Tyrone down to meet him, and detained him there until word came that Docwra was fairly well established. Then, after a skirmish in the Moyry Pass on the road to Dundalk, he returned to Dublin. Tyrone marched back to threaten Derry, but did not venture to attack.

We cannot, unfortunately, go very deeply into the complicated and amusing relations of Docwra with the local magnates, which he has himself so graphically described.

We have spoken of his merits; we must now mention his weakness, which was gullibility. It has to be realized that his only regular means of communication with the outside world was by sea. Supply ships brought him from time to time powder and shot, kettles and tools, flour and beer. Fish were abundant. But for meat he was dependent on what cattle he could buy or get driven in from the lands of his neighbours. It was therefore doubly important that he should obtain Irish allies: first, to break up Tyrone's confederation; and, secondly, to feed his force. Surely enough, the allies appeared. On the eastern side of the Foyle there was for long no sign from Donnell Ballagh O'Cahan, Lord of Coleraine, but his brother Rory arrived with a detachment. There were likewise offers of assistance from south and west. First, Sir Art O'Neill, son of Tirlagh Luineach, came in from Dunalong, bringing few men but—true chip of the old block—an enormous thirst. His modest price for his support was possession of all the dominions of Tyrone. Then there was a friendly approach from Sir John O'Dogherty, Lord of Inishowen, as thirsty as Art but rather more useful because he possessed plenty of cattle. More interesting and promising was the appearance of two brothers who seemed to represent the power behind O'Dogherty: two delightful young men whose handsome and patently honest countenances won the Governor's heart —Hugh Boy and Phelim Reagh MacDavitt. Finally, after some delay, there appeared a fighting man more formidable than all the rest put together, the truculent, gallant, ambitious and boastful Neill Garve O'Donnell.

So, for a time, there was no shortage of cattle; many a head being driven in from Hugh Roe O'Donnell's herds by his kinsman Neill Garve. Yet Docwra soon began to discover that his Irish allies were not all they might have been. Sir Art was useless, but at least he gave no trouble, speedily drinking himself to death. Then, however, the Governor found that the charming Hugh Boy was plotting with O'Dogherty to deliver Culmore Fort into the hands of Hugh Roe. Strange as it may appear, Docwra forgave him as a reward for other services, and soon believed in him as strongly as ever. O'Dogherty eventually followed Art to a drunkard's grave. Art himself was replaced by his brother Cormac, greatly superior to him but with the same great expectations. Neill Garve, Cormac, and Hugh Boy hated one another like poison, and each constantly accused the other of treacherous designs, quite possibly with truth.

We may smile at Docwra's disillusionments, but we must not forget the magnitude of his achievements. Before the year was out the whole peninsula of Inishowen was completely under his control, and this without the usual wasting with fire and sword; for it was covered with corn and flax. He had captured from Hugh Roe the fortress of Lifford, the gateway across the Foyle river between Tyrone and Donegal, and had established Neill Garve there. He had sent a party across the Swilly and seized the old monastery of Rathmullan in the country of the MacSwineys, vassals of Hugh Roe, the maintenance of this place being a striking example of the impotence of the Irish against walls. In the following year he or his Irish allies captured Castlederg, Newtown (now Newtownstewart), and Omagh, in the very heart of the enemy's country, and garrisoned them. He had bearded and humiliated Tyrone and O'Donnell at their own doors.

Chichester at Carrickfergus had meanwhile also had his successes, though of another sort. His policy was for the moment one of extermination pure and simple. Though, by comparison with Docwra, he had a small force and could not afford garrisons, he speedily made himself master of all

South Antrim and North Down. During the winter of 1600 he built a fleet at Edenduffcarrick on Lough Neagh, his biggest boat being a 30-tonner. In May 1601 he began to raid Tyrone across the huge lough.

" I have launched the great boat, and have twice visited Tyrone with her, and often with lesser," he writes from Massarene to Mountjoy in May. " We have killed, burnt, and spoiled all along the lough within four miles of Dungannon, from whence we returned hither yesterday; in which journeys we have killed above one hundred people of all sorts, besides such as were burnt, how many I know not. We spare none of what quality or sex soever, and it hath bred much terror in the people, who heard not a drum nor saw not a fire there of long time. The last service was upon Patrick O'Quin, whose house and town was burnt, wife, son, children, and people slain, himself (as is now reported unto me) dead of a hurt received in flying from his house, and other gentlemen which received blows in following us in our return to the boat; and Tyrone himself lay within a mile of this place, but kept himself safe, sending 100 shot to know the matter, which he seemed to marvel at."

The savagery of this letter needs no comment. It is to be recalled, however, that Chichester's methods were those of his age, especially when the enemy practised guerrilla warfare. They are hardly more repulsive than the callousness or timidity of Tyrone, who let a small party — Chichester's whole fleet would carry only sixty men—thus destroy one of his adherents without coming to his aid. They certainly weakened the Earl's prestige. That of a successful rebel gathers strength like a snowball, but often declines as swiftly in adversity. It was significant that " every catching knave " in the neighbourhood was now volunteering for service against Tyrone. Chichester did not think that they were in general worth their pay, but at least if Irishman fought Irishman then all the casualities would be Irish, in his view the most satisfactory sort of warfare. After a victory in Upper Clandeboye, gained chiefly with the aid of native *bonaghts*, over Tyrone's people, he wrote with grim humour that " it was good service on both sides; for never an honest man was slain."

Meanwhile the Lord Deputy's field army had swung like a pendulum up and down the country. Leinster he had completely brought to heel. He had made expedition after expedition into Ulster, though he had never yet brought Tyrone to a general action, the latter preferring to evacuate the strongest fortified positions rather than risk an English attack. The stiffest fighting was during the return from one of these campaigns, when the Irish attempted to dispute the way at Carlingford and were very roughly handled. In June 1601 Mountjoy garrisoned Armagh, chased Tyrone back from his lines on the Blackwater, and built a new fort on the river. The one and only Captain Thomas Williams was left in command, though his leg was broken and in splints. In Lecale the Lord Deputy left Colonel Sir Richard Moryson, brother to Fynes, with 500 men. Members of the clans of MacMahon, Magennis, and O'Reilly came in, though some of them were refused pardons till they had done work to merit them. Affairs were certainly improving, though Tyrone had still 4000 men in his own country alone, as large a force as the Deputy's field army.

From Munster, too, the news was good. Everywhere Carew was breaking up the rebel bands, whose remnants were hiding in the woods. The Sugane Earl and the MacCarthy More were prisoners in the Tower. Four thousand men had come in to receive pardons. In short, it seemed likely that the rebellion would everywhere be extinguished within a little—if the Spaniards did not come. If they did come, who could say what would happen, how much of the work of the last two years would be undone in a day?

That was the crux of the situation. For years now the rebels had been enduring with the hope of Spanish aid. So far all that Philip III had done for his allies had been to send two ships with gold and munitions, but letters so non-committal that O'Donnell raved with fury when he read them. Other messages in plenty passed between Tyrone and Philip or Irish priests in Spain, and some were captured. Spies brought frequent news of the assembly of fleets at Cadiz or Corunna. It was much put about that the Spaniards would sail in May 1601, but there was no sign of them then. Cecil, whose intelligence was good, thought they would come that year, but to a number of not more than about 5000. He held troops and shipping ready to move to Cork or Waterford, not sending them only because the Spaniards might after all try Limerick, or even Galway.

News that a large fleet was at sea reached Cecil on the 12th August, but it was then lost to sight and not heard of again for a month. The weather was very bad, and possibly the fleet, or part of it, put back into Spanish harbours in the interval.[1] In any case it could not be taken for granted that it was bound for Ireland; it might be for the Low Countries, where active operations were in progress. On the 14th September Carew had word that it was close at hand. Then on the 23rd, when Mountjoy and Carew were staying together for a conference at Ormonde's Castle of Kilkenny, a messenger rode in to say that the long-delayed

[1] Cecil's letter of the 12th from Windsor did not reach Carew at Cork until the 4th September: an exceptionally long time. The delay was doubtless due to the storms which troubled the Spanish fleet.

invasion was come at last. A large Spanish fleet was off the Old Head of Kinsale. The first question that flashed into the mind of Mountjoy was how long it would take to send down into Munster supplies sufficient for the biggest army he could put into the field, including the reinforcements now on their way. Carew coolly replied that all the year's supply of biscuit in his province was intact; he had, in modern jargon, issued his troops with money " in lieu of rations ", in anticipation of just this emergency. At the news the delighted Mountjoy jumped up from his chair and embraced him.

The Spaniards made for Cork, but, the wind falling off as they entered the great harbour, they ran out again and put into Kinsale. Once again the elements had favoured Elizabeth. The capture of Cork with its supplies would have been disastrous, though the city had a garrison big enough to make a fight of it. At Kinsale there was no question of opposition. The little garrison evacuated the place, and the Spaniards began to land on the 23rd, the very day that news of their arrival reached Kilkenny. They were a well-equipped, highly-trained force of over 4500 men under a distinguished commander, Don Juan del Aquila. They brought ashore a few guns and great quantities of supplies and equipment, including 1600 saddles on which to mount their cavalry when the Irish had provided horses. Then their fleet set sail for Spain.

They had come rather late. Not till they landed did they learn that the Sugane Earl and the MacCarthy More were prisoners and that the heart of the rebellion in Munster had been broken. However, Tyrone had vowed that he would at once hasten to their aid, so, while awaiting his coming, they set about the fortification of Kinsale with the customary skill of their nation. Their commander issued a proclamation to the Irish that Elizabeth had been

71

deprived of her sovereignty, and her subjects absolved from fidelity to her by the Pope.

The spirit of Mountjoy was one of calm, unboastful confidence. He bade Cecil not worry about what happened anywhere in Ireland except at Kinsale.

"If we beat them," he wrote, "let it not trouble you though you hear all Ireland doth revolt, for (by the grace of God) you shall have them all return presently with halters about their necks: if we do not, all providence bestowed on any other place is vain. . . . I apprehend a world of difficulties with as much comfort as ever poor man did, because I have now a fair occasion to show how prodigal I will be of my life in every adventure that I shall find to be for the service of my dear Mistress, unto whom I am confident God hath given me life to do acceptable service, which when I have done I will sing *Nunc dimittis.*"

And a few days later, having painted the blackest possibilities, an invasion of England by combined Spanish and Irish forces, he added:

"And now, Sir, that you know (as I hope) the worst, I cannot dissemble how confident I am to beat these Spanish Dons as well as ever I did our Irish Macs and Os."

The essential was that Mountjoy should be at Kinsale before the arrival of the Ulster rebel army. In this he very easily succeeded. He had his forces concentrated at Cork by mid-October. At the end of the month an English fleet under Admiral Sir Richard Leveson arrived with heavy siege guns and entrenching tools. The Queen forgot her penury for once and used Mountjoy nobly. Two thousand troops arrived with the squadron, followed by another thousand under Lord Thomond. Mountjoy began the siege in earnest, simultaneously bombarding Kinsale and fortifying his own camp against intervention by Tyrone.

What, meanwhile, were the Ulster leaders doing? O'Donnell, indeed, set out fairly quickly. But, after he had been ferried across the Shannon and had entered Tipperary, he sat down to wait for Tyrone, who he very reasonably expected would soon be on his heels. To pass away the time, his eulogists the Four Masters tell us, his men "continued plundering, burning, and ravaging the country round them." Then, by a daring night-march over a frozen bog, he slipped round Carew, who had been sent to intercept him, and moved down into Cork.

At least he had shown some initiative, which was more than could be said for Tyrone. Never was the latter more timorous than at this hour when all his hopes were crowned. He havered and debated whether or not he should go in person. Finally he decided to, but he did not move at all till November, nor arrive on the scene of action till December. By that time affairs were going none too well for the Spaniards. One great sally by half their force had failed after initial success, and they had been beaten back with loss. They had plenty of biscuit and rice, but little other food, and were galled by an unceasing cannonade. Meanwhile another expedition had sailed, but a portion of it had been driven back by unfavourable winds. Six small ships had turned up, but, finding the English fleet in Kinsale harbour, had made for Castlehaven, where they landed 700 men. Leveson went round with four ships of war and promptly sank five out of their six vessels, but was unable to effect a landing.

With Tyrone's arrival besiegers became besieged, and Mountjoy's position was truly an anxious one. In front of him was the Spanish Army, which still had nearly 4000 men on their feet, whose vigour and determination were shown by almost nightly sorties; behind were Tyrone and O'Donnell with 6500, including 200 Spaniards from Castlehaven under Alonzo del Campo; his own numbers were now reduced by sickness, battle casualties, and some desertions, to 6000. Worse still, he was cut off from Cork, his main supply depot, and was so short of forage that when the crisis came he was on the point of sending away his cavalry. A lesser man would have abandoned the siege. Mountjoy put aside for the time being the project of storming Kinsale, but he fought grimly on, never ceasing to bombard the town with guns mounted on high platforms, though his trenches were flooded, his men were dying at the rate of fifteen a day, and belts had to be drawn tighter and tighter.

Aquila had no difficulty in getting messages through to Tyrone, urging him to attack and promising that he would at the same time fall upon the English with his whole strength. The notion of offensive action was, as usual, abhorrent to the Earl. He would rather have sat down and continued to blockade the besiegers till they were forced to draw off. There was, however, a good deal of risk in this; for Mountjoy's and Leveson's guns were playing havoc with Kinsale. O'Donnell, too, declared that he could no longer endure the shame of leaving the Spaniards in the lurch. Eventually it was decided that the English camp should be assaulted simultaneously by Tyrone and the garrison of Kinsale at midnight on the 23rd December.

Treachery and love of liquor have marred many an Irish plan, and they combined to do so here. Very few Ulster notabilities had followed Tyrone and O'Donnell, but in their camp was one who is an old acquaintance of ours, Bryan MacHugh MacMahon, the unsuccessful candidate for Monaghan in Fitzwilliam's day. Bryan MacHugh was athirst, and the whisky was out, as well it might be in a wet and stormy December. He recalled that his boy had once been page to the Lord President, also that he knew a commander named Taaffe in the English camp. He sent over a lad to ask Taaffe to procure a bottle of aquavitæ from Carew, who he supposed was likely to be well provided. Looking at Carew's portrait we see that Bryan MacHugh was a good judge; the Lord President was certainly one who would not let himself run short of such little comforts. The bottle was sent. In return came a message of gratitude, bidding the Lord President stand upon his guard, and announcing the hour of the attack.

The English stood to arms, and a flying column a thousand strong was drawn up ready for an instant move. But the hours passed without sign of the enemy. The Spaniards in the town evidently concluded that there would be no relief and that the Irish had failed them; they remained quiet. It was a clear night with flashes of sheet-lightning, more suitable to midsummer than to midwinter. A little before dawn the scouts saw the glow of the Irish matches, while ever and anon the lightning played upon a pikehead so that it burned like a torch. What had happened was the Irish guides had gone astray and the army had arrived some six hours late.

Leaving Carew in command of the siege, the Lord Deputy moved out with 400 cavalry and the flying column, followed later by some further troops, in all perhaps 2000 men, to meet the enemy. For the first time since the rebellion had begun the two sides were about to try con-clusions in the open, and Mountjoy must have felt a grim satisfaction, even if the odds were three to one against him. On the other hand, Alonzo del Campo, the Spanish com-mander with Tyrone, was delighted when the dawn showed him the weakness of the English, and urged Tyrone to launch an instant assault. Again that fatal hesitation!

75

O'Donnell, the rear-guard commander, was still wandering about lost, and, the Earl alleged, his own men were disordered by their night march. Instead of attacking he retired, to put a bog between himself and the English. The withdrawal increased the disorder. Suddenly the Marshal, Sir Richard Wingfield, in command of the English cavalry, and young Lord Clanrickard, making a detour round the bog, dashed against the Irish horse. The latter standing firm, Wingfield, following cavalry tactics not then uncommon, wheeled at the last moment and drew off. Then, hoping that the enemy's nerve had been shaken, he charged again. This time the Irish cavalry, though composed of the heads of septs and other gentlemen, broke shamefully and seems to have ridden into its own infantry. After that the fight was quickly over. A blind, crazy panic seized the Irish, and the apparently first-class army which Tyrone had taken years to form and train, fled wildly from the field. The Spanish contingent, less fleet of foot and living up to their reputation for steadiness, stood and fought it out, at first aided by some of Tyrrell's mercenaries, then, when these too had fled, alone. This stand must have saved the lives of many of their allies, but it was fatal to themselves. Finally, all were killed but about forty, who surrendered. Then the English cavalry rode after the flying mob, hacking and hewing, cutting them down in swaths. A full twelve hundred were killed outright; the number might have been doubled but that the English horses were nearly starved, and were ridden to a standstill after a pursuit of a mile and a half. The total English casualties were about a dozen.

Next day Tyrone fled northward at such a speed that he littered his route with dead men and horses, while the kinsmen of those he had butchered on his way down had the sweet satisfaction of treading his wounded and stragglers down into bogholes. O'Donnell and some other notables embarked at Castlehaven on a newly-arrived Spanish ship and sailed for Spain. Within a week Aquila was treating with Mountjoy. On the 2nd January he undertook to surrender not only Kinsale, but Castlehaven, Baltimore, and Dunboy, which were held by detachments of the second expeditionary force. He was soon on the best of terms with the victors, making merry at the expense of his former allies. He had been sent by his royal master, he said, to support two *Condes* (Tyrone and O'Donnell). Now he found no *Condes* in *rerum natura*; they had dissolved. He was therefore relieved from his mission. Irish writers down to the present day have dubbed him coward and traitor, but there is very little doubt who failed at Kinsale.

The terms to the Spaniards were the most honourable. They were shipped off to Spain as soon as Spanish ships could be sent for the purpose, merely undertaking not to bear arms against the Queen before they actually reached home. Almost immediately after their surrender Mountjoy intercepted a letter from Philip to Aquila, bidding him hold out because a fresh expedition was about to sail. The news from Ireland put a stop to that.

There is little more to tell until we reach the scene of the prologue. Carew had to finish off the business in the south, and had hard fighting. The Lord Deputy returned to Ulster in the summer, and again during the winter in 1602. With the aid of Docwra and Chichester, with a fresh chain of forts, he gradually reduced Tyrone to the last gasp. Elizabeth had long been determined to fight Tyrone this time to a finish, but as she felt death drawing nigh she relented. Perhaps towards the end her mind was slightly deranged; certainly one postcript in her own hand to a letter addressed to the Lord Deputy reads like it.

Anyhow, this war had cost an impoverished kingdom a million and a half of money, and probably the lives of hundreds of thousands. In Cheshire there was hardly a family that had not to mourn a husband or a son. She was weary of the slaughter. And after all, she could afford to be generous because she had won; she had beaten Spain in Ireland as she had beaten Spain upon the seas. There was, of course, still anxiety in Ireland lest another Spanish fleet should appear, but Cecil declared that the Spaniards would not come again. "The Queen," says Sir Thomas Stafford, editor of Carew's history, "did seal up the rest of all her worthy acts with this accomplishment, as if she had thought that her task would be unfinished, and tomb unfurnished, if there could not be deservedly engraven thereon, 'PACATA HIBERNIA.'" Despite all her errors, that could now be written. She could die in peace.

# Book Two

## THE FLIGHT OF THE EARLS

---

### I

### TYRONE IN ENGLAND

THE greater part of Ulster, when the Earl of Tyrone returned to the north, lay in the silence of exhaustion after one of the most terrible of wars. In the eastern parts famine had followed upon the devastations practised by Mountjoy and Chichester. The corpses of folk who had starved to death lay upon the highways. From Fynes Moryson we have that famous and gruesome story of the band of old hags who enticed little girls to their company, killed them, and ate their flesh. Only the kites and the wolves were fat, and the wolves had become so emboldened by lack of resistance that they pulled down grown men in the open country and in broad daylight. This land would take several years to recover, especially as many of the inhabitants had drifted south in search of food and showed no signs of returning. Tyrone must have reflected that his financial prospects for some time to come were not good. It has been alleged that the famine conditions described by Moryson and others extended over all Ulster, but there is no proof that they existed beyond Down, South Antrim, and East Tyrone.

The Earl of Tyrone, at least, had no difficulties to face apart from the miserable state of his country and the defiant attitude of some of his own vassals; for he had no rival.

In Donegal and Fermanagh the case was different. In the former there was Sir Neill Garve O'Donnell—recently knighted by Mountjoy for gallant service in the field— insistently demanding his reward. In the latter Connor Roe, once the "Queen's Maguire," and now since the Queen's death generally known as the "English Maguire", expected the lordship of the county and perhaps an English title too. He had deserved well of the Government, even if his exploits had not equalled those of Neill Garve. But were the appointments which they considered they had merited likely to be popular, to make for future peace? That was the question which concerned Mountjoy. For Fermanagh there was also a "Rebel Maguire" candidate in the person of the late Hugh's brother, Cuconnaught, as handsome and dashing a young man as Hugh had been. Here the Lord Deputy did the best he could, and not too ill perhaps. He provisionally divided the country between Connor Roe and Cuconnaught, allotting to each three and a half of its seven baronies.

Had he done as well by Sir Neill Garve in Donegal his honour would have benefited, and some future troubles might have been averted. Neill Garve had never left any doubt as to the prize he was playing for in his support of Docwra's Derry settlement. Without him that settlement could scarcely have continued to exist. His merits, too, had been emphasized by the behaviour of others. Poor Docwra's disillusionments had indeed been cruel. Cormac O'Neill, son of Tirlagh Luineach, had gone over to Tyrone. Then a certain MacGilson, "trusted and beloved of all men", who had taken over Cormac's Irish troops, suddenly turned on the English soldiers with whom his followers shared the garrison of Newtown and murdered them to a man. Another of Docwra's Irish captains made an attempt to seize Castlederg, but fortunately failed. "The mere instigation of the devil!" declared the astounded Governor. The devil may have had a hand in it, but the main factor was undoubtedly the Spanish landing, of which the Irish had heard and Docwra had not. Hugh Boy MacDavitt, once again the apple of the Governor's eye, had behaved none too well, but had not gone as far as active treachery. What would have happened in his case we do not know; for he was soon afterwards murdered by a band of outlaws, to Docwra's great grief. He left an equally charming younger brother, Phelim Reagh, whom we shall meet again.

So, all the favourites had failed. Meanwhile the un-popular, the mistrusted, the "rough" Neill Garve had been the intelligence agent, the caterer, and—outside walled forts—the fighting arm of the force based on Derry. With his own hand he had slain Manus, Hugh Roe's brother, and routed his followers. In May 1601 he had given warning that Tyrone was on his way to raid the cattle grazing about the fort of Dunalong. He had then gone out himself and ambushed the assailants, killed a large number of them, and personally chased their leader for six miles, his lance almost pricking the rump of the Earl's horse, while pursuer howled insults at pursued, bidding him turn and strike one blow an he were a gentleman. Tyrone, who had no false pride in such matters and was, to do him justice, old enough to have been O'Donnell's father, had been saved by his horse's legs. Then again, in August, Neill Garve had with the aid of three English companies occupied Donegal Castle and gallantly stood a siege by his kinsman Hugh Roe until the latter marched off to the aid of the Spaniards at Kinsale. Neill Garve was restless, he was uncouth, he was importunate, and he was not wholly trustworthy; but he was indispensable. So much so, that the Lord Deputy had definitely promised him the succession to Donegal, with certain reservations. That we have in writing.

Of course, there was " the public good ". Hugh Roe O'Donnell's next brother Rory had been a rebel, but not a very prominent one, and it seemed possible that Donegal would lie quieter under him than under the headstrong and turbulent Neill Garve. Hugh himself had died in Spain, probably of poison, in the summer of 1602. While the Lord Deputy was considering the situation, Neill Garve very unwisely proclaimed himself " the O'Donnell " in Donegal. Rory attacked him, and he was forced to take refuge with his old patron Docwra in Derry, where the Deputy ordered that he should be confined. Given his parole by the kindly Docwra, he broke it, galloped away, and disappeared. Mountjoy now had the excuse for which he had probably been waiting. He decided to recommend Rory as the heir to Donegal.

" The public good—the old song ! " said Docwra afterwards of this and other like matters. If it was old then, it is older still now. It is not by any means exclusively English, as readers of Monsieur Bergeret will realize, but it has been sung *ad nauseam* by the English in Ireland. The viceroys of the sixteenth and seventeenth centuries are linked to those of the early twentieth, and their chief secretaries, by the detestable and useless practice of buying off enemies at the expense of friends. They thus earned only the contempt of their enemies and the disgust of their friends, while, as time went on, the latter became harder and harder to find.

Neill Garve afterwards made his peace and, two years after these events, under the administration of Chichester, was assigned 13,000 acres, mostly ancestral lands, in the Finn valley, but excluding the new town of Lifford. To a man of his ambitions, and indeed of his achievements, this was a preposterous reward. He was converted from a warm friend to a bitter enemy of the Government by the Government's ingratitude and failure to stand by its word.

This episode was unfortunate if for no other reason than that it disgusted and discouraged Docwra, whose honour was affected by it. He was next to be hit by failure to implement a joint promise made by himself and Chichester. Donnell Ballagh O'Cahan, Lord of Coleraine, had taken part in the early stages of Tyrone's rebellion, but had come in before him. By the terms of his submission he was to be free of Tyrone's overlordship; and he now, therefore, repudiated all claims the Earl had upon him as *uriaght* or chief vassal. Once again Mountjoy, as representing the Government, was inclined to favour the new protégé, Tyrone, despite the strong protests of Docwra. This matter was, however, left unsettled pending the return of Tyrone, who was to pay a visit to the King in England.

The drama of the rebellion was over, and the chief English actors, Mountjoy and Carew, were eager to make their bows and quit the stage. The trouble in Munster having subsided, there was nothing to keep either of them any longer in Ireland, since the former was intensely anxious to return to his mistress, and Cecil was equally anxious to have Carew by his side. The Lord Deputy, while still in the south, had been informed that he had been created Lord Lieutenant and chosen one of the Privy Council of England, and that, having appointed a Deputy, he was to return, bringing Tyrone with him. On the 1st June 1603 Sir George Carey,[1] the Treasurer at War, was sworn Lord Deputy in the Church of the Holy Trinity. Next day

[1] Not, of course, to be confounded, as he sometimes is, with Sir George Carew, Lord President of Munster, who had already gone. The two names were pronounced alike. It is also to be noted that Carey was not Mountjoy's "deputy", though the first intention seems to have been that he should be, but the King's.

Mountjoy sailed for Holyhead with Tyrone, Rory O'Donnell, and their suites in the naval pinnace *Tramontana*.

After so many perils of the wars, in which members of his Staff had been constantly hit by his side, his very greyhound shot dead as it trotted at his horse's feet, his horses killed under him, Mountjoy came very near to a grave beneath the seas in that crossing. As the *Tramontana* ran under all sail through a dense mist there was on a sudden a harsh outcry of multitudes of gulls and a flapping of wings about the ship. Straining his eyes forward the captain saw looming above him the great black rocks of the Skerries. He bellowed to the helmsman: " Aloof (luff) for life! " By instant obedience the helmsman saved the ship, which just slipped past unharmed. So close was the shave that the boat slung over the stern actually struck a rock. Preserved from destruction, the *Tramontana* found her way round the north coast of Anglesey into Beaumaris Bay.

The party then set out for London, the Lord Lieutenant having to protect Tyrone from the Welsh populace, and especially from women mourning husbands and sons lost in the Irish wars, who pelted him with stones and mud. They stopped at Mountjoy's house at Wanstead to recover from the journey, and then went on to Hampton Court.

Their reception was splendid. To Mountjoy the spoils of the victor were not stinted. He was sworn to the Privy Council, appointed Master of the Ordnance, given a grant of £400 a year—the equivalent of at least eight times that amount to-day—and granted lands in Lecale with other estates in the Pale which would fall to the Crown on the death, without heirs male, of the Countess of Kildare. He was created Earl of Devonshire, Tyrone being present at the ceremony in the great hall. He was promised the full superintendence of Irish affairs, all despatches to and from the Lord Deputy passing through his hands as Lord Lieutenant. As he was also to draw the major portion of the Deputy's stipend, he might reckon himself nobly done by. He had, as it proved, less than three years to enjoy these honours and emoluments.

So much for the victor. The vanquished had no reason to complain. Tyrone was most graciously received by the King, who confirmed his pardon and the restitution of his lands, including—not specifically but by implication—the disputed territory of Coleraine. So much was made of him that those who had served against him, and recalled how the Government had fulminated against " the Traitor Tyrone ", could scarce believe eyes or ears.

" I have lived," exclaims Sir John Harrington, " to see that damnable rebel Tyrone brought to England, honoured, and well liked. Oh, what is there that does not prove the inconstancy of worldly matters ? How I did labour after that knave's destruction ! I adventured perils by sea and land, was near starving, ate horseflesh in Munster, and all to quell that man, who now smileth in peace at those who did hazard their lives to destroy him; and now doth Tyrone dare us old commanders with his presence and protection."

Rory O'Donnell did well too. On the 4th September he was created Earl of Tyrconnell and granted the county of that name, except for the Church lands, the castle and town of Ballyshannon, and a thousand acres adjoining the fishery in the Erne. In his case, however, it was a condition of the grant that he should renounce all claims to over-lordship of O'Dogherty's country, the peninsula of Inish-owen, to which his ancestors pretended. Young Sir Cahir O'Dogherty, son of that Sir John who had died at Derry, had also repaired to Court to plead his cause. He profited by the King's benignant mood, receiving a patent for all such lands as had been granted by Queen Elizabeth to his father, the Church lands again excepted, to be held by knight's service. James was especially gracious to him. The fort at Culmore was excepted from the grant, as it was required for the defence of Derry, but the King gave his royal promise that in time of peace and " so often as the castle of Culmore shall be relinquished by the King or the governors of the said castle, the said Sir Cahir and his heirs shall have the *custodiam* of the castle and lands and fishings, without rent." The atmosphere of the Court could not have been more genial: for the past, oblivion; for the present, friendliness; for the future, hope. There was just one empty seat at the festal board to which some eyes may have turned. Cuconnaught Maguire might have come if he would, but he was not of the stuff whereof repentant prodigals are made.

And yet all was not quite so happy as appeared on the surface. While Tyrone was being fêted he was also being watched. When the Court was at Hampton he lodged at Kingston. Evidence, sworn before a Justice of the Peace, was brought to Lord Devonshire that a certain Father James Archer, of the Society of Jesus, had been seen to dismount at Tyrone's door, and that " sometimes in the apparel of a courtier, at other times like a farmer ", he frequented the company of other Irishmen then in England, including some who were lodged in the Tower.

Now, the fact that the Earl saw a priest would not in itself have been noteworthy; there were plenty of English Catholics who did so without incurring displeasure. But Archer was no ordinary priest. He was considered by the English the most dangerous of his cloth. It was by his instrumentality that, just after Mountjoy's arrival in Ireland in 1600, Ormonde had been kidnapped during a parley with the rebel leader, Owney O'More.[1] Father Archer's warm admirer and co-religionist, Philip O'Sullivan Bear, admits that he was " very bitter against the heretic enemy" and infinitely useful to the rebel leaders, including Tyrone, " by his zeal, advice, pains, and industry ". If, therefore, the visitor who was alternately courtier and farmer was really Father Archer, he was bad company for the Earl; if he was not, the Lord Lieutenant had none the less been led to believe that he was and could not fail to be unfavourably impressed.

The season of festivity and reconciliation was now over, and the Earls went back to Ireland and to hard realities. Tyrconnell, arriving in Dublin apparently in early September 1603, celebrated his return by marrying Brigid, daughter of the 12th Earl of Kildare—a fine match. He was, however, for some time unable to return to his own country, where Sir Neill Garve had established himself. He had therefore to remain in the Pale, " very meanly followed ", a sad disillusionment to a new-made peer. In Fermanagh also there was unrest, the rivals Connor Roe and Cuconnaught Maguire being engaged in a quarrel virtually amounting to open war.

There was no such obstacle in the path of Tyrone, but the misery of his country and the flight of many of his tenants to better lands made his old quarters at Dungannon appear unattractive, and in the spring of 1604 we find him temporarily settled in Drogheda, outside his own territories. Thence there issued a stream of complaints. He was at odds with his half-brother Sir Tirlagh MacHenry O'Neill,[2] who

---

[1] Possibly no treachery was intended on the priest's part, but one can hardly doubt that it was on that of O'More. Carew, who had just landed, was present, and narrowly escaped. Ormonde's immense prestige secured him from ill treatment, and after strenuous attempts to convert him to Roman Catholicism he was released.

[2] Tirlagh MacHenry was the son of Ferdoragh Lord Dungannon's widow and Sir Henry O'Neill.

had been exempted from his overlordship. He wanted the Government to order his tenants back, though the Government considered that they " had rather been strangled than returned unto him ". The old fear that a sheriff would be appointed in Tyrone was troubling him. None was appointed in 1604, but he could not hope to escape one for long. We need not condemn him. He was growing old and could not reconcile himself to new ideas. He stood for mediævalism against modernity, and he could do no other. It must also be recalled that there were still garrisons in Tyrone, and that seventeenth-century troops of occupation did not behave like the British Army of the Rhine.

Sir George Carey, Mountjoy's successor in the office of Lord Deputy, did not stay long, and no event of great importance from our point of view occurred during his viceroyalty. His most notable achievement as Treasurer had been the debasement of the Irish coinage; his outstanding measure as Deputy was its restoration. The other chief event of his time, the disbandment of a large proportion of the Army, was an automatic measure outside his control. He was old, weary, on bad terms with the Lord Lieutenant in England, and on all three counts eager to be gone. It was also alleged by his enemies that he had warmly feathered his nest. There was some delay in meeting his demand, chiefly because his office was a beggarly one while Mountjoy drew two-thirds of the emoluments. Eventually it was decided that his successor, Sir Arthur Chichester, should draw £1000 a year and an equipment allowance in addition to his third of the salary. On the 24th February 1605 Chichester received the Sword, which he was to hold for the exceptionally long period of eleven years.

During the viceroyalty of Carey a new and much more interesting and attractive personality appeared on the Irish scene. In November 1603 there arrived in Dublin as

Solicitor-General a young lawyer, who was in his fashion
as remarkable a character as either Mountjoy or Chichester.
John Davies, born in 1569, was a Wiltshireman of Welsh
descent. As a lawyer he was brilliant, though rather erratic
and not quite in the first rank at a moment when the
standard was set by his friend Bacon and by Coke; but
he was also scholar, poet, wit, and—what has most endeared
him to historical students—an admirable writer of official
despatches. Mountjoy, Chichester, Carew, and Docwra
wrote excellent letters, but Davies outshone them all.
From them we have faithful and often graphic records of
events; from him, records of events in which ever and
anon a vivid personal touch conjures up a whole scene
before our eyes. He was the fifth English poet associated
with Ireland within a few years; the others being Raleigh,
Spenser, Wotton, and Harrington, the last two of whom
had served under Essex.

John Davies had had to conquer himself and his own
violent temper. Disbarred for breaking a cudgel on a
fellow-barrister's skull at table in the hall of the Middle
Temple, he had occupied the period of enforced idleness
and disgrace by writing his most celebrated poem, which
bore the significant title of " *Nosce Teipsum* ".

> If aught can teach us aught, Affliction's looks—
> Making us pry into ourselves so near—
> Teach us to know ourselves beyond all books,
> Or all the learned schools that ever were.
>
> This mistress lately plucked me by the ear,
> And many a golden lesson hath me taught;
> Hath made my senses quick, and reason clear,
> Reformed my will and rectified my thought.

His will reformed and his thought rectified, he was
readmitted to the Middle Temple and found favour in the
eyes of the new King, who had read his poem in Scotland.

His industry was prodigious. Apart from doing nearly all the Law Officers' work—first, as Solicitor, with an elderly and sickly Attorney, then, as Attorney, with a drunken and idle Solicitor—writing voluminous reports to Cecil and framing the Plantation scheme, he found time to learn Irish and to study Irish history, law, and custom. His *Discovery of the True Causes why Ireland was never entirely subdued* and other historical tracts are masterly pieces of work. His legal appreciations, such as that on the custom of tanistry, can be found fault with by modern historians, but they can never be dispensed with. Going on circuit as a judge, covering hundreds of miles every year on bad roads, and often sleeping in a tent, prosecuting as Law Officer in Dublin, building up a large and lucrative private practice, poring over dusty rolls among the archives, writing immense letters in his delightful prose, visiting London to draw up the scheme for the Plantation, pleasing Chichester in Ireland and enchanting Cecil in England, his labours were those of half a dozen ordinary men. Yet he grew portly on them.

## II

## GROWING DIFFICULTIES

OUTWARDLY Ireland was quieter than within living memory. Davies was astonished, as many English newcomers have been, to find that, politics apart, the Irish were a more law-abiding race than the English. One of Chichester's early measures, on the 20th February 1605, was to recall all commissions of martial law, except to the governors of certain towns and to a few great noblemen, whereof the Earl of Tyrone was the only one in Ulster. On the same day he issued another proclamation, forbidding the wearing of arms to all persons travelling, on pain of forfeiture and imprisonment. It was not only an important step towards the appeasement of the country, but clear proof that the English writ ran where it had never run before. The virtual disappearance of the Army had a similar significance. In July 1604 it was still at a strength of 374 horse and 3900 foot. By April 1606 it had fallen to 234 horse and 880 foot—little more than a police force. The peace with Spain was, of course, contributory to this great reduction.

Chichester's most serious difficulty was, in fact, the shortage of money. The Irish revenue was quite insufficient. The subsidies from England came late. Again and again we find the Lord Deputy complaining of his miserable situation in this respect. On one occasion, out of £8000 remitted, more than £5000 had at once to be paid out to lenders. Chichester had to pledge his own credit, and even then the Army, reduced as it was, was always waiting for

91

its pay. Forty thousand pounds were owing to it, largely to men dead or disbanded, and of this little was ever paid.

Munster and Connaught, under very different administrations, gave no trouble. In the former province Carew's successor as Lord President was a fierce and repressive but humorous veteran, Sir Henry Brouncker, who enforced the law against priests and recusants so thoroughly as to disquiet the Council in England, and gleefully reported that he had hanged "many fat ones" for aiding and abetting an outlaw. In Connaught the young Earl of Clanrickard, appointed President during the viceroyalty of Carey, was a great success, ruling rather as a mild and benignant Irish chieftain than as a governor appointed by the English. Clanrickard had married the widow of Essex, previously the wife of Sir Philip Sidney. Few women have been able to write beneath their correspondence such successive signatures as Frances Walsingham, Frances Sidney, Frances Essex, and Frances Clanrickard. Almost as remarkable was her transportation from the Court of England, where her whole life had been passed, to what must have seemed the wilds of Galway. Yet she appears to have been happy. She was, says Davies, after a visit to the President at Athlone in the winter of 1604, "very well contented and every way as well served as when he saw her in England." Clanrickard is said to have borne a strong personal resemblance to the luckless Essex, which one would have expected to be a painful reminder to the lady. Possibly, on the other hand, it assisted her to forget and to skip one husband in her reckoning. In the same letter Davies remarks that in Galway he found the people better behaved than in the Pale, and that Clanrickard's affability and good temper had made him universally beloved and respected.

Ulster was less satisfactory. It is true that the County Tyrone was quiet and orderly. There was, however, intermittent unrest in Cavan, while Donegal was the most unruly county in Ireland. The chieftains of the north-west were all dissatisfied. Tyrone, especially, complained time after time of encroachments, of prying into the terms of his patent, and of his poverty. The loss of his fisheries in the tidal waters of the Bann and in Lough Foyle, the latter of which had been granted to Sir Henry Docwra, were his chief grievances, as these fishing rights represented a large source of income. In Fermanagh the two Maguires were on scarcely better terms than before, any more than were the two rival O'Donnells in Donegal. In June 1605 Tyrconnell put in a serious of demands, the chief of which were that the garrison of Lifford should be removed and the town should be handed over to him; that the abbey lands and fisheries should be restored to him; and that he should be given the right to nominate the sheriff of Donegal. In the first two he failed; as regards the third he was reasonably met, it being decreed that he should send annually the names of six freeholders to the Lord Chancellor, from whom the latter would choose the sheriffs in accordance with the statute.

In the summer of 1605 Chichester and representatives of his Council made a tour in the north, beginning at Armagh. Here they found the church in a ruinous condition and a number of priests holding their prebends by " Bulls from Rome ". Having set that matter right, they then, after a conference with the Earl of Tyrone, divided the county into six baronies, allotted lands to the forts of Mountnorris and Charlemont, and heard a dispute between Tyrone and his kinsman Sir Henry Oge O'Neill, Shane's grandson. To Sir Henry they allotted considerable lands on both sides of the Blackwater, in performance of what

93

they took to be the true meaning of promises given by Mountjoy.

Going on to Dungannon, they persuaded Tyrone to create a number of freeholders. Here they found many gentlemen claiming a right to lands possessed by them and their ancestors, which the Earl strongly denied, alleging the whole country to be his own. They ordered that these men should continue in possession of their estates until time could be found to investigate their claims. Only in the case of Tirlagh MacArt O'Neill, son of Docwra's bibulous ally at Derry and grandson of old Tirlagh Luineach, did they definitely allot a ballybetagh (about 900 acres) of his own choosing, finding him "a poor young gent of some hope". For the remainder of what he professed to have been promised by the late Queen they left the poor and moderately hopeful young gent to make out his case.

At Lifford they took a step which, natural as it was, gave umbrage to two powerful men. Both Tyrconnell and Sir Neill O'Donnell laid claim to the new township. Its strategic position, covering the ford between Donegal and Tyrone, seemed to Chichester too important for it to be allowed to fall to either. They decided that it should be kept in the King's own hands, and should be made a corporate town, suggesting that the town itself and certain lands allotted to it should be settled with soldiers, and that merchants should be encouraged to resort to it—which they certainly would not were it in the hands of either of the O'Donnells. They found that in Donegal, as in Tyrone, the chief proprietor had forced ancient freeholders to surrender their lands, and persuaded him to reinstate them. Next they visited Derry, now growing into a fine town.

From Derry they passed by Newtown-Limavady, where they established a weekly market, via Coleraine, to Carrickfergus, Chichester's old post, on which he always looked with affection. There they divided Antrim into eight baronies. In the course of the journey the judges held assizes in Armagh, Tyrone, Donegal, and Antrim. The Council made arrangements or suggestions for the building of forts at Coleraine, Massarene, Toome—the vital ford on the Bann north of Lough Neagh—and Inishloughlin.

The trouble they had stirred up at Lifford was not long in making itself heard. On the very day on which Chichester sent in his report, the 30th September, Tyrconnell wrote to Cecil, now Earl of Salisbury,[1] earnestly demanding that the town should be restored to him.

Over Chichester there was coming a remarkable change, which continued throughout his viceroyalty, so that by the end of it he is hardly to be recognized as the relentless Governor of Carrickfergus. There is some excuse for regarding him as an inhuman monster in those early days, but historians who persist in picturing him as such when he was Lord Deputy cannot have read his letters, or are deliberately concealing their good side. This affair of Lifford is an early example of his new attitude. With only a handful of armed forces at his disposal, it was for him a vital matter to hold the main strategic points in country where unrest was probable. Four days after his proposal we find him writing again to Salisbury to say that he had found the Earl of Tyrconnell not unreasonable, and suggesting that in exchange for Lifford some of the abbey lands in Donegal should be passed to him. Chichester may have made mistakes, but the charge that he deliberately strove to force the northern Earls into revolt is moonshine.

Unfortunately there was the religious question, which, while it did not really touch Ulster, undoubtedly con-

---

[1] Honours fell thick upon Cecil after the accession of James. He was created Viscount Cranborne on the 20th August 1604, and Earl of Salisbury on the 4th May 1605. In 1608 he became Lord High Treasurer, while still retaining the office of Principal Secretary of State.

tributed to the disaffection of the great lords in that province. Here Chichester was carrying out the orders of the King and Privy Council in London, though we need not suppose that they were in marked conflict with his own views. One cannot always restrain a feeling of indignation as one reads what followed in Dublin, but it is to abandon all historical sense if one represents this business as a phase of English persecution in Ireland. It was, in fact, an example of the application of contemporary religious policy, which in the reign of James I was infinitely more drastic to English than to Irish Catholics. So much, indeed, was this the case that English priests, threatened with banishment, were flocking over to Ireland, where they expected to be allowed to remain. Let us curse intolerance, that vice parading as a virtue, that cruelty practised in the name of righteousness; but let us not see in this affair any particular malignity of the English in Ireland.

On the 4th July 1605 the King published a proclamation against toleration in Ireland. There had been, he indignantly declared, a false rumour that he purposed to give liberty of conscience to his subjects in that kingdom, contrary to the statutes. This was an imputation upon him, as though he were less careful of the Church of Ireland than of the other Churches whereof he was the head. He now proclaimed that there would be no toleration to exercise " any other religion than that which is agreeable to God's word and is established by the laws of the realm ". He therefore ordered his subjects to attend their parish churches on Sundays and Holy Days. He further decreed that all Roman Catholic priests should quit the country before the 10th December following. The legality of the order to attend church could not be disputed, but it was otherwise respecting the banishment of the priests. No law to this effect had ever been passed by an Irish Parliament, and it had not previously been contended that Acts of the Parliament of England applied to Ireland. Poynings Act of 10 Henry VII (1495), which decreed that all Acts of the English Parliament were good in Ireland, was, as regards this clause, purely retrospective.

The machinery for compelling attendance at church was available. It consisted in a fine of 12d. for non-attendance, and was fairly effective with the people when put into force by Brouncker in Munster, where the experiment was first made. But a fine of that size was obviously only a trifle to a wealthy citizen such as the Dublin alderman, and he was now the objective. Accordingly, on the 13th November a royal mandate was addressed by name to each of the aldermen, requiring them to attend their parish churches on the Sunday following sight of it, or else to accompany the Mayor when he repaired in state to the cathedral. The object was to convict them, if they refused, of contempt of the King's command and thus bring them within reach of the Court of Star Chamber. Once again it was from the constitutional point of view a doubtful and arbitrary proceeding.

Finding that no notice was taken of the mandate, the Council sent for the aldermen and some other prominent citizens and strove to persuade them to comply. On their refusal they were summoned to appear in the Court of Castle Chamber, the Irish equivalent of Star Chamber, where the aldermen were fined £100 and three others £50 apiece. It was also decreed that the recusants should be confined to the Castle during the pleasure of the Court. The result was that several aldermen took to attending the services, and that the Dublin churches were better filled than at any time during the last dozen years.

So far, so good. But the Catholic nobility and gentry of the Pale, without waiting for the judgment of the Court

97

of Castle Chamber, framed a petition of protest, averring that the King, " moved, as it should seem, by some sinister information ", had foully impugned their honour and loyalty. Every Catholic of note in the Pale put his signature to this document, but, as usual in such cases, the real authors were but a handful: Lords Gormanston and Louth, Sir Patrick Barnewall, Richard Netterville, and a few more.

Chichester was angry, and reproved the petitioners for interference in a matter that had not yet touched them. It was, indeed, a most awkward moment for them, when men's tempers were inflamed and their nerves on edge; for on the 13th November news was received in Ireland of the discovery of the Gunpowder Plot. The coincidence struck Chichester as remarkable, especially when the leaders among the petitioners pressed him for a reply in a manner which to his mind bordered on insolence. He began to wonder whether the two affairs had any connection. Pending further inquiry, he committed to the Castle Gormanston, Barnewall, their legal adviser, Christopher Flatsbury, and afterwards one or two others. The arrest was marked by a dramatic scene. When Barnewall heard he was committed, he remarked across the Council table: " Well, we must endure, as we have endured many other things."

It was one of those defiant mutterings in which it is hard to find definite offence, but which give the speaker the satisfaction of having the last word; but Chichester was not the man on whom to practise it. At once he demanded sharply: " What mean you by that? "

" We have," said Barnewall, " endured the rebellion, and other calamities besides "—obviously not what he had meant, but all that he dared to say. Even that would not do for Chichester.

" *You* endured the misery of the late war? " retorted the Deputy. "No, sir, *we* have endured the misery of the war; we have lost our blood and our friends, and have indeed endured extreme miseries to suppress the late rebellion, whereof your priests, for whom you make petition, and your wicked religion, was the principal cause." He thereupon committed Sir Patrick to the Constable.

The affair eventually blew over. The prisoners one by one expressed regret and were set free. Barnewall, who had taken a high tone and had also made a personal attack upon Sir James Ley, the Lord Chief Justice, was sent over to England and for some time confined in the Tower; but it was mainly due to his pluck and obstinacy that the system of procedure by mandate was dropped. No trace of any fore-knowledge of the Gunpowder Plot was ever discovered in Ireland, and tempers began to cool. The Privy Council of England, in a letter significantly addressed not to the Deputy and Council but to Chichester alone, laid down that a moderate course should be followed, neither yielding any hope of toleration on the one hand, nor startling the multitude by general or rigorous compulsion on the other. Only prominent persons who boasted of their disobedience were to be singled out for punishment. Even priests were to be banished in accordance with the proclamation only if they came into the open; no particular search was to be made for them. The policy suited Chichester, who had no itch for persecution. But the result was that in the different provinces the laws were differently enforced. In Munster, as has been stated, Brouncker delighted in the harrying of both priests and recusants. In the Pale things were rather easier, except perhaps in Dublin; in Connaught easier still; and in Ulster the question hardly arose. It cannot be doubted, however, that the incident had the effect of increasing the suspicions of Tyrone and Tyrconnell, and perhaps still more of Cuconnaught Maguire, who came of a family always particularly devoted to the Church. Barnewall was a friend and kinsman of Tyrone's and had, it will be recalled, been the matchmaker when the Earl eloped with Mabel Bagenal. Davies thought the Government policy mistaken. In his view it would have paid better to leave the big men alone and concentrate on the masses, as it seemed to him that the latter were less firmly bound to Rome than the former. At any rate, according to his evidence, never before had so large a proportion of the poor in the Munster towns attended Protestant worship. According to Brouncker, the women were the foremost champions of the Roman Catholic Church, for which they fought with the weapons of Lysistrata. The death of the President of Munster on the 3rd June 1607 gave the Government a welcome excuse to slacken the rigour of his ecclesiastical policy.

Chichester had set secret inquiries afoot throughout the country to discover whether there had been any correspondence between the authors of the Gunpowder Treason and their co-religionists in Ireland. As has been recorded, nothing came of them, but a curious state of affairs in the Earl of Tyrone's family was revealed. The Lord Deputy had noticed when in Ulster during the summer of 1605 that the young Countess of Tyrone seemed to be ill-pleased with her lord; and it had occurred to him that if the Earl were engaged in that or any other plot against the State she might prove a useful channel of information. He therefore instructed one of his captains in the north, Sir Toby Caulfeild, to sound her. It was not an edifying business. In a letter of the 26th February 1606 Chichester owned

SIR TOBY CAULFEILD, FIRST LORD CHARLEMONT

to Devonshire that it was "a very uncivil and uncommendable part to feed the humour of a woman to learn the secrets of her husband"; his only excuse was his zeal for the King's safety and that of the charge committed to himself.

During the winter Sir Toby had gone to Dungannon two or three times without being able to have private speech with Lady Tyrone. At last in January, the Earl being absent, his opportunity came. Lady Tyrone spoke in very bitter terms of her husband, declaring that he mistreated her when he was drunk and that she was weary of life with him. Sir Toby gently suggested that she should buy protection against his tyranny by giving information if she discovered that he was engaged in any plot against the peace of the kingdom. She answered that, if any such knowledge came to her, much as she hated the Earl, she would not be known to accuse him of anything that would endanger his life. She then swore that she knew of nothing for certain, adding that, had there been a plot, she was the last to whom he would have confided it. She believed, however, that Henry O'Hagan—who had gone to visit the Earl's second son Henry, serving in the Spanish Army in the Netherlands—had been sent on some business which his master did not dare commit to writing. She admitted that she had heard him, when in the company of Tyrconnell and Cuconnaught Maguire, "talk angrily against the King". Finally, she denied that there had been any connection between the Gunpowder traitors and her husband, and promised to inform Sir Toby if anything serious came to her ears. He for his part swore that her communications with him should be kept secret.

There was nothing much in all this except that the Earl of Tyrone was discontented, that he used high words in his cups, and that his Countess was unhappy, all of which Chichester knew already.[1]

Having toured Antrim, Down, and Tyrone and looked into the affairs of Donegal the previous year, the Lord Deputy, with representatives of the Council and Judiciary, set out on the 19th July 1606 to investigate those of Monaghan, Fermanagh, and Cavan. They began with the Essex estate of Farney in Monaghan. From that time forward they had to camp in the open, there being no town considerable or clean enough for their lodgment. Their total escort was about 130 infantry and 50 cavalry, whereas in the most peaceful interludes of Tudor days no Deputy had ever adventured into Ulster with less than eight hundred men. In Monaghan they found that Fitz-william's settlement [2] had not survived. His freeholders had relapsed into the condition almost of serfs. On the other hand, the half-dozen MacMahons among whom the county had been divided had forfeited their grants either by rebellion or non-fulfilment of the conditions. Chichester restored the majority of these men, among whom was Brian MacHugh Oge of Kinsale notoriety; but he insisted upon their restoring to their lands such of the freeholders as had survived the wars. Lands in the neighbourhood of the village of Monaghan, which had belonged to men killed in rebellion, he allotted to discharged soldiers settled

[1] As a not untypical example of how Irish history is written from the Nationalist point of view, the account of this incident given by the Rev. C. P. Meehan in *The Fate and Fortunes of Hugh O'Neill, Earl of Tyrone, and Rory O'Donnell, Earl of Tyrconnell* is worth study. Father Meehan was no ordinary historian. He was clever and painstaking; he wrote before the State Papers of this period had been calendared and gave in full several documents which are only summarized in them. In this case he took care not to do so. After enlarging upon the infamy of Chichester's approach to Lady Tyrone, he states that the interview was barren of results, which is more or less true, but omits all mention of her complaints of her husband's brutality and drunkenness, of her suspicions, and of her offer to inform against the Earl if she discovered anything, so long as her name was kept out of the affair.

[2] See p. 21.

in the village, thinking that they would prove a useful reinforcement to the little garrison in time of trouble.

Neither of those two great events which were on the horizon, the Flight of the Earls and the Revolt of O'Dogherty, had any effect upon Monaghan. This county was therefore settled in accordance with what had been observed during the tour in question, and was untouched by the Plantation of Ulster. The settlement was recorded in detail in a volume known as *The Book of the Division of the County of Monaghan*, the preamble to which consisted of a proclamation signed and sealed by Chichester and his Council on the 12th March 1607. It is an interesting document, almost unique of its kind, though from its great length unsuited for inclusion in an account like the present. A short consideration of it is, however, of value, especially as it enables us to wipe the county off the slate so far as the Plantation is concerned.

Generally speaking, there was no " plantation " in Monaghan in the sense that settlers were brought in from outside. We find one great English landlord, Sir Edward Blaney, who, as Seneschal, Constable of Monaghan Castle, and the chief military authority in the county, had received large grants of land. We find also a handful of smaller ones, doubtless for the most part those ex-soldiers whose presence Chichester had welcomed. Finally, in one barony only, that of Donamaine, formerly known as Farney, there was the great Essex estate of perhaps 15,000 acres—which was left undisturbed and unrecorded by the Commissioners —and in addition the termon lands which had been forfeited to the King and were now let by him to large tenants at a rent of 1s. per six acres.

All the rest of the county was in Irish hands, mainly in those of the MacMahons, with considerable portions allotted to members of minor septs, such as the O'Duffys and M'Cabes. The head of the great house of MacMahon, Ross Bane, might be no longer " the MacMahon " or a ruling prince; but he could struggle through life and keep a good coat on his back with five ballybetaghs (4800 acres) in demesne and 8½ ballybetaghs (8000 acres) in chiefry. His rival, Bryan MacHugh Oge, now Sir Bryan, having been knighted for his many misdeeds and his fortunate thirst at Kinsale, had no need to feel himself pinched on five ballybetaghs in demesne and twelve in chiefry, four-fifths of the whole Barony of Dartry. In that of Cremorne, Ever MacCooley MacMahon—the very man whose imprisonment had started the trouble in Fitzwilliam's day—could still scrape along on three bally-betaghs in demesne and 5½ in chiefry. But the normal holding was about 120 acres, a small one for the Ireland of those days. The following extract, taken almost at random, shows the disposition of two ballybetaghs in the Barony of Monaghan:

### IN THE BALLIBETOGH CALLED BALLINAC-I-GOWNE [1]

| | |
|---|---|
| Owen M'Brian M'Mahowne, in demesne, four tates | Ballaghiland<br>Tregane<br>Killenecleagh<br>Dromgale |
| Hugh M'Corbe M'Con M'Mahowne, in demesne, four tates, viz. | Gortmore<br>Dromeshenny<br>Rathe<br>Naghill |
| Conn M'Gill Patrick M'Mahowne, in demesne, one tate, viz. | Coretagher |
| Hugh M'Owen M'Brien M'Magowne, in demesne, one tate, viz. | Killcorragh |

[1] The original spelling is followed. Measurements varied, but in Monaghan they were the tate, roughly 60 acres, and the ballybetagh, containing generally 16 tates.

Art, brother to Patrick M'Hugh M'Mahowne, in demesne, two tates, viz. } Carnebane Aghenebracke

Wm. Field, a servitor for that the first patentee died without issue, in demesne, two tates } Cornestowe Cabbragh

Art M'Hugh Roe M'Mahowne, in demesne, two tates, viz. } Dromegarve Greaghhane

### In the Ballibetogh called Ballireaghe

Art M'Mannes FitzPhillip M'Mahowne, in demesne, two tates } Cromelin, two tates so-called

Rory and Edmond, the two sons of Gilleduff FitzPatrick M'Mahowne, in demesne, four tates } Drom Rottagh Culmulkilly Killonserlie

James M'Mahowne, in demesne, two tates, viz. } Mullaghmore Cowledaghe

Toole M'Mahowne, in demesne, two tates } Dirrey Collrey

Brian FitzJames M'Mahowne, in demesne, two tates } Tollenore Kiltedoe

Art FitzMannes M'Mahowne, in demesne, two tates } Carne Kilmultaghie

Art M'Rory FitzOwen M'Mahowne, in demesne, two tates } Cavan Reagh Liskarney

Every one of these was an existing tenant, an Irishman, and a MacMahon, with the exception of William Field, who was a servitor, or servant of the Crown, and who had been granted two tates because the previous holder had died without issue. Occasionally we find an entry such as this in the Barony of Dartry:

Conn M'Owen M'Ross M'Mahowne, in regard of his honest deserts, the former patentee having been slain in rebellion, in demesne, two tates } Maghenenekillie Dromeyacke

Otherwise the Commission had sought to compromise between the establishment of existing rights and tenancies and an even distribution of Irish farmers throughout the Shire. It was not hard dealing. One of its results was that thirty-five years later, when the Plantation was well established throughout the rest of Ulster, Monaghan was the poorest and most backward county in the province. In the rebellion of 1641 the MacMahons, though a few kindly ones appeared among them, did not show themselves notably less bloodthirsty than the natives of neighbouring counties, where the Irish had had far harsher treatment. In fact, by comparison with the O'Reillys of Cavan, they were savages.

We now return to Chichester and his party. Painfully making their way through woods and bogs which almost held up their carriages and wagons, they passed on via the ruined abbey of Clones to the shore of Lough Erne, opposite Devenish Island, where the Sessions were to be held within the walls of an ancient abbey, a ruin then, but existing to this day.[1]

Fermanagh was in a curious condition. The people were not for the most part fighting men, and their lord when in rebellion had generally employed outsiders; consequently, few had been killed in revolt or attainted, and there was no question of their lands having been forfeited to the Crown. The county had, as will be recalled, been provisionally

---

[1] Davies says that they came to the "south side" of Lough Erne. Strictly speaking there is no south side here, as the lough runs south and north. A little further to the north it bends west, so that the west shore becomes the south, and it is frequently so described all along the lower lough. But, coming from Clones, Chichester and his party cannot have reached this shore. It is, in fact, a practical certainty that they encamped on a small shelf above the lake at the foot of a steep hill, on which shelf there now stands Little Derryinch House. The writer may be pardoned for this digression when he mentions that his father dwelt at Little Derryinch until quite recently, and that he himself passed many happy days there. The ruined abbey on Devenish, beside the famous round tower and the little house of St. Molaisse, is in view of the windows.

divided between Connor Roe and Cuconnaugh Maguire, but the important question for Chichester and the Council was what freeholds there were, according to Irish tenure, and what rents and services they rendered to the Maguires. It was here that Davies made his fascinating inquiries into the lands of the *corbes* and *herinaghs*, but, interesting as are these ecclesiastical functionaries, they are rather outside the scope of our present purpose. What does concern us is the economic situation of the chieftain, and this is hardly less interesting.

Here they were very lucky in their search. Everyone whom they questioned spoke of a roll or chronicle in the possession of O'Bristan, the Chief Brehon of Fermanagh, who dwelt not far away. They therefore sent for him. He was so old and feeble that he could scarce stagger to the camp, but he arrived at last. Questioned about the roll, he appeared much troubled, admitted that he had had it in his keeping, but declared that it had been burned by English soldiers during the rebellion. Some of the on-lookers at once struck in that this was not true, and that they had seen the roll in his hands since the war. Archbishop Jones, the Lord Chancellor, then put him upon his oath and seriously charged him to tell the truth about it. The poor old man, fetching a deep sigh, answered that he did indeed know where it was, but that it was dearer to him than his life, and that he would never deliver it unless the Lord Chancellor likewise took an oath to return it to him. The latter then smilingly gave him his word and hand that it should be restored when a copy had been taken, where-upon the Brehon drew the tattered document from his bosom.

The gist of the Council's discovery was that the mensal lands of the Maguire, which yielded him his pork, meal, and butter, were between three and four thousand acres;

that he had a yearly rent of 240 beeves from the seven baronies of the county; and that at Enniskillen itself he had another 800 acres cultivated by his own people. Beyond this he had nothing according to the Brehon law, and in time of peace he exacted no more. But, adds Davies, "marry in time of war he made himself owner of all, cutting what he listed and imposing as many *bonaghts*, or hired soldiers, upon them as he had occasion to use."

The lawyers then investigated all claims to freehold, barony by barony, and drew up a complete record of them; but Chichester made no decision regarding them. In the whole county there was not even a village, and the Deputy was in some doubt as to where it would be advisable to establish a market, court-house, gaol, and school—the usual basis of a corporate town. He decided that Lisgoole Abbey was the best site. There, at least, he did not see into the future; for it was on the historic island of Enniskillen that the county town was to stand, and from a tall neighbouring hill that Portora Royal School (*cuius alumnus indignus sum*) was to look down upon it.

The party then moved on to Cavan, camping beside the then wretched little town of the same name. Here a jury empanelled for the purpose found that, since the lands seized by the O'Reillys before the rebellion had been forfeited by the death of most of them in revolt, the greater part of the county was now vested in the Crown. Yet, conceiving it to be the King's pleasure that the natives of the county should be established in the possessions they held before the war, Chichester had the same inquiries made as in Fermanagh. Again, he deferred the final settlement until his return to Dublin. The key to his intentions is probably to be found in a passage from a letter from Davies to Salisbury:

" For the common good, not only of these parts, but of all the kingdom besides, His Lordship in this journey hath cut off three heads of that hydra of the North, namely, MacMahon, Maguire, and O'Reilly; for these three names of chiefry, with their Irish duties and exactions, shall be utterly abolished; the customs of tanistry and gavelkind, being absurd and unreasonable as they are in use here, and which have been the cause of many murders and rebellions, shall be clearly extinguished. All the possessions shall descend and be conveyed according to the course of the Common Law. Every man shall have a certain home and know the extent of his estate, whereby the people will be encouraged to manure their land with better industry than heretofore hath been used, to bring up their children more civilly, to provide for their posterity more carefully. These will cause them to build better houses for their safety and to love neighbourhood. Thence will arise villages and towns, which will draw tradesmen and artificers. So as we conceive a hope that these countries in a short time will not only be quiet neighbours to the Pale, but be made as rich and as civil as the Pale itself."

It will be observed that, while the conditions in Monaghan, Cavan, and Fermanagh differed among themselves, they had, in the view of Davies, a certain likeness which made them differ far more sharply from those of Tyrone and Donegal. In the latter counties, one chief, the native lord of the soil, had in each case been allotted in the settlement made by Mountjoy and confirmed by James an altogether predominating position. That settlement could not be questioned now, however unwise it seemed—and, Devonshire having died suddenly that April, Davies was bold enough to hint that it had been at least precipitate. But in Monaghan and Cavan the paramountcy of the MacMahons and O'Reillys was gone for ever; in Fermanagh, although

two of the Maguires had been allotted the leading rôle in
the county, it was the intention of Chichester and his
legal adviser that this rôle should not exceed that which
was revealed in old O'Bristan's chronicle.

These projects were not likely to be attractive to headstrong Cuconnaught Maguire. And, indeed, at the very
moment they were being considered, some disquieting
news of him came to the camp near Devenish. It was
reported that he and Tyrconnell had gone to an island on
the Donegal coast, ostensibly to see if there were any wine
for sale there, actually, it was suspected, to look for a ship
which would carry them, or one of them, to France or
Spain. A fortnight or so later one, Gawen Moore, of
Glasgow deposed that Tyrconnell had come aboard his
boat and demanded if she were fit to sail to either of those
countries. Moore apparently replied that she was not,
which was not extraordinary, seeing that she was only a
12-tonner. Salisbury made a note on the report of Moore's
examination expressing his disbelief that Tyrconnell was
about to flee the country; it was much more likely, he
thought, that he was seeking a passage for Maguire.

At the beginning of 1607 there occurred an event of no
great import on the face of it which was yet to have mo-
mentous results. George Montgomery, Dean of Norwich
and rector of Chedzoy in Somerset, had been two years
earlier, in accordance with the general ecclesiastical policy,
appointed Bishop of three Sees which had never yet been
in the hands of the Reformed Church: Derry, Clogher,
and Raphoe, comprising all western Ulster. Despite the
extent of these dignities, the new Bishop had shown no
disposition to come over and begin his sacred work of
conversion and reform. For one thing, he had a nervous
wife, who had heard that Ulster was a wild place. She
was to find that it could be wild enough on occasion. She

mentioned in a letter that George had three bishoprics, but could remember that of Derry only, the names of the others being so strange; she supposed he would have to visit them once anyhow, but certainly did not contemplate living in Ireland. At last, however, the Bishop responded to the many pointed reminders of Chichester and took up his residence at Derry, which Mrs. Montgomery at first found more civilized than she had expected. There was good company there and in the neighbourhood, though Irish visitors sometimes left a louse behind. Unfortunately— very unfortunately, as will shortly appear—Sir Henry Docwra was gone. Disgusted with his own prospects and with the treatment of his protégés at Derry, he had got permission to hand over his governorship and his company and to dispose of his grants to Sir George Paulet. We shall see little more of the worthy Docwra, though he afterwards returned to Ireland as Treasurer, ended his life with the fitting title of Baron Docwra of Culmore, and was buried in Christchurch Cathedral, Dublin, in 1631.[1]

There was one neighbour with whom relations were hardly of a social kind, but none the less important for that. Mention has been made of the disgust of Sir Donnell Ballagh O'Cahan, Lord of Coleraine, that he should be the vassal of the Earl of Tyrone. On the Earl's return from England, flourishing his patent, O'Cahan, who was an illiterate man, apparently took it that his case had gone against him and made the best terms he could with his overlord, who was also his father-in-law. The arrangement was that Tyrone should hold one-third and O'Cahan two-thirds of the broad and fertile lands of Coleraine.

---

[1] The writer had always believed that Docwra was represented in the well-known "servitor" family, the Brookes of Colebrooke, County Fermanagh, through the marriage of his daughter Elizabeth to Sir Henry Brooke. It appears, however, that their descendants died out.

It was purely temporary and terminable by either at will. Reflection had not left O'Cahan better pleased with his side of the bargain, nor, for that matter, the Earl with his.

When the Bishop of Derry arrived he was shocked to find that the revenues of his bishopric were almost non-existent. Tyrone was in possession of all the Church lands in both the counties of Tyrone and Coleraine. At Derry Paulet had his hands upon the land of the bishopric on the island itself and, worse still, the very bishop's house. This was a pretty business. Montgomery had not left his snug deanery of Norwich and his pleasant rectory at Chedzoy for the wilds of Ireland to live without a stipend and sleep in a hovel. Finding that O'Cahan was likely to be easier to deal with than Tyrone, and had besides considerable knowledge of the extent, rents, and tenure of the Church lands, Montgomery thought he would be a useful ally. As a *quid pro quo* he gave him some encouragement and advice regarding his old claim against his overlord.

We may briefly set out the views of the three parties concerned, O'Cahan and Tyrone, the contestants, and the legal adviser of the Crown, the intervener. O'Cahan deposed that for " the space of three thousand years and upwards "—doubtless he would have said since the day his ancestor married Noah's daughter, had it occurred to him— his family had been possessed of " O'Cahan's Country ". For it they had paid no more than a small head rent of 21 cows annually to the O'Neill, and undertaken to aid him in war with 100 horse and 300 foot. When, in the late war, he came in nine months before Tyrone, he was promised that he should hold his lands directly from the Queen.

Tyrone denied that there was a country called " O'Cahan's Country ". O'Cahan and his ancestors had held it but as " tenants at sufferance ", servants and followers, to the

O'Neills. If there had been any promise such as O'Cahan alleged, it was countermanded by the patent granted to himself by King James.

Davies, for his part, had been reflecting upon his discoveries in Ulster in the summer of 1606 and especially on O'Bristan's chronicle. Until he had seen that document he had always considered that Tyrone had the freehold of both Tyrone and Coleraine. But he had found that in Fermanagh Maguire " had only a seigniory consisting of certain rents and duties, and had withal some special demesnes, and that the tenants or inferior inhabitants were not tenants at will, as the lords pretended, but freeholders, and had as good and large an estate in their tenancies as the lords had in their seigniories." He was now inclined to the belief that the counties of Tyrone and Coleraine were in the same situation. The Earl of Tyrone's patent granted him only what his grandfather, Con Bacach, had had. What had Con Bacach, then? Only a seigniory and certain means? If so, all the rest was by the Statute of the 11th of Elizabeth vested in the Crown, but those who dwelt upon these lands were to be regarded as freeholders under the Crown. Davies made no suggestion that the settlement should be upset as regards the County Tyrone, but as regards Coleraine he was strongly of opinion that the Earl's claims should be resisted. It is to be noted that his view more or less coincides with that of Irish Nationalist historians when they are reproaching the English with making grants to the chiefs over the heads of the tribes, but which they forget when they come to consider this particular episode!

In May the two claimants came up to Dublin to argue their cases. Carried away by passion, Tyrone forgot his usual respect for the Viceroy. Snatching a paper from the hand of O'Cahan, he tore it across. Chichester contained himself, though, as he admits, against his nature. He allowed the incident to pass with but a slight reproof, but made the Earl understand that he had done amiss. It was decided that the provisional arrangement between the two rivals should continue until the affair could be fully thrashed out in England, and in July the King directed that they should come over for the hearing of the case in the following Michaelmas Term. The case was never to be heard.

## TYRONE SAILS FROM LOUGH SWILLY

O N the 18th May 1607 an anonymous letter addressed
to the Clerk, Sir William Ussher, was pushed under
the door of the Council Chamber in the Castle. It
began with the traditional patriotic flourish of the informer :

" Sir—My zeal for my country, lately on fire, and my
love to you for loving the same, will show you by this
relation, though I am far from you in religion, how near
I come to you in honesty."

The writer went on that he had lately found himself in
the company of some Catholic gentry, who informed him
under pledge of secrecy that they intended to murder
Chichester and the most formidable of his officers, Sir Oliver
Lambart, by poison or other means. They would then
surprise the Castle and rush, or starve out if they could not
be rushed, the smaller garrisons. The towns were for them,
and " the great ones " in the North were ready to strike in
their cause. Spanish aid had been promised if required, but
they did not think it would be, counting on the fact that
Ireland was denuded of troops and on James's known dislike
of war. Having seized power, they would elect a Governor
and Council of their own, and then despatch submissive
letters to the King begging him to grant complete freedom
of religion. They expected that he would do so ; if not,
they would have ample time to fortify their maritime towns
and fall back upon Spanish aid. The informer concluded
that he had consented to join the conspirators, but had been

tormented by remorse ever since. While not desiring to betray his friends, he was determined to give the Council a chance to avert the danger.

When this letter came into his hands Chichester was considering a personal message from Salisbury, which he had been directed to keep to himself, that a plot was being hatched in Ireland and in the Spanish Netherlands. Salisbury's informant was Christopher St. Lawrence, son of Lord Howth. St. Lawrence was what we should call to-day an " unsatisfactory " young man who would not settle down, but there seems to have been nothing more than that against him; indeed, he had a good record in the wars. His company had since been disbanded, so, like many other sons of the Irish Catholic nobility, he had gone to Flanders with the intention of seeking service in the Irish Regiment commanded by Colonel Henry O'Neill, Tyrone's second son. On the 11th May his father had died, and he was now on his way back to assume his title and his patrimony.[1]

In June Salisbury sent the new Lord Howth over to Dublin, where between the 29th of that month and the 25th August Chichester had a long series of private interviews with him. It was a difficult situation; for Howth would not speak in the presence of a third party, still less give public evidence, so that the Lord Deputy's hands were tied. The fact that Cuconnaught Maguire had suddenly and secretly gone abroad was disquieting, and seemed to support the tale. On the other hand, Howth was so shifty and contradictory

[1] Father Meehan states that the anonymous letter addressed to Ussher was written by Howth, but this is obviously a mistake; Howth was in England at the time it was received, on his way home from Flanders. A curious complication was that Chichester had under arrest at the time a man named " Howth ", who had confessed to being engaged in a plot to seize the Castle, and that this man had given to an associate the name of Christopher St. Lawrence, of whom he was doubtless a kinsman. It is perhaps idle to speculate as to the authorship of the letter, but Lord Delvin is a possible writer.

in his statements that Chichester did not know what to make of him.

"I like not his look and gesture when he talks with me of this business, which, together with his words, I set down in writing immediately upon his departure from me," the Deputy reported to Salisbury. "I wish I had the assistance of a third person when I speak with him, for I like not the business, especially to deal with him alone therein." If Howth lied as he sat cheek by jowl with that terrible countenance, like a Chinese mandarin's with its thin drooping moustache and high cheek-bones, and frozen to the same impassivity, but burning beneath the ice with enormous vigour and ruthlessness, then he was indeed a very brave man.

According to his story, the plot was first discussed about Christmas 1605. One of the conspirators, Lord Delvin, then almost wrecked it by his absolute refusal to have any part in the murder of Chichester. The following August Howth went to Flanders, where he was told that many of the Irish in the Spanish service were engaged in the affair. He made a special trip over to England to inform Salisbury, and then returned to Flanders for a short time. He professed to have learnt on this occasion that, within twenty days of the outbreak, 10,000 Spaniards under the great commander Spinola were to land in Ireland. He implicated Tyrconnell, Cuconnaught Maguire, and Sir Randal Macdonell of Antrim; also a few magnates outside Ulster, such as the Catholic Butler Lord Mountgarret, and Sir Thomas Burke. He had no evidence against Tyrone, but believed that he was in it. There was, he said, no immediate anxiety, as the Spaniards would not be ready until the following year.

Was all this rubbish or not? Chichester became more and more inclined to believe that there was something in it, but he did not see how to act. Tyrone was once more seriously upset because his nephew Bryan MacArt, the most gracious

117

and popular of all the O'Neills, had just been arrested for a murder in the house of Sir Tirlagh MacHenry and—for fear of a rescue—had been brought to Dublin for trial in the King's Bench; yet Chichester did not believe that the Earl either had lent or was likely to lend himself to any such scheme. Of Tyrconnell, who was vain and unbalanced, he was by no means so sure, and he thought of having him arrested. He was still undecided when, on the 7th September, word was brought to him that Tyrone and Tyrconnell, with almost all their kindred, had fled the country.

. . . . .

The news was bewildering. A week before Chichester had actually been staying with Tyrone under the same roof: that of the Flemings at Slane Castle, in Meath, where they had been regally entertained. This sudden secret flight would have been disturbing at any time; on top of the Howth affair, it came like a thunderbolt. The Deputy rode back post-haste to Dublin that same night and at once summoned his Council to him. Then, one by one, from the Castle gateway couriers clattered out to carry without stint of spur his urgent messages to all quarters. Orders to every harbour that the fugitives should be detained if driven in by weather; orders to Galway and the Munster ports that all available ships should be manned and should put out at once in an attempt to cut them off from Spain; proclamation to the people of the counties affected, bidding them remain quiet; commission to the military commanders and the gentry to preserve the peace; warning to Argyll in Scotland; directions to secure Tyrone's infant son Con, who had been left behind because his *creaghting* foster-parents could not be found in time. Warders were placed in Tyrone's castles at Dungannon, Newtown, and Dunalong, and in Tyrconnell's at Donegal and Asheroe. Suspects were dragged in for examination. Sir Cormac MacBaron O'Neill, Tyrone's brother, who had brought the first news of the flight, was promptly put under lock and key in the Castle. He came in, full of virtue, with the tale that Tyrone had begged him to accompany the party to Spain, and that he had refused; now, for reward, he desired to be given charge of his brother's lands. Chichester discovered that the two had been together at Dunalong just before the Earl sailed, and that Cormac had withheld the news from the garrisons of Lifford and Derry until he was clear away. It looked very like a put-up job. Sir Cormac's suit to have the *custodiam* of his brother's country might well be, as Davies remarked, " to his brother's use, by agreement betwixt them ". For this and other suspicions, the witty Attorney reported, " the constable of the Castle of Dublin has the *custodiam* of him ".

This is what had happened. On the 28th August Tyrone received at Slane a letter informing him that a ship was awaiting him in Lough Swilly, and that Cuconnaught Maguire, disguised as a seaman, was aboard. Tyrone was at the moment nervous and discouraged. If there was a plot of any sort, he almost certainly knew of its existence, even if he knew nothing else about it. But it is not necessary to suppose any such thing in order to explain his worry. He had begun to realize finally that his day as an independent chieftain was over. He had heard a rumour that it was proposed to create a Presidency of Ulster, on the lines of those of Munster and Connaught, and the prospect could not fail to be extremely distasteful to him. He did not want to go to England. It turned out that Lord Delvin had, in Chichester's vivid phrase, " put buzzes " in his ear, recounting to him some idle gossip about a Sir Patrick Murray remarking to King James that Tyrone was an honest man, whereupon the King was said to have replied : " Patrick,

119

I pray God he prove so ". It was quite in James's portentous manner, but what did it amount to? Tyrone seems to have feared that, once in London, he would be confined in the Tower, though nothing was further from probability. Cuconnaught had heard the same story in Flanders from the lips of exiles eager to stir up trouble. He had, with money given by the Spaniards, procured in Rouen a 60-ton ship, and come over in her, with nets and some tons of salt aboard so that he might make pretence that it was a fishing venture. Now he urgently counselled Tyrone to flee with him to Spain.

The Earl did not hesitate. He finished his business with Chichester, told him that he would be in England by the time appointed, and bade him a friendly farewell; though the Deputy afterwards recalled that he seemed more highly strung than usual. Yet his actions were cool and without sign of haste. He even stayed another two days at Slane after the arrival of the letter, doubtless to give his messengers time to reach their destinations, and then rode on to spend a night with his friend, Sir Garret Moore, at Mellifont. There he said a sad farewell, blessing every member of the great household in turn. This caused some astonishment; for though it was a fairly common Irish custom, it was not at all in keeping with his usually reserved manner. He then rode north, via Dungannon, picking up his wife and family. According to the tale related to Davies, Lady Tyrone slipped down from her horse in the course of a night ride, burst into tears, and declared that she was too weary to go farther; whereupon her husband drew his sword and vowed that he would kill her there and then if she did not ride on, and with a more cheerful countenance. Though this is only hearsay, it seems possible, knowing what we do of the relations between the Countess Catherine and her lord, that her action was a ruse to avoid going over seas with him. The women of septs such as that of Magennis were not as a rule easily tired by a journey.

Despite the secrecy of the Earl's move, the Governor of Lifford heard of his approach to Lough Foyle, and sent him an invitation to dinner. He excused himself, and rode on to Rathmullan, on the western shore of the Swilly, where Maguire's boat lay at anchor. Here Tyrconnell and his family joined the party. Next day, the 3rd September (o.s.), they sailed, and the three Ulster princes left Ireland for ever.

There were ninety-nine persons aboard the French ship, of whom modern scholarship has accounted for the names of more than half and all of the smallest importance. We have to concern ourselves with a few only. There were the Earl of Tyrone and his Countess; Lord Dungannon, his heir; Shane and Bryan, his young sons by his present wife; Art Oge, his nephew, son of the Sir Cormac who remained behind; the Earl of Tyrconnell and his brother Caffar or Cathbar, with the latter's wife Rose, née O'Dogherty, and their son Hugh, aged two years; Tyrconnell's sister Nuala, who had left her husband, Neill Garve; Cuconnaught Maguire, who had come over in the ship; and, last but for us not least, the historian Teig O'Keenan, from whom we have the record of their voyage and of their wanderings.

It was an exodus of almost all the native nobility of Tyrone, Fermanagh and Donegal, with their seed, and is not to be contemplated without emotion. The lament of the Four Masters, in a translation quaint to English ears but retaining the spirit of the original, still rings out mournfully like a death-knell :

"That was a distinguished company for one ship. For it is most certain that the sea has not borne nor the wind wafted from Ireland, in the latter times, a party in any one ship more eminent, illustrious, and noble than they were in point of genealogy, or more distinguished for great deeds, renown, feats of arms, and valorous achievements; and would that God had granted them to remain in their patrimonies until their youths should arrive at the age of manhood! Woe to the heart that meditated, woe to the mind that planned, woe to the council that decided on the project of their setting out on that journey! "

Fearing to be intercepted, the master stood out far to sea once he had passed Sligo Bay. Almost at once a great storm arose. Tyrone's device of towing in the water a gold crucifix containing a portion of the True Cross seemed to bring some relief, but they were terribly buffeted. The wind had not only the force of a gale but was contrary, and day after day they made little way. Soon they had completely lost their bearings. At last they spoke with three Scandinavian merchant ships running north from Spain, and learnt from them that they were still in the Channel. Provisions were running short, their overcrowded little vessel was battered, and the condition of a company containing a good many women and children, even infants in arms, became ghastly. They therefore decided to give up all hope of reaching Spain and to make for the coast of Normandy. On the 23rd September they reached Quillebœuf with scarcely a drop of water left aboard.

They were received well if not enthusiastically. At Lisieux they were met by the Duc de Montpensier, Governor of Normandy, with a friendly greeting. They were not invited to Paris, and Henri IV showed no desire to meet the soldier for whom he had professed so much admiration. At Arras, in Spanish territory, their welcome was much warmer. They moved on, by way of Douai, where they stayed at the Irish College, to Enghien. Here Tyrone met his son Henry, Colonel of the Irish Regiment quartered at Bruges, who presented his officers. Among these was the

Earl's nephew, Owen Roe, a youth of about seventeen, destined to fame as great as his own in Irish annals.

England, now at peace with Spain, maintained not only an ambassador at Madrid but also one at Brussels, the capital of the Spanish Netherlands. The task of the latter, Sir Thomas Edmonds, was a delicate one. He had, in brief, to prevent too much honour being paid to the fugitives, without taking a high tone or appearing to threaten. At the outset he was not very successful. The Spanish authorities replied to his representations, reasonably enough, that no military aid would be given; that Tyrone, Tyrconnell, and Maguire, by the very fact of their flight, had ceased to be a menace to King James; and that they must be received with the respect and courtesy due to their rank and their ancient friendship with the King of Spain. In fact, the Spaniards could not have done more for them than they did. The Commander-in-Chief, the Marquess Spinola, perhaps the foremost of living soldiers, drove to Enghien to invite the Irish to a banquet at Brussels, sent carriages to bring them there, and gave them a magnificent entertainment, with musicians and dancers. The Regent, the Archduke Albert, then sent his carriages to Nivelles, to which they had moved, and conducted them to his palace at Binche, where their reception was equally noble. Edmonds heard to his great annoyance that Tyrone had been permitted to remain covered in his host's presence, and though this was afterwards denied, there was no doubt that the Archduke had gone out of his way to pay the greatest possible measure of respect to his visitors. They were then allotted quarters at Hal and entirely maintained by the Spaniards, having no great funds of their own.

However, Sir Thomas Edmonds, who was an able man and a very persistent one, soon reaped the fruits of his discreet labours, strongly seconded by those of his colleague,

Sir Charles Cornwallis, in Spain. Salisbury's instructions to Cornwallis are typical of the Secretary. He began by directing that too much should not be made of the affair. The Ambassador was to set out the full circumstances from the English point of view, but to make no particular proposition, leaving the action to be taken to King Philip and asking only for a friendly message. He was to point out quietly that the refugees, without the aid of the King of Spain, were of no account; if the King took a hand in their schemes, his Majesty of England could find a spot where the Spaniards would be sorry to see the English. Cornwallis was also to make it clear that upon the departure of the Irish lords not a man had stirred.

The upshot was that the Irish were prevented from going to Spain. Tyrone, finding that no military aid was to be had from the Archduke, was anxious to put his case to Philip in person. Leaving the ladies at Louvain, he set out in November with the rest of his party, intending to travel overland, but had got no further than Namur when he was recalled by a messenger from the Archduke. Sadly he returned to Louvain, where he spent Christmas, he and his friends striving, as Edmonds maliciously noted, to drown their sorrows in sherry. Another rebuff came from Pope Paul V, who informed the Earls that they must not expect a subsidy, because the Papal Treasury was empty, and that no promises made by the Irish Roman Catholic Archbishops were binding upon the Holy See. His Holiness would extend to them his paternal goodwill so far as his means allowed; no more.

In December the two Earls drew up formal " Declarations of Grievances " addressed to the King of England, whose faithful subjects they still professed to be, though now without doubt and almost without concealment making suit to Philip of Spain to restore them by force of arms.

There was, of course, no mention in these documents of the plea, which they had put in the forefront of their appeal to the Spaniards, that Tyrone was to have been clapped into the Tower when he went to England. Even if they believed that tale, they obviously could not suggest to James himself that his intentions had been treacherous.

The main headings of Tyrone's protest were the following : He alleged that he had not been allowed to hear Mass in his own castle at Dungannon ; he complained of his treatment in the case of O'Cahan, of his loss of lands to Sir Henry Oge and Sir Tirlagh MacHenry O'Neill, and to Docwra, and of the Bishop of Derry's claim to the Church lands ; of the loss of the Bann fishery ; of the behaviour of the garrisons ; of the fact that he had been, as he alleged, deprived of authority in his own county, though Lieutenant of it, and that a sheriff had been brought in from outside. He put forward again his suspicion that a President of Ulster was about to be appointed. Finally, there was the affair of his nephew, Bryan MacArt, which has already been mentioned. All that had happened, said Tyrone, was that Bryan's servant had given a man with whom his master had quarrelled " some three or four stabs with a knife ", and the master had followed this up with another stab for luck, " through which means the man "—careless fellow that he was— " came to his death ". A jury had then been forced to bring in a verdict of murder against that good and faithful servant, while Bryan MacArt, as we have seen, was await-ing his trial in the King's Bench. A pretty thing that a member of the ruling house of the O'Neills should have to stand his trial like a common malefactor for punishing an insolent rogue with a knife-thrust !

O'Donnell made the best point, and it is significant that he put it first on his list. He protested against the per-secution of the priests. His other complaints were chiefly of the depredations of the garrisons, though he also urged as grievances that Lifford had been withheld from him and that, at the general settlement, the ancient—and rather stale— O'Donnell claim to dominion over Sligo had been disregarded. No notice was taken in England or Ireland of these documents.

If Spain was barred, Rome was not. On the 17th February 1608 the wanderers set forth again, but now in a smaller party, many of the subordinates of military age having taken service in the Irish Regiment. It was a bad time of year for travel, especially for the passage of the Alps, and it was evidently owing to the steady pressure exerted by Edmonds that the Spaniards moved them on without letting them wait for the spring. Passing through the Dukedom of Lorraine in order to avoid French territory, they were hospitably entertained by the Duke at Nancy. On the 12th March they crossed the Saint-Gotthard, and four days later were in Milan, the capital of Spanish Lombardy. Here the Governor, Count Fuentes, a soldier second in fame only to Spinola, received them, and invited them to a banquet.

Directly they set foot in Italy they came into the sphere of the Ambassador to the Republic of Venice, Sir Henry Wotton, an old acquaintance of Tyrone's, who, as Secretary to Essex, had taken part in the conferences of 1599. Wotton did not wait for instructions, but immediately attached to their company a spy, doubtless in the guise of a servant, with instructions to follow them wherever they went. He also protested to his Spanish colleague against the magnificence of the reception given to them, as did Cornwallis in Spain. But their stay in Spanish territory was not a long one. On the 29th April they made a state entry into Rome, which exceeded in splendour aught that had gone before. Two miles outside the city the party was met by a column of state coaches, to each of which eight horses were harnessed, sent by the leading Cardinals. The Pope placed a palace at the disposal of his guests, and gave Tyrone two private audiences during the early part of May.

Before returning to the Irish scene we may finish with the lot of the exiles, which was calamitous enough to recall the last act of one of the English tragedies of that day, wherein the corpses of the personages, stabbed or poisoned, lie all about the stage. Before the summer was out all the most important of the party, with the exception of Tyrone himself, were dead. Tyrconnell was the first to be taken, in July. His death was followed by that of his brother, Caffar. Cuconnaught Maguire, restless as ever and unable to endure the monotony of life in Rome, made in the course of August a trip to Genoa, where he likewise was struck down. Then came a terrible blow to Tyrone. In September his son and heir, Hugh Lord Dungannon, died also, and was buried with the O'Donnells, his uncles. There were rumours of poison, as so often in the case of sudden death in that age, and Tyrconnell's death was actually attributed to the Pope. But it is as certain as such matters can be that these four men, transported to a new climate, caught fever, which they probably treated with over-liberal doses of wine and spirits.

The tough Earl of Tyrone had another eight years to live, during which, but for a trip to Naples, he never left Papal territory, as no other State would receive him. All the time he was carefully watched by Salisbury, and after the latter's death, by Somerset. O'Neill never admitted that he had given up hope of returning to his country, backed by Spanish arms and especially by those of the Irish in Spanish service. As late as 1613 Robert Lombard, nephew to the titular Archbishop of Armagh, having turned spy, reported to Wotton's successor, Sir Dudley Carleton, that when the old man was *vino plenus et ira*, as he commonly was every night, he would declare that it was his resolute purpose to die in Ireland. Few now believed that, and it is doubtful if he did so himself. At the last he became feeble and nearly blind. He died on the 20th July 1616 and was given a state funeral, the Spanish Ambassador and three members of the highest nobility of Rome carrying the pall.

· · · · ·

When the news of the Flight of the Earls was announced in Ireland the previously discredited, or only half-credited Lord Howth said with emphasis: " I told you so! " Confirmation of his tale was forthcoming from an associate in the alleged plot. Richard Nugent, Lord Delvin, was a young Irish peer of much the same type but rather more character. Like Howth he had in the past served the Crown, but was now impoverished by an unfortunate law-suit and discontented; besides being, as Davies remarked, compounded of " the malice of the Nugents and the pride of the Geraldines "—his mother's family. Chichester laid hands upon him and shut him up in the Castle, where in November 1607 he made a full confession, very closely bearing out the story told by Howth. At Christmas 1605, he declared, the Earl of Tyrconnell informed him in the garden at Maynooth that he had learnt from Spain of the English intention " to cut them off one after another," and that they must therefore take measures for their own safety. Soon afterwards Tyrconnell disclosed to him a scheme for surprising the Castle, and stated that he had written to the King of Spain, asking for the aid of 10,000 troops.

Delvin escaped from the Castle, but after long wanderings in woods and bogs suddenly appeared in the Council Chamber and made humble submission. O'Dogherty's revolt had by then taken place, but it was clear that he had had no part in that. He was accordingly pardoned. He afterwards became the chief champion of the recusants, despite which he was created Earl of Westmeath towards the end of the reign.

From the tragic company which sailed with Tyrone from Rathmullan, one important figure had been missing. Lady Tyrconnell had been staying at Moyglare, and had been left behind with her infant daughter because her husband had fled in such haste that he had not had time to fetch her from so near Dublin. Chichester turned to her in hopes of shedding fresh light upon the affair, but with little success. She declared that she had no fore-knowledge of the flight, and had been saddened by it because she thought at first that Tyrconnell had left her for want of affection. In September, however, a well-known Franciscan friar named Owen Magrath had come to see her, bringing gold from Tyrconnell—and gold not minted in these islands, as Chichester pointed out in sending a specimen piece to Salisbury. The friar suggested that she should rejoin her husband, and had another priest at hand to act as her guide and ghostly father on the journey. She had no intention of going. In fact, she told Chichester that she would inform him if any news of treason came to her ears, and even went so far as to pray God to send the Earl a fair death rather than that he should rebel against his prince. It is a grim reflection on her prayer that within less than a year Tyrconnell, a young and vigorous man, was dead.

Chichester sent Brigid over to England, where she was received by the King, who expressed wonderment that her husband should have left so fair a face behind him. She must indeed have been beautiful; for James was not as a rule attracted by feminine charms. She was, by Chichester's good offices, granted a pension of £300 a year from

Tyrconnell's forfeited estates, and shortly after his death married Lord Kingsland.

Some other evidence was collected, but it was inconclusive. There was talk of naval preparations in Spain, but neither Cornwallis in that country, Edmonds in Flanders, nor Salisbury in England, seem to have had any serious apprehension of a new Spanish invasion of Ireland. In a private letter written in May 1608, Edmonds declared that even the rumour of troops of the Irish Regiment in Flanders disbanding in order to go to Ireland secretly was untrue. On the contrary, he said, their colonel was doing all he could to prevent any of them from obtaining passports. Salisbury was indeed watchful, even suspicious; but the most he feared was that if there were an Irish rising some small aid might be sent in the Pope's name, just possibly with the connivance of Spain. Even that was only an outside chance. Spain was genuinely pacific now, even friendly, where England was concerned. Philip III had gone so far as to give secret instructions to the Count de la Villa Mediana, one of the peace delegates of 1604, to propose a match between Henry, Prince of Wales, and the Infanta Anna—a proposal, as every schoolboy knows, to be revived years afterwards with Charles substituted for Henry, dead, and Maria in the place of Anna, married to Louis XIII of France. Spain had extended courtesy and generous hospitality to the Irish fugitives, but nothing more than that, and seems to have been glad to be rid of their presence on Flemish soil. Had she given undertakings to aid an Irish rising, some trace of them must have been left. There is none.[1]

[1] The writer has examined such Spanish historical works and calendars as were available without finding a hint of Spanish plans for intervention in Ireland. Nor do the most authoritative English writers on this period seem to have discovered anything of the sort. It is to be noted, too, that though Howth spoke of Spanish aid having been promised unconditionally, and the writer of the anonymous letter declared that it had been promised in case of need, Delvin merely said that Tyrconnell had written to ask for it.

What, then, was the cause of that major historical mystery, the Flight of the Earls? Are we to believe that there was no Irish plot, but instead an English conspiracy to ruin the Ulster magnates or drive them from Ireland? That, too, is incredible. The historians who suggest it certainly attribute to Chichester and Davies not merely ingenuity, of which they were indeed doubtless capable, but a positively satanic inspiration, when they picture them carrying through such a conspiracy and leaving " not a rack behind ". That they should have done so is the more unlikely because their most secret thoughts on kindred matters—not by any means always creditable to the English in Ireland—are revealed by correspondence, some of it partly in cipher.

The most reasonable explanation seems to be the following: Tyrconnell and Maguire, moved by wrongs real and imaginary, by the persecution of the Roman Catholic Church, and most of all by the discovery that their day as independent princes was over, had been engaged with certain others in plotting, or at least talking, treason. There may have been little more than talk; for Tyrconnell was not a man of strong character and Maguire was extremely impulsive. The element of Spanish aid was largely aspiration; if they believed in it, it was because their hopes cozened them into doing so. They may have had vague promises, perhaps through some of the Irish priests, whose zeal for the Church deluded them, but not from any responsible person. Spain had long been the ally of rebel Ireland, and they had not sufficient knowledge of the international situation to realize how unlikely it was that she would again intervene in her favour. Then they took fright. Rumour spread, as such rumours often do in a band of conspirators—and this we know contained at least two, Howth and the writer of the anonymous letter, who had not their hearts in the business—that the Government intended to " strike them down ". Maguire fled abroad and was told in Flanders that Tyrone's summons to England was a trap. He got the money from the Archduke, for old times' sake, bought his ship, and brought her over. Tyrone, who was a disappointed man, considered himself badly treated, was growing old, and had probably lost his nerve, was rushed into joining the fugitives. He, too, doubtless hoped that he could persuade Philip to restore the house of O'Neill to its ancient grandeur.

At all events, the Ulster lords were gone. James and his advisers, genuinely disquieted at first, speedily determined to turn the situation to their own advantage. They would carry out a colonization of the Ulster counties concerned, avoiding the mistakes of their predecessors and planting the roots deep in the soil. On the 3rd September 1607, less than four weeks after the flight, the Lords of the Privy Council addressed a letter to Chichester giving him an outline of the project. There was to be a judicious mixture of inhabitants, Irish, English, and Scottish. The Irish were to be chosen from those who had shown their loyalty, the English rather from servants of the Irish Government than newcomers. But there was to be no haste, and the King was determined to check every step personally. And, first of all, there were certain legal formalities to be fulfilled.

Just before Christmas of 1607 Sir John Davies and other Commissioners went north for the purpose of obtaining an indictment of the fugitives for high treason, in both the counties of Donegal and Tyrone. At Lifford the Donegal jury numbered twenty-three, thirteen Irish and ten English, with the youthful Sir Cahir O'Dogherty, the chief landowner now remaining in the county, as foreman. On the main charge the jury had some scruples. However, after it had been explained by the Attorney-General that an indictment was an accusation, not a conviction, it found a true bill against the Earls and their followers on the charges of "conspiring and practising to deprive the King of his Crown of Ireland " —a point on which there was no positive evidence—and of robbing and despoiling the King's faithful subjects—which, without a shadow of doubt, they had done for the provisioning of their ship. The Commission then crossed the river to Strabane, where a jury of nineteen, mostly Irish, with Sir Henry Oge O'Neill as foreman, indicted Tyrone of having assumed the forbidden title of " the O'Neill "[1] and of having murdered several men.

Such was the situation when, on the 22nd April 1608, a scared survivor rode into Dublin to report a great disaster. Sir Cahir O'Dogherty, Chief of Inishowen, had surprised Derry, slain the Governor, and burnt the place to the ground.

[1] The document on which the indictment was framed began : " O'Neill bids O'Quin to pay . . .", but was signed " Tyrone ", so would not appear to have been particularly good evidence. The jurors, however, declared from their personal knowledge that Tyrone in his dealings with his own followers insisted on the Irish princely title, and that none dared address him otherwise. In any case, this was to a great extent a legal form ; for there could be no doubt that Tyrone was now engaged in treasonable correspondence.

## IV

## THE REVOLT OF SIR CAHIR O'DOGHERTY

I F Sir Henry Docwra had remained Governor of Derry it is almost certain that Sir Cahir O'Dogherty would not have gone into rebellion; had he by any chance done so, it is impossible to believe that Derry would have been surprised and burnt. Docwra's successor, Sir George Paulet, was the last man whom Chichester would have chosen for this important post. The Lord Deputy could understand and sympathize with a governor who ruled by kindness, as Docwra had done, though his own method at Carrickfergus had been terror. If the Irish neither loved nor feared their ruler there was likely to be trouble. Paulet was even detested by his own men, not because he was a strict disciplinarian—for he was slack in this respect—but because he was bad-tempered and brutal. He was also without any considerable military experience. Chichester had long been disquieted about the situation at Derry; but Paulet was a rich young man of family imposed upon him from above, and not easily removed. All the Deputy could do was to warn and reprove the Governor, and report to England that he was dissatisfied with him. He had already done both.

Sir Cahir O'Dogherty was deeply indebted to Docwra. On the death of his father, Sir John O'Dogherty, in 1600, when he himself was in his early teens, Hugh Roe O'Donnell had appointed Sir John's younger brother to be Lord of Inishowen. But the boy Cahir had two powerful adherents: the brothers Hugh Boy and Phelim Reagh MacDavitt,

mentioned more than once in this record, who were bound
to him by the closest of all Irish ties, that of fosterage.
The brethren countered O'Donnell's move by repairing to
Docwra and persuading him to back Cahir against his uncle.
Docwra was pleased to do so; apart from the well-tried
principle of *divide et impera*, it was good policy to put the
chiefry of Inishowen into the hands of a youngster who
could be moulded. It was also in accordance with the
English law of inheritance. The choice seemed a good one.
The lad was bright, attractive, and affectionate; bereaved
of his father, his relations with Docwra were soon filial.
He was also a little cockerel to fight. In one smart affair
at Augher he stood to it so stoutly by his patron's side that
the latter obtained for him the honour of knighthood at the
hands of Mountjoy. We have seen that at the settlement
James had restored to Sir Cahir his father's lands. He had
since married the sister of Lord Gormanston, and lived in
some state at his castles of Birt, Elagh, and Buncrana.

His relations with Paulet were bad from the first. It is
said that the Governor struck him with his riding-whip
during an altercation, and though the sole evidence for this
is the record of the Four Masters, who wrote in the next
reign and were not then in Donegal, so caddish an insult
rather accords with what we know of Paulet. Sir Cahir
had, however, a more material grievance. Just before the
settlement of 1603 Mountjoy had leased Inch Island in Lough
Swilly, which contained the best lands of Inishowen, to
Sir Ralph Bingley. Docwra had protested vigorously that
the rights of O'Dogherty were infringed by this transaction,
but without effect, and Bingley had remained in possession.
This state of affairs continued despite direct instructions
issued by the King to Mountjoy—or Devonshire, as he had
become—that the lease was to be cancelled. Again the
King's attention was drawn to the matter, and on the 18th

April 1608, the Lords of the Council wrote to Chichester directing that the lands should at once be restored. It was too late; the letter is endorsed: " Re. after he entred into rebellion ". At least one Irish historian has suggested that the letter was purposely held back, but this is absurd. Letters from Whitehall to Dublin normally took five or six days, and often more.

It will thus be seen that O'Dogherty had been badly treated in the matter of Inch Island. It must not be forgotten, however, that he was, even without it, in one important respect better off than ever his father had been; for he paid no head rent to the house of O'Donnell. His conduct had lately been suspicious. At the end of October 1607, he suddenly and without warning landed a party of armed men on Tory Island, and it was reported that he meant to " stand upon his keeping " and await the return of Tyrone. In his absence Paulet rode to Birt, intending to seize the castle, but found it barred against him and did not venture to attack it. O'Dogherty sent the Governor a gentlemanly letter, complaining of hard treatment at his hands, but subscribing himself, " Your loving friend ". Paulet replied bidding him disperse his men and lay down his arms, adding, like the fool he was : " Wishing confusion to your actions, I leave you to a provost marshal and his halter." Indeed, Paulet was not the type of young man suitable for the maintenance of an " outpost of empire " in the twentieth century any more than in the seventeenth.

O'Dogherty then made a wise move. He rode straight in to see Chichester himself, and to deny formally that he had any intention of either fleeing the country or going into revolt. Chichester bound him to appear upon twenty days' notice, one of his two sureties being his brother-in-law Gormanston, and let him go, not because he trusted him completely, but because his detention would have scared others and created unrest. That was towards the end of November. A month later, as we have seen, Sir Cahir was foreman of the Donegal Grand Jury—on which his enemy Paulet also sat—who found a true bill for treason against the fugitive Earls and their followers. In February 1608 he was so far from contemplating immediate rebellion that he addressed a letter to the young Prince of Wales, begging for the position of Gentleman of the Privy Chamber. Perhaps the fact that his demand got no satisfaction was the last ounce that tipped the balance and drove him into his futile and puerile revolt.

If strategically the revolt deserves these adjectives, the tactical methods employed were skilful. To capture Derry Sir Cahir needed arms, and he actually contrived to get them from a garrison much more alert than that of Derry, and under a much sounder commander than Paulet. Despite his quarrel with Paulet he was still on the most friendly terms with the latter's subordinate, Henry Hart, the Governor of Culmore Fort, who was godfather to his son. On the 19th April he invited Hart and his wife to dinner at Buncrana, ensuring the latter's company by the clever plea that Lady O'Dogherty came of a great family of the Pale and was lonely without the society to which she had been used. The Harts were hospitably entertained. Just before it was time to go O'Dogherty took Hart upstairs for a private word. He then complained to him of Paulet's treatment, informed him that he was his prisoner, and vowed that he would have him put to death if he did not surrender Culmore. This Hart steadfastly refused to do ; nor was he shaken in his resolution when Sir Cahir brought in Lady O'Dogherty and his own wife to implore him to agree.[1]

[1] The writer had the honour of serving with his descendant from those very parts, who was killed in the Battle of the Somme. He was a silent, steady man, who in like case would have suffered himself to be cut in pieces without betraying his trust, but who would have refused in the least dramatic manner.

Mrs. Hart was then removed and told by Sir Cahir that her husband would instantly be killed if she refused to obey his orders. She, poor soul, gave way. It was about nightfall when O'Dogherty set out with a strong party for Culmore, taking her with him. On reaching the fort she was sent forward to call to the sentries that her husband was lying in a ditch with a broken leg. The gate was thrown open and a party came out to rescue their captain, whereupon the Irish rushed forward and speedily overcame the little garrison. By this means Sir Cahir obtained possession of the fort, the stands of arms in it, several guns, and two sailing-boats drawn up on the strand below the walls.

Sir Cahir, who was a humane man enough, killed none of his prisoners. He then wasted no time but marched with one hundred men through the night to Derry, only six miles away, arriving at 2 a.m. on the 20th. The whole town was asleep, which was all the more negligent on the part of its Governor, because it was not surrounded by a wall, but only by a ditch and bank. The settlement had grown like a mushroom since the day of Docwra's arrival, as is proved by the fact that it contained nearly a hundred able-bodied men, exclusive of the garrison of about the same number. The defences consisted of a fort at either end: a big one where the Governor and the bulk of his company lay, and a small one containing the powder-magazine. O'Dogherty divided his force into two, in order to attack each fort simultaneously: his redoubtable foster-brother, Phelim Reagh, leading one party against the big fort, while he himself assaulted the minor one.

Despite the complete surprise, there was some resistance. Paulet broke through the assailants as they entered the door of his fort and reached the house of Ancient Corbet, where they both gallantly defended themselves. Corbet engaged Phelim Reagh in single combat and wounded him, but was struck down from behind. His wife promptly slew her husband's slayer, and was herself slain. Paulet was killed by a member of the O'Dogherty family—or, according to another report, by Phelim Reagh. Another officer, Lieutenant Gordon, rushed out naked and killed two men before he was himself struck on the head by a stone and then hacked to death. At the second fort another Englishman came near to accounting for the leader of the revolt. He fired his pistol point-blank at Sir Cahir, but that young man, with great presence of mind, grabbed hold of one of his own followers and held the living buckler in front of him. The kerne it was that died, but the Englishman did not long survive him. Meanwhile the centre of the straggling township had not yet been attacked, and the momentary respite inspired one bold spirit, Lieutenant Baker, to attempt the recapture of the lower fort. He was, however, badly seconded by the handful of townsmen whom he had gathered together, was wounded in the arm by Sir Cahir, and fell back to the neighbouring houses of the Bishop of Derry and the Sheriff, where he and his party barricaded themselves in.

The Irish, who loved nothing less than a storm, failed to dislodge the defenders; but when a gun was brought from Culmore and trained on the house, Baker realized that his chances were poor. He then obtained a written promise that he and his men should be allowed to depart with their arms. This promise was kept, and O'Dogherty's former friend, Hart, was ferried across the Foyle with his wife so that they might make their way to Coleraine. Lady Paulet and Mrs. Montgomery were, however, carried off by the raiders. Only about a dozen on either side were killed, which shows that the resistance of the garrison was largely confined to its officers. Phelim Reagh, judging

Derry to be untenable by such a force as O'Dogherty could yet muster, burned the houses, including the Bishop's, in which his valuable library was destroyed. Then, throwing most of the guns into the bay, Phelim put the others into the two captured boats and made off for Culmore.

So far all had gone well enough with Sir Cahir; nor did fortune immediately desert him. He surprised and captured Dogh Castle on Sheep Haven. The little garrison of Dunalong was alert, but dared not await his coming, and escaped to Lifford, where the Governor, Sir Richard Hansard, was also strengthened by the arrival of some Scotch settlers from Strabane, who fled in haste across the river. There success came to an end; for though the rebels increased in numbers to not far short of a thousand, hardly a man of position joined them. Sir Cahir's attitude was certainly not that of a conqueror. Placing Phelim Reagh with thirty men in Culmore and other small garrison in Birt Castle, where he left Lady Paulet, Mrs. Montgomery, and his own wife, he crossed the Swilly into the wild country of the MacSwineys. Here he was joined by the only really prominent adherent whom he ever secured. Shane MacManus O'Donnell, an uncle of the late Hugh Roe and of Tyrconnell.

The old ferocious Chichester of the days of Carrickfergus replaced the moderate statesman who presided over the Council in Dublin Castle. He declared that the repression of the revolt should be " thick and short ", and he fulfilled his promise. He put a price of £500 on the head of Sir Cahir, and one of £200 on that of Phelim Reagh MacDavitt. No other rebel was placed beyond hope of pardon, but none could gain it without bringing in another rebel, alive or dead. It appears to us a ghastly policy, but it paid. In the days to come scores of O'Dogherty's adherents were to be stabbed to death by their fellows, and this horrible struggle on the pattern of that of the Kilkenny Cats saved the forces of the Crown much trouble. Realizing that Sir Neill Garve O'Donnell would be able to deal with the revolt before his own forces were on the scene, he authorized him to raise a force of 100 foot and 25 horse at the King's charge. As a reward for services expected, he let him know that he was applying to the Privy Council in London for a grant of more lands. At the same time he removed Sir Neill's son from Trinity College and lodged him in the Castle as a hostage for his father's good behaviour. He then sent out a small relief force under his two best fighting men, Sir Richard Wingfield, the Marshal, and Sir Oliver Lambart, to march as quickly as possible to Lifford, which was holding out without difficulty, though somewhat short of supplies, and then to Derry. A cannon would be needed to batter a way into the fortresses held by O'Dogherty; but in order not to delay the force he sent Sir Ralph Bingley with a demi-culverin round to the Foyle by sea.

The relief force reached Derry on the 20th May, to find the place a complete ruin, except that the little cathedral church was undamaged—probably because it was dedicated to St. Columba—and that the stone chimneys of the wooden houses were intact. The inhabitants began trickling back and putting up huts to sleep in, while the troops swept in cattle from Inishowen to feed them. Phelim Reagh did not await an attack by Wingfield, but evacuated Culmore, burned what of it would burn, and slipped out of the Foyle in his two boats, taking with him several small guns. The fort was roughly repaired and garrisoned, its commander being that Lieutenant Baker who had fought so stoutly at Derry.

The forces under Wingfield had now been joined by three of the local Irish notabilities, Sir Neill Garve O'Donnell,

Sir Henry Oge O'Neill, and Sir Tirlagh MacArt. There was little doubt as to the loyalty of the two latter, but Neill Garve had been behaving in a very peculiar manner. He had first of all refused to come in to Lifford when requested to do so by Sir Richard Hansard. He had then removed the Lifford garrison's cattle under pretence of saving them from O'Dogherty, and now showed no signs of returning them. Still, just as servant-maids who steal sweets are often quite honest in other respects, so no Ulster chieftain was to be judged by his behaviour when cattle were in question. Neill Garve obtained a "protection" from Wingfield and accompanied him into Donegal. Meanwhile a small force under Lambart had been left in front of Birt, a strong castle, to await the arrival of the demi-culverin. When it arrived the garrison was summoned. The defenders were ingenuous folk, like most of the men of Inishowen, and were not quite sure whether they were holding Birt for O'Dogherty or for the King of Spain, but they answered that they would fight it out. They also announced that if a breach were made they would put Mrs. Montgomery into it. Poor lady, her foreboding that Ulster was a wild place had after all been correct. How she must have longed for the sanctified peace of Norwich Cathedral Close or the mild and gentle rusticity of Chedzoy! However, she was spared that last trial. No breach was made; in fact, the two rounds fired by the demi-culverin made little impression on the stout masonry. But the garrison had had enough, and Lady O'Dogherty came forth to announce its surrender at discretion. She was taken aboard that historic ship the *Tramontana*, which was lying in the Swilly, and Mrs. Montgomery was, as the report went, "returned to her owner" the Bishop. Inishowen was completely cleared of the rebels.

In northern Donegal Sir Cahir made no fight of it. His

character, indeed, is ruthlessly exposed by his conduct in the days that followed. He had shown himself a brave man under the leadership of a Docwra, and a bold one with the backing of a Phelim Reagh. Left to himself he was without initiative. His one success smacked of assassination. Like Vandamme on the eve of the Waterloo campaign, Sir Henry Oge refused to sleep in the camp, but repaired for the night of the 5th June to a house outside it. Here the enemy broke in upon him, killed him in his sleep, and wounded one of his sons so grievously that he afterwards died. At Dogh Castle, a place even stronger than Birt, another detachment under Sir Henry Folliott, the Governor of Ballyshannon, was dropped to await the all-important demi-culverin. Sir Thomas Ridgeway, the Treasurer, who seems to have accompanied Wingfield in the first place as a volunteer, because the affair was too good to be missed, and Neill Garve led about 150 men in pursuit of Sir Cahir towards Glenveagh.

It was a district into which English troops had probably never penetrated before, and as wild as any in all Ireland. The narrow gorges dividing steep-sided hills were thickly wooded, and it was found that every path had been barricaded. Had Sir Cahir at last decided to fight, Ridgeway with his little force would have been powerless to dislodge him. But Sir Cahir did not fight. Instead, he slipped away to Fermanagh, leaving his cattle behind. Neill Garve heard about the cattle and promptly asked for two days' leave, his object being to dispose of them in his own fastnesses. As the quarry had escaped, Ridgeway let him go.

During the absence of Neill Garve his two brothers came to Ridgeway with a strange tale. Neill Garve, they said, had been in communication with Sir Cahir throughout the march. He had warned him of the English advance and had actually offered to take charge of his cattle and return them to him afterwards. More—one can see Ridgeway's growing stupefaction as the story developed—Neill Garve had known all about the revolt from the first. He was its instigator, though he had failed to carry out the part which he had promised Sir Cahir to fulfil. So that was how it was! Ridgeway began to understand many things hitherto obscure. Now he knew whose was the brain that had contrived the daring *coups* at Culmore and Derry. Now he could account for Sir Cahir's hesitations and half-heartedness after his bold beginning. It was because his ally had failed him and only half the job was done. Ridgeway realized that the apprehension of Neill Garve was even more important than that of O'Dogherty; but after he had the former in his hands it would not be safe to stay with so small a force in this wilderness, so near the prisoner's own country in the Finn valley. He therefore waited only until Neill Garve returned, arrested him, hurried back to the shore of Lough Swilly, and put him aboard the *Tramontana*.

O'Dogherty had meanwhile done nothing but march aimlessly about Ulster. He penetrated as far as Armagh, then suddenly turned and made his way back to the neighbourhood of Dogh Castle, having gained scarcely any fresh adherents. Probably it was his intention to relieve Dogh. On the 5th July there was a brush with the besiegers hardly deserving the name of a skirmish, in the midst of which Sir Cahir O'Dogherty was killed by one of his own men. The £500 price upon his head had proved too tempting. That sum was paid out of the Irish Treasury, but we know not to whom; and the head was sent to Dublin to welcome arrivals over one of the gates. Such was the end of a young man who had once appeared to be the most hopeful and fortunate in Ulster. We need waste no tears upon him, while admitting that there were many less attractive figures on both sides. His lack of courage

DOGH CASTLE, SHEEP HAVEN, COUNTY DONEGAL

after the capture of Derry would deprive him of our sympathy even if we approved of that action.

The demi-culverin arrived at Dogh almost immediately after his death, but the castle stood a good pounding without surrendering, and in the end Shane MacManus O'Donnell and most of the garrison escaped by boat. Towards the end of July Phelim Reagh MacDavitt was discovered hiding in a wood. He defended himself fiercely, but was captured and sent in to Lifford for a trial that could have but one result. Chichester himself was coming north with the judges, and his mood was grim. At Dungannon, a brother of Sir Donnell O'Cahan named Shane Carragh, who had taken the opportunity of O'Dogherty's revolt to come out in Coleraine and murder some personal enemies, was tried by a completely Irish jury and condemned to death by hanging, drawing, and quartering. The natives of Tyrone had never seen this gruesome punishment carried out and were duly impressed by the methods of civilization. The party then moved to Coleraine through the forests of Glenconkeine, where, said Davies, "the wild inhabitants wondered as much to see the King's Deputy as the ghosts in Virgil wondered to see Æneas alive in hell." At Coleraine a score of those who had either been in rebellion themselves or harboured rebels without compulsion were hanged. As he went forward the fruit of Chichester's proclamations dropped into his hands; for from all sides rebels were brought in by their associates, often by their close kindred. At Lifford Phelim Reagh met his fate, and a full twenty swung with him. Before he died he testified that O'Dogherty had, prior to their flight, disclosed to him the "treasons and conspiracy" of Tyrone and Tyrconnell.

It was not only where the revolt had been extinguished that the proclamations were of value. In western Donegal, where Sir Henry Folliott stamped out the last embers, they were also useful. Folliott returned to Glenveagh, where some of the O'Gallaghers were holding out, and they promptly turned their swords against one another. He had some difficulty owing to bad weather in reaching Tory Island, where Shane MacManus had left a dozen men in a little fort, but when he did the process was repeated. The constable of the fort killed three of his own men; a fourth killed the constable and was then stabbed to death by a fifth. Seven heads in all having fallen, Folliott pardoned the remainder. That was the end of the revolt of Sir Cahir O'Dogherty, though one unimportant outlaw "stood upon his keeping" until the following year.

It only remained to deal with Sir Neill Garve O'Donnell and Sir Donnell O'Cahan, who had also been arrested on the charge of complicity in the revolt, though he had been in custody when it took place. Regarding Sir Neill Garve there could be no doubt. Overwhelming evidence was produced not only by his brothers but by Lady O'Dogherty, by Phelim Reagh before his execution, and by Ineenduv O'Donnell. That hag's testimony against the son-in-law whom she hated would not have amounted to much unless it had had strong corroboration, but she probably stated a truth, and an important one, when she declared that he had avoided open revolt because his son was in Chichester's hands. Neill Garve was the begetter of the whole plot. He had told Sir Cahir that while the latter was capturing Culmore and Derry he would be getting possession of Lifford by collusion with Sir Richard Hansard. He had urged O'Dogherty to exterminate the two garrisons. He had actually lent him some men for the attack. His part had been played with a mixture of that skill in intrigue and blind recklessness as to the future which were elements in his strange character. We have urged that he was a wronged man, but no wrongs that he had suffered can excuse his double treachery.

If, however, the case against him was clear, the manner of procedure was not. Davies, with a strict regard for legality that did him credit, would bring against him no charge on the score of any action prior to the protection granted by Wingfield, holding that that covered all wrongful acts already committed. There remained therefore only his treasonable correspondence with Sir Cahir after the protection had been granted. A grand jury in Donegal found a true bill, but the grand jury exhausted all the principal Irish gentry of the county, and the common jury which was called in June 1609 was composed of men of no position. This was fatal to hopes of a conviction. Then, as in the last days of English rule in the twentieth century, the lower in the social scale the jury, the harder it was to obtain a conviction against a prominent political misdemeanant. The judge clattered up in his carriage with his mounted escort; to him impartial justice seemed easy and natural. But it was the poor juryman who had to go home through the lonely bog, whose pools of black water would never yield up a secret; it was his windows that received the charge of buckshot; his cattle that were driven off; his stallion that was maimed. Contrary to established belief, one of the main causes of failure to obtain an honest verdict in cases of political crime in Ireland was failure or inability to protect honest jurymen. Though the idea seems strange to us, one of the arguments for the Plantation of Ulster was that it would provide jurymen not likely to be intimidated. In this instance, though the jury was shut up until it was almost starved, it would not convict. It was therefore discharged without reaching a verdict, and Sir Neill Garve O'Donnell was sent to London for confinement in the Tower.

Chichester and Davies decided not to risk a fresh fiasco by bringing Sir Donnell O'Cahan to trial in Ireland. He was therefore sent to the Tower with Sir Neill Garve, to join a third fallen Ulster magnate, Tyrone's brother, Sir Cormac MacBaron O'Neill. They were treated as first-class prisoners, with liberty to take what exercise they pleased within the walls, to write letters, and even to see their friends; but they never regained their liberty in upwards of twenty years, Neill Garve dying in 1626 and Donnell O'Cahan apparently in 1628. Neill Garve's son, Nachten, a clever boy with all his father's brains, far more than his scholarship—having been at Oxford as well as Trinity—and a full share of his wicked temper and malignity, shared their captivity for a brief period, and was then released.

Whatever Neill Garve's wrongs, he had, as has been stated, got no more than his deserts, and no one has ever sympathized with Cormac; but one cannot feel so confident about O'Cahan. The chief evidence of his complicity in the revolt was that of his brother Shane Carragh, who may have testified against him in an effort to save his own life. Docwra, who was, of course, not in Ireland at the time of the revolt, thought he was guilty, but that all the trouble had in his case arisen " from the breach of my promise with him ".

# Book Three

## THE PLANTATION

---

### I

### THE SETTLEMENT OF ANTRIM AND DOWN

THE flight of the Earls had made available for an Anglo-Scottish Plantation the counties of Tyrone, Donegal, Armagh, and Fermanagh, in greater or less degree, while Cavan was also considered to be in the same situation. From what has already been written it will appear that the circumstances of these counties differed considerably.

Of Tyrone itself a clean sweep could be made equitably as well as legally, so long as the fidelity of the house of Tirlagh Luineach O'Neill, now represented by his grandson Sir Tirlagh MacArt, and certain others was borne in mind. In Donegal also the paramount chief was gone abroad and attainted, but the barony of Inishowen had been expressly removed from him. In Armagh, where Tyrone's base brother, Art MacBaron, had acted as chieftain, the Earl's legitimate half-brother, Sir Tirlagh MacHenry, had large claims, but the county as a whole was escheated. In Fermanagh the flight of Cuconnaught Maguire had condemned at least half the county, but there still remained Connor Roe, who had been nominally faithful, and Cuconnaught's younger brother Bryan, who had at least remained quiet. Here it was evident that a large proportion of the county would have to be left in Irish hands.

The case of Cavan was rather different, because it had not been affected by the Flight of the Earls. On the other hand, the O'Reillys had received no such regrants of territory as had the Earls of Tyrone and Tyrconnell, so the rebellion of the chiefs in the reign of Elizabeth could still be used as a handle to effect the forfeiture of the county. "Philip (O'Reilly) at Cavan aforesaid, was slain in actual rebellion, by reason whereof all the said territory or county of Breny O'Rely . . . did come into the hands of the said late Queen Elizabeth, and are now in the actual possession of His Majesty." It was hardly fair that this should have been raked up against the inhabitants of Cavan years after the rebellion, since when their behaviour had been on the whole good. The O'Reillys had not only shown more disposition to loyalty than any other Ulster clan; they were also ahead of the rest in civilization and manners. As a matter of fact, it will appear that for this very reason Chichester had no intention of planting Cavan on the same scale as some of the other counties, and that there was no considerable transportation of the Irish as a result of his action. What he wanted was the power to bring in a number of English and Scottish colonists as a measure of security, and to set an example in agriculture to the natives, who, for the rest, he hoped to settle on small parcels of land as in Monaghan. Nevertheless, Cavan was technically added to the list of the " escheated counties " which were subject to the new scheme.

Since the revolt of Sir Cahir O'Dogherty there had been added the small but rich county of Coleraine, and the barony of Inishowen. In Donegal, too, the broad lands of Sir Neill Garve O'Donnell reverted to the disposition of the Crown, because he had not yet received a patent for them. (He could have had it, but had, as we have seen, been disgusted because the grant was not greater, and had been waiting for a better offer.) So, the whole of Ulster, but for Monaghan, the case of which has been fully described, and the eastern counties of Antrim and Down, were actually or theoretically open for plantation. O'Dogherty's revolt, however, had had a moral as well as a material effect. It had hardened Chichester's views and steeled his heart. Had it not taken place, the Plantation would probably have been very different, and modern Ulster might not have come into existence. Chichester's original project, immediately after the Flight of the Earls, was simply to divide up the lands among the natives and force them to become agriculturalists. Owing to *creaghting* and miserably backward methods of agriculture the lands were but half populated, so that if the " mere Irish " were closed up on to farms of limited size, there would still be estates left over on which to plant not only deserving officials and soldiers, but also a considerable number of colonists from over the water. After O'Dogherty's revolt the Lord Deputy's scruples in part disappeared, and he had less hesitation in supporting the much more radical plan of settlement that was being prepared in London. We shall find, however, that he never became one of the extremists from this point of view, and that in general he acted as a brake upon the scheme of the Plantation.

Before we consider this scheme and its fulfilment, we must first take note of the situation in Antrim and Down. When we speak of the " Plantation of Ulster " we commonly include the changes which took place in these counties under that heading. Actually, they did not come into the Plantation proper, yet a great series of grants and purchases had very much the same effect, and the future of no county was more deeply influenced by Anglo-Scottish settlement than theirs, certainly than that of Antrim. This process had been at work prior to the Flight of the Earls, having, in fact, begun immediately after the accession of James I. We have therefore to go back a few years to discover its origins.

It will be recalled that in 1595 the Earl of Tyrone had fallen out with the Macdonnells. He had subsequently come to terms with the head of the clan in Antrim, Randal, son of Sorley Boy. Randal had accompanied him to Kinsale, but with a following of only a few hundred, a great proportion of whom seem to have been killed. The Macdonnells were, indeed, at that time in low water in Antrim, which had been ravaged by Chichester, and they were further weakened by quarrels with the head of their house in Scotland. They had likewise to reckon with the personal hostility of Chichester, whose brother and predecessor as Governor of Carrickfergus they had slain. However, Randal MacSorley was a cautious and discreet man, who had also the luck to be a Scottish magnate, a useful advantage when a Scottish king mounted the throne of England and Ireland.

Randal's first move had been to desert Tyrone in the autumn of 1602. It was a step for which he could hardly be blamed. He had helped the Earl as long as he well could, keeping him supplied with food and whisky when a hunted fugitive in Glenconkeine. Now Tyrone's cause was doomed, and further adherence to it might well mean the extinction of Clandonnell in Ulster. Randal was received tolerably well by his old foe at Carrickfergus, and warmly by Mountjoy, to whom Chichester presented him. The Lord Deputy, in pursuance of his general policy of reconciling the existing chiefs—unexceptionable in this case, where there were no pledges to be broken as in Donegal—knighted the Scotsman, and recommended him to King James immediately on his accession. James, who had long known him, granted him by patent deed, dated the 28th May 1603, the Route and the Glynns, the whole coast region of Antrim from Larne to Coleraine, considerably over 300,000 acres, without regard to the claims of his Scottish kinsfolk. It was a magnificent estate, of valuable though at the moment almost deserted land. And yet, for several years Sir Randal had a hard row to hoe. He had to repopulate and recultivate a devastated and famine-stricken country-side, to keep his clansmen quiet, to allay the continued but gradually clearing suspicions of Chichester. His marriage about 1604 to a daughter of Tyrone's turned out to be disadvantageous, good match though it appeared at the moment, as Tyrone became less and less in favour with the Government.

In the summer of 1607, only a few weeks before Tyrone's flight from Ireland, an event occurred which greatly benefited Randal, and incidentally helped to give the population of the Antrim coast the characteristics which endure to this day. In 1599 the Macdonnells had headed an unsuccessful Highland revolt in Scotland. One of the conditions of their submission was that they should remove their clansmen from Cantyre, which was then repeopled by the Earl of Argyll with Presbyterian Lowlanders from Renfrew, Dumbarton, and Ayr. In 1607 there was another Highland revolt, in the midst of which the aged Angus Macdonnell, who was Randal's uncle but at the same time his foe, came down upon Cantyre like a wolf on the fold. The sheep, that is, the Lowland settlers, did not await the arrival of the indignant lord of the soil. Putting their household goods and what cattle and horses they could into boats, they made off across the water to Antrim. Presbyterians though they were, they were a godsend to their new Catholic master, as they were able to stock the farms which he allotted to them.

Sir Randal had already proved that he was prepared to march with the times by granting farms with long leases, in some cases so long as to be virtually freeholds, to well-behaved Irish tenantry. Now, to his own Macdonnells, to Irish O'Haras, O'Dowds, and hibernicized Scottish Magees, were added Scottish Boyds, Kennedys, Dunlops, and Sloans. He could not have better pleased the Government, who were always striving with little success to induce the native chiefs of Ulster to do the same thing. And, as the Plantation proper was carried out, more and more Lowlanders came to Antrim, where conditions were fairly settled. Sir Randal not only kept quiet himself, but restrained his Irish neighbours during O'Dogherty's revolt. From the English point of view he was a good landlord; that is to say, he settled on his lands tenants of the sort of which the Government approved, and also introduced modern methods of farming, though not to the extent of his neighbours in Down. In 1618 he was rewarded with a viscounty, and in December 1620 he was created Earl of Antrim.

As regards the rest of the country, Chichester himself was allotted a large grant in the neighbourhood of Belfast Castle; the O'Neills of Northern Clandeboye were not neglected; and the head of the greatest native clan, Rory Oge MacQuillan, obtained 60,000 acres about Galgorm. This huge estate passed by purchase into the hands of the founders of three notable Ulster families, the Reverend Alexander Colville, Sir Robert Adair, and Chichester's nephew and biographer, the well-known soldier Sir Faithful Fortescue. A footing within the country was also obtained by a Scottish settler named James Hamilton, who had been allotted a considerable estate in the neighbouring county of Down.

That leads us to a consideration of Down, the fate of which was rather more complicated than that of Antrim. The Clandeboye O'Neills were the lords of Southern, or Upper Clandeboye, where they owned over 60,000 acres.

Various members of the clan had been involved in rebellion and dispossessed. In 1601 Chichester had installed a young man who appeared to be innocuous, Con Bryan Fertagh O'Neill, as chieftain of this great area. He remarked in his sardonic way that if Con were hanged the King and the world in general would be no heavy losers, but that it was worth while to give him a chance. He even induced Mountjoy to pardon his lapse in going over to Tyrone when the Spaniards landed at Kinsale, and reinstated him. At the beginning of 1603 Con and his retainers, after a drunken orgy at Castlereagh, attacked the garrison of Belfast Castle. They were beaten off, but the luckless young chief was seized and imprisoned at Carrickfergus. On the accession of James and the advent of peace, he was allowed to walk about the town and even to entertain his friends in the taverns, a privilege of which, from what we know of his character, he was likely to avail himself to the full.

Sharp eyes were watching Con from over the water. They were set in the dour and clever head of Hugh Montgomery, Laird of Braidstane, elder brother of the George Montgomery who was to become Bishop of Derry, and equally painstaking in his own advancement. Hugh employed his kinsman Thomas Montgomery, owner and master of a vessel trading between Scotland and Carrick-fergus, to propose to the prisoner that he should rescue him and bear him to England. There the Laird of Braid-stane would use his considerable influence to obtain for him a free pardon from the King. The return demanded was not modest; it was, in fact, the cession to Hugh Montgomery of half the lands of Southern Clandeboye. Con was, none the less, willing, and the escape was carried out, with some pretty romantic by-play on the part of Captain Thomas, who won the heart of the town marshal's daughter in the good old style. Con was shipped off, hospitably entertained at Braidstane, and taken to Court, where the second part of the scheme went through, Con getting his pardon and Montgomery his grant.

Among the birds of prey there are some great ones which make a practice of seizing the spoils taken by the lesser. There was another watchful Scot, James Hamilton, who had opened a Latin school in Dublin fifteen years before, had become a Fellow of Trinity College on its establishment, and had acted as agent for James VI. Hard and unscrupulous but a brilliant organizer and endowed with the true spirit of the pioneer, Hamilton was in many respects a great man. On James's accession to the English throne he repaired to London, where he was knighted by the King. He now came forward and suggested that Montgomery's grant was too large, and that he himself should have a share. He must either have been very convincing, or have put James very deep in his debt; for the King promptly cancelled Montgomery's grant and replaced it by one of the whole of Southern Clandeboye to James Hamilton. There was, however, a proviso that he should hand over one-third of the lands to Montgomery and one-third to Con. Montgomery was annoyed, but could reflect that he had got on the wrong side of the law regarding Con's escape and that his grant was still a fine one, of excellent, though, as in the case of Antrim, completely devastated land. Con was probably bewildered, but at least he was pardoned, free, and in possession of a large estate, while his right to Southern Clandeboye had not in the first instance been any too convincing.

Unfortunately for himself, Con was " a drunken sluggish man " and a weakling, who found himself elbow to elbow with two neighbours very far from sluggish or weak and well able to hold their liquor. His lands were desolate,

SIR JAMES HAMILTON, FIRST LORD CLANEBOYE

almost worthless as they stood, and he had neither the means nor the energy to repeople and restock them. Gradually he sold them to the two enterprising Scots. Finally, in 1616, he disposed of the last of them, together with his ancestral home of Castlereagh, to an officer of the army named Sir Moyses Hill. That was the end of the O'Neills of Southern Clandeboye. Con's son Daniel became a personage of some celebrity, a Royalist officer in England, a negotiator between the Viceroy Ormonde and Owen Roe O'Neill in Ireland, and a Court official after the Restoration. His petition for the return of his father's lands failed, but he received large grants in England, married the Countess of Chesterfield, died rich, and "left his old lady all ". His epitaph was written by Charles II in a letter to Madame his sister : " Poor O'Neale died this afternoon of an ulcer in his gutts; he was as honest a man as ever lived."

The above is perhaps not a pretty picture. Yet it cannot be said that either of the Scots adventurers failed to merit his good fortune or his subsequent honours; for James created Montgomery, Viscount Montgomery of the Ards; and Hamilton, Viscount Clandeboye, or Claneboye, as it was then usually written. Nowhere in Ulster was plantation carried out with such zeal and efficiency. They received or bought a wilderness and they made of it a garden.

Hamilton established himself at Bangor, and Montgomery repaired the old castle of Newtownards as a temporary shelter for himself and his allies in the great venture, Boyds, Moores, and Catherwoods. From these headquarters they set about their work with astonishing speed.

Chichester once exclaimed in a letter to the King, that it was a finer work to repopulate and retill the deserted lands of Ireland than to colonize Virginia. The life of the early settlers was not unlike that of those who crossed the

Atlantic, with lurking wood-kerne in place of Red Indians as a constant menace. The big men like Hamilton, Montgomery, and their chief associates might patch up some old castle to dwell in, and would certainly begin the building of a strong house at the earliest possible moment. The little man, the under-tenant farming a few acres at a rent of a boll of barley the acre, might have to dwell for years in an " Irish house "—a frame of unsquared boughs through which wickerwork was woven, banked up outside with sods, and with a rush-thatched roof.

Yet towns sprang up like mushrooms; or, as the Montgomery annalist puts it more prettily, rose out of the ground like Cadmus's colony. By 1611 Bangor consisted of " 80 newe houses, all inhabited with Scotyshmen and Englishmen." Hamilton himself had built there " a fayre stone house ", 60 feet long by 22 in breadth, and was about to build another for his private residence at Holywood, three miles away. Here there were already twenty houses for his tenants and servants. The year before he had purchased from the Whytes, an Anglo-Irish family long settled there, the vast estates of Dufferin on the western shore of Strangford Lough, containing 1600 cottages and nearly 30,000 acres. At Killyleagh, in this new demesne, he speedily built himself, possibly on the basis of a ruined shell, " a vera strong castle, the lyk not in the North."

Meanwhile Montgomery had not been behind his rival. He too had built himself " a princely mansion ", at Newtown, and that town had beaten Bangor in its development; for it had, according to the Plantation Commissioners, one hundred houses, all peopled with Scots. He made a jetty at Donaghadee, between which port and that of Stranraer in Scotland a prosperous trade was established. He was blessed with a wife who proved a true helpmate, a farmer, and a first-class gardener. In every parish she built a water-mill, so that the tenants should not have the toil of grinding their corn with the primitive hand-worked millstones of the country. A chronicler, looking back upon her over the span of three-quarters of a century, was moved to lyric exaltation by the bucolic idyll:

" Now everybody minded their trades, and the ploughs, and the spade, building, and setting fruit-trees, etc., in orchards and gardens, and by ditching in their grounds. The old women spun, and the young girls plied their nimble fingers at knitting, and everybody was innocently busy. Now the Golden peaceable age renewed, no strife, contention, querulous lawyers, or Scottish or Irish feuds, between clans and families, and surnames, disturbing the tranquility of those times."

Yet not quite that. The many Irish who remained on the lands as labourers—Gibeonites, hewers of wood and drawers of water, as the same writer put it—" hated the Scottyshe deadly," so much so that they even began to hold the English in affection. The cause was partly the greater energy of the Scots, which made them the more formidable and the less likely to be displaced, and partly their dourness and severity. As for absence of family feuds, there was one sufficiently bitter—though falling short of violence—between the two great colonists them-selves. Hamilton's cousin of the same name, who was created Earl of Abercorn, and was one of the leading undertakers in Tyrone, did his best to heal their quarrels. Writing from Bangor in October 1614, he declared that, " having spent this thre wekis passit in trying and clering all maters questionabill betwixt my cousing Sir James Hamilton & Sir Hew Montgomerie als weill in the marchis of their landis as vtherwayis," he thought he had succeeded. He had perhaps patched up a peace of sorts, but it was not until the next generation that there was any friendship between the houses of Hamilton and Montgomery.

The southern and south-western districts of Down remained Irish, by far the greatest proprietor being the native chief Arthur Magennis, who was created Viscount Iveagh. The Irish element is fairly strong here to this day.

## II

## THE PROJECT FOR THE ESCHEATED COUNTIES

WHEN the plantation of the escheated counties was taken in hand, the men who were responsible for it had to bear in mind that two previous projects in Ulster, those of Thomas Smith and of the first Earl of Essex, had completely failed. Outside Ulster they had before their eyes two more instructive examples of what to avoid. These were, first, the plantation of Leix and Offaly, later Queen's County and King's County, in Leinster, and, secondly, that in Munster, to both of which there has been some reference here.

The Leinster colonization is always spoken of as Marian, because the decision to carry it out was taken under Mary and Philip, and the counties concerned were renamed in their honour. Actually, the colonists did not for the most part arrive until after the accession of Elizabeth. The motive for bringing them over went back to the reign of Edward VI, when the O'Moores and O'Connors broke out into insurrection just when the country seemed to be settling down after the revolt of Silken Thomas. By the terms of his grant each grantee undertook to maintain his principal dwelling on his estate, to use English language and dress, to keep in his employ or as a tenant no Irishman able to bear arms who was born outside the county, and not to part with any of his lands without the consent of the Lord Deputy. He also admitted that every female of his family who married an Irishman should forfeit her jointure or dower.

161

Broadly speaking, the new colonists were gentry only. Apart from a few personal servants, and in some cases a dozen Scottish mercenaries for defence, they brought none from over the water with them. There was a change in the nationality of the landlords, but the tenants remained practically all Irish. These Marian settlers did, however, build strong castles, and it was owing to their foresight in this respect that many of them survived Tyrone's rebellion, though their lands were thoroughly ravaged.

Apart from that rebellion, the O'Moores of Queen's County, one of the most stubborn and unruly septs in all Ireland, were constantly out during Elizabeth's reign. Their official record of eighteen revolts must, in fact, have made even the O'Byrnes of Wicklow not a little envious. Finally, under Chichester, they were made the subject of an experiment in transplantation which is mentioned by but few historians. By persuasion and force intermingled they and other turbulent tribes were moved to Kerry, where a large grant of land on which to settle them was made to one Patrick Crosby. A certain number were also sent to Thomond, or Clare.

In the Munster colonization, after the Desmond rebellion had been put down in 1584, an attempt was made to remedy the defects of that in Leinster. The conditions in Cork, Waterford, Limerick, and part of Tipperary differed from that of the earlier plantation in that the lands were grouped into seigniories of 6000 or 12,000 acres, so that the colonists might not be dispersed, and that they were not allowed to have any Irish tenants or servants, even drawn from the native population of the counties. This latter condition was completely disregarded and would, indeed, have been hard to fulfil. Nor did the planters build as well as their predecessors in the midlands. The consequence was that in Tyrone's rebellion the whole colony was swept out of existence in a few days. It was to have been an improvement upon the Marian settlement, but when its testing time came it was found to be not nearly as strong. It had not only failed, but failed disgracefully. There must be no repetition of that fiasco.

The procedure with regard to Ulster may at first sight seem slow, complicated, and obscure. We shall, however, simplify the task of understanding it if we recognize that its framework was three separate Royal Commissions, in 1608, 1609, and 1610, which may be described as commissions of inquiry, of survey, and of settlement respectively, and had thus quite separate rôles.

The first commission, that which had to inquire into the conditions of the escheated lands, did its work during the summer of 1608, simultaneously with the suppression of O'Dogherty's revolt. The results were embodied in a long document in the form of instructions from Chichester to Sir James Ley, the Chief Justice, and Sir John Davies, the Attorney-General, who were sent with it to England. In these notes, dated the 14th October, the Lord Deputy dealt with each of the six counties separately and in detail. He described the conditions, made suggestions as to the sites of forts and of future corporate towns, stated what were the claims of Irish and in some cases English inhabitants, and gave the names of certain prominent Irishmen whom it would be well to conciliate by favourable treatment. The two lawyers made an extraordinarily good impression in England. To Ley, in fact, the King took such a liking that he refused to let him out of his sight in future. Ley therefore remained in England with the appointment of Attorney-General of the Court of Wards, and Sir Humphrey Winch, then Chief Baron of the Court of Exchequer in Ireland, was made Chief Justice of the King's Bench in his stead. Ley was to rise to far higher offices, to be created Earl of Marlborough, and to be immortalized by Milton as:

> . . . that Good Earl, once President
> Of England's Council and her Treasury,
> Who lived in both unstained with gold or fee.

With Davies, King and Council alike were equally pleased. James appointed him Serjeant, and directed that a grant of land of the value of £40 a year should be made to him as compensation for his loss of practice during his six months' stay in England. Doubtless the Attorney could have got a good post in England also, but his not unremunerative lot was now cast in Ireland, and he had certain promising plans for his future there.

To Ley and Davies were added five men who were either then serving in Ireland in some capacity or had experience of the country, including our old acquaintances Sir Henry Docwra and the Bishop of Derry, to form a special committee which was to advise the King and Council and to be responsible for the framework of the scheme.

On or about the 6th March 1609, Chichester received two documents, one, the "Project for the Plantation", being instructions addressed to himself, and the other, "Orders and Conditions to be observed by the Undertakers", being for publication, and in some degree a prospectus. In the latter the King's intentions were clearly set out. It was announced that James,

> of his Princely Bounty, not respecting his own Profit, but the public Peace and Welfare of that Kingdom, by the civil Plantation of those unreformed and waste Countries, is graciously pleased to distribute the said Lands to such of his Subjects, as well of *Great Britain* as of *Ireland*, as being of Merit and Ability shall seek the same, with a Mind not only to benefit themselves, but to do Service to the Crown and the Commonwealth.

The " Project " is very important, because, despite many changes, it is the ground-work on which the great scheme was eventually carried through. It therefore deserves our study in some little detail.

It was laid down that there were to be three classes of tenants in chief, with large holdings on which sub-tenants were to be settled: " undertakers ", or colonists from England and Scotland; " servitors ", or officers of the Army; and Irish. All were to be nominated by the King, and were to cast lots for their holdings. They were to be allotted portions of 2000, 1500, and 1000 acres, according to their means and position, which they were to settle within two years. The undertakers must have English or *inland* Scottish tenants—there were enough marauders in Ulster already, without introducing any more Scots from the Isles or the western seaboard. They were to pay £5, 6s. 8d. English per ־ט00 acres after the first two years, when it was expected that they would have begun to get some return from their holdings. Servitors were permitted to have Irish tenants, as they were accustomed to dealing with the Irish and would know how to defend themselves, but were to pay £8 per 1000 acres settled with Irish, and only the same amount as the undertakers where they had English and Scottish tenants. The Irish, who would have none of the preliminary expenses of the other two classes, were to pay £10, 13s. 4d. per 1000 acres. In their case, however, they and their tenants were absolved from·the Oath of Supremacy required of the undertakers, and, in practice, were absolved also from the conditions as regards building.

These last were that holders of the largest portions (those of 2000 acres) were to build within two years a strong castle, together with a *bawn* or court for the protection of live stock, and the smaller tenants in chief to provide for the protection of themselves and the sub-tenants on a lesser scale. The system of tenure was to vary according to the size of the portion. Those with 2000 acres were to hold by knight's service *in capite*; those with 1500 acres, by knight's service as from Dublin Castle; and those with 1000 acres, in common soccage. The distinction was a serious one. Knight's service *in capite* (from the King himself) subjected the tenant to vexatious and expensive burdens, especially as regards marriage and wardship. Tenure " as from Dublin Castle " was also from the King represented by his Government in Ireland, but not so directly from the source of honour, and was therefore less onerous. Common soccage, which had originally entailed certain services, such as ploughing and hedging, to the lord of the fee, now entailed none that were more than nominal.

It is proof of the acuteness of Chichester's intellect and of his practical cast of mind that he was able to subject this scheme to most damaging criticism, drawn up though it had been by the best brains, legal and lay, and approved by the King and Council. The lottery he utterly condemned, though, doubtless with his eye upon his royal master, who was so learned in the Scriptures, he paid tribute to the model, which was that of the Hebrews in the Land of Promise. In this case there were native lands on which it would be impossible to put settlers; besides, it would be a mistake to separate friends and kinsfolk, who would provide mutual society and support. He strongly objected to tenure by knight's service *in capite*, and hinted broadly that few undertakers or servitors would come forward if that condition were maintained. The time limit of two years for building, settling, and the payment of rent was, he said, too short. He considered the fixed portions too theoretical, and would have preferred that their extent should have been decided in accordance with each man's worth and quality. Finally, he feared that too little land was to be assigned to the natives, if he were to judge by a detailed plan for County Tyrone, which he had received some weeks earlier.

The results of his expostulation were that the lottery dropped out of the programme; knight's service *in capite* was not required from any tenant; the time limit was extended; the colonists were invited to group themselves in "consorts" of friends and kinsmen; and, though his hint that there should be specially large portions created for great noblemen was disregarded, persons of importance were placed in control or as patrons of the "consorts".

The "Orders and Conditions" contained a reproof to importunate suitors who were asking for greater portions than they were able to plant. We know nothing of these proposals, but if they are to be judged by one put forward in the following July, they were not of undue modesty. That of Lord Audley, who came of a very ancient family with possessions both in Ulster and Munster, almost takes away one's breath. He announced that he was prepared to undertake 100,000 acres in Tyrone and Armagh. He would divide this portion into thirty-three lots, on each of which he would within a space of four years build a castle and a town of thirty families; he would also erect iron-mills and make glass. Chichester was tickled by this proposition. Lord Audley, he explained, was an elderly nobleman inclined to bite off more than he could chew. As his one castle in Munster was not decently maintained, the prospects of his thirty-three castles in Ulster were poor. Besides, he was "near to himself", or close-fisted, and not given to hospitality, which would make a bad impression. If, went on the Deputy, the provision for the natives was not better than he had reason to believe, they would "kindle many a fire " in Lord Audley's buildings before they were half finished.

One would have liked to hear the view of Davies, had he been able to regard the application detachedly. Unfortunately, however, his sense of humour was blunted by the fact that he had recently married Lord Audley's daughter, whom he had met on circuit when staying at her father's shabby castle. He therefore professed himself delighted to hear that Audley was living up to the spirit of his august ancestors, one of whom had been a Lord Marcher in Wales, while another had accompanied John de Courcy to Ulster and settled in Lecale. Yet one cannot avoid the belief that, son-in-law of the applicant though he was, the Attorney had his tongue in his cheek when he wrote these words. Alas for ambition! Lord Audley eventually got no more than one of the 2000-acre portions. At least his blood still flows in the veins of several prominent Ulster families, which take pride, generation after generation, in naming either a son or daughter Audley to commemorate his kinsman Audley Mervyn.

In May 1609 Davies returned to Dublin, full of enthusiasm, to find Chichester less sanguine. The view from London was undoubted rosier than that from the Castle, and, as so often happens in like cases, the man on the spot saw ugly little details invisible to the men at Whitehall, fascinated by contemplation of their own regular and beautiful designs. Worst of all, Chichester had discovered that a survey begun the previous year was so bad that there was nothing for it but to do the work all over again, and to delay the colonization until it was ready. Those responsible for the survey had been Ridgeway, the Treasurer, and Sir Josias Bodley, who would to-day be described as " Engineer-in-Chief"; and the qualifications of Ridgeway at least seem to have been but mediocre. Bodley had distinguished himself in the wars at Kinsale and elsewhere, and has another title to fame as the brother of that Sir Thomas who endowed the University of Oxford with the great library that bears his name. He took a hand in the new survey, assisted this time by the official surveyor, William Parsons, and one or both of them produced an admirable and beautiful set of maps of the escheated counties.

At the moment the keenest " planter " of them all was the King himself. His reputation for wisdom was deeply engaged, and there was nothing he prized so much. The colonization must go forward. " Foreign estates do cast their eyes upon it," he remarked to Chichester, " and the ill-affected at home and abroad will be ready to take advantage of anything omitted or neglected therein." He was not perturbed by difficulties or mistakes already committed, but was determined that the edifice should stand upon a sound base. He therefore issued a new commission, dated the 21st July, to make a fresh survey, fixing the boundaries of ballybetaghs and other sub-divisions of counties; to distinguish carefully between temporal and Church lands, which the last commission had failed to do; and to mark out sites on which the undertakers were to build. The commissioners numbered no less than twenty, and included Chichester himself, the Lord Chancellor and Archbishop of Dublin, the Primate and Archbishop of Armagh, Ridgeway, Winch, St. John, Lambart, and, of course, Parsons, the Surveyor-General; but five of them formed a quorum.

Chichester went north at once. He had been waiting impatiently for the commission, fearing to lose the season and be caught by wet weather with his train of carriages and wagons on the bottomless highways of Ulster. Like the good soldier he was, he had established a ration dump at Newry, which, if the journey were put off, could be used by the Ulster garrison. His forethought was rewarded, and the commissioners were back in Dublin by the beginning of October.

Of all the various progresses through Ulster connected in greater or less degree with the Plantation this was the most important, and it is therefore interesting to note its methods of procedure. Chichester reached Dundalk on the 31st, and there drew up the programme. In each county he decided to summon assizes, and, in addition to the grand jury, to empanel a "jury of survey or inquiry" in each barony, to discover what lands belonged to the King and what to the Church. In each district men who knew the boundaries were to be detailed to accompany Parsons and Bodley on their map-making. Quiet though the country seemed, these prudent men took a guard with them on their excursions. "Our geographers," said Davies, "do not forget what entertainment the Irish of Tyrconnell gave to a map-maker about the end of the late rebellion; for, one Barkeley being appointed by the late Earl of Devonshire to draw a true and perfect map of the north part of Ulster (the old map of Tyrconnell being false and defective), when he came into Tyrconnell the inhabitants took off his head, because they would not have their country discovered."

On the 3rd August the commissioners set out from Dundalk. It was a foul day, and one can imagine their great column—first, cavalry; then the carriages of such as chose to journey in them; the rest on horseback; a train of wagons bearing food, tents and their furniture, ammunition, and stationery; and finally a rear-guard—lurching along, of course at a foot pace, with oaths and cracking of whips beneath such a downpour as Ireland knows how to spill. On the 5th they pitched their tents four miles from Armagh, and remained there two days, hearing the claims of the Primate. At Armagh itself they stayed from Monday the 7th to Saturday the 12th, each section devoting itself to its particular duty. The assizes were light; in fact, Ulster had never, in the belief of Davies, been so peaceful since the days of the Norman invasion. Simultaneously they recorded what lands in the county could be disposed of to undertakers. Of the five baronies, two were almost entirely available, but Tyrany was held by the heirs of the Sir Henry Oge O'Neill, who had been killed on the Government side in O'Dogherty's revolt, and by the Primate, in virtue of his office; the Fews were mainly the property of Sir Tirlagh MacHenry O'Neill, and the Church held a share here too, leaving only 6000 acres over for plantation; and the barony of Armagh was largely in the hands of Dublin University and the Church again, leaving only 4500 acres. These Church lands were definitely held in demesne, and there was no possible claim to their possession by the Crown. But the third important feature of the commissioners' activities was the inquisition into the *termon* lands, that is, those assigned for the endowment of a church or monastery, and with regard to these the verdict went against the Church. An almost entirely Irish jury, which included Sir Tirlagh MacHenry, found that these lands did not belong to the bishops in demesne, and that their only claim upon them was certain " chiefries " or duties; the *termon* lands must therefore be considered as vested in the Crown by the Act of the 11th of Elizabeth.

On Saturday the 12th August the commissioners moved on from Armagh to Dungannon, and at once began the same procedure for the County Tyrone. Here there were none of the complications that had to be faced in Armagh over Church lands, since neither the Primate nor the Bishop of Derry had mensal or demesne lands there, though the latter was recommended by Davies to the King's grace in this respect. Except, therefore, for a few hundred acres of glebe and abbey lands and some territory granted to Sir Henry Oge O'Neill and his heirs, the whole county, said the jury, was now in " the real and actual possession of His Majesty, by reason of the attainder of treason of Hugh, late Earl of Tyrone, and by the Statute of the attainder of Shane O'Neill, made in the 11th year of the reign of the late Queen Elizabeth, and by reason of either of them." Chichester could not have hoped for a clearer case or a cleaner slate.

On the 24th August they set forth for Limavady. In order to avoid the Sperrin Mountains and Slieve Gallion they were obliged to go by Glenconkeine, and even then had to camp three nights among its woods while covering some sixty miles. But it is convenient to leave them to their arduous journey and turn to glance at what was happening on the other side of the Irish Sea, where the colonization scheme had become the topic of the day.

.    .    .    .    .

Applications for the escheated lands were coming in fast, the undertakers grouping themselves into " consorts " under some powerful or popular leader, and thus taking a leaf from Chichester's criticism of the original scheme. The process of weeding out must have been severe; for only about one-sixth of the names found in the first lists appear in those of the undertakers who finally secured portions. One big consort, under the patronage of the Lord Deputy's brother, Sir Thomas Chichester, and almost entirely drawn from East Anglia, offered to settle all the available lands in Fermanagh. This list was evidently referred back by Ley's committee; for we find next a very much shorter and more modest one for that county, still East Anglian in composition. This may be given as a specimen of the rest, showing the type of Englishman who engaged in the venture. Against the names of all but two—of whom one, Sir Henry Hobert, was probably a wealthy man—their annual incomes are given.

Sir Henry Hobert's consort, viz. :

Sir Henry Hobert
John Thurston, Suffolk, 600*l*. per annum.
Arthur Everard, Norfolk, 300*l*. per annum.
Henry Honing, Suffolk,
Thomas Blenerhassett, Norfolk, 120*l*. per annum.
Robert Bogas, Suffolk, 240*l*. per annum.
Thomas Flowerdew, Norfolk, 200*l*. per annum.
John Archdale, Suffolk, 200*l*. per annum.
Richard Harte, one of His Majesty's Servants, Suffolk, 50*l*. per annum.
Sir John Aldridge, Norfolk, 200*l*. per annum.
John Colby, Suffolk, 200*l*. per annum.
Isaac Thompson, Norfolk, 100*l*. per annum.
William Strutton, Suffolk, 100*l*. per annum.
Thomas Cheyney, Suffolk, 60*l*. per annum.
Roger Dersley, Norfolk, 110*l*. per annum.

Perhaps we may describe Thurston and Everard as well-to-do squires, the rest, with the exception of Cheyney and Harte, simply as "squires", Cheyney as a yeoman, and Harte as a Government official. Only five of these names appear in the list of grants in Fermanagh. We have given the applications for that county as an example, but those from England were largely for portions in Armagh, which was more accessible, was considered less savage than the west, and had the extra advantage in case of trouble of being conveniently near the Pale.

From north of the Tweed, too, there was brisk competition, in response to a proclamation by the Privy Council in which we hear the authentic voice of Scotia. The suggestion that the English would have got all the booty but for his sacred Majesty's unspeakable love and affection for his original subjects is particularly pleasing.

"Forsameikle as the Kingis Maiestie haueing resolued to reduce and setle vnder a perfyte obedience the north pairt of the Kingdome of Ireland, which now by the providence of Almichtie God, and by the power and strength of his Maiesties royal army, is fred and disburdynit of the former rebellious and disobedient inhabitants thairof, wha, in the justice of God, to their schame and confusion ar overthrawin, his Maiestie, for this effect, hes tane a verie princelie and good course, alswell for establischeing of religioun, justice, and ciuilitie within the saidis boundis, as for planting of coloneis thairin, and distributeing of the same boundis to lauchfull, ansuerable, and weill affected subiectis, vpon certane easie, tollerable, and proffitable conditionis, and although thair be no want of grite nomberis of the cuntrey people of England, who, with all glaidnes, wald imbrace the saidis conditionis, and transport thame selfiss, with thair famileis, to Yreland, and plenische the saidis haill boundis sufficientlie with inhabitis, yit, his sacred Maiestie, out of his vnspeikable love and tender affectioun towards his Maiesties antient and native subiectis of this kingdome, quhome his heynes wald haue to communicat with the fortunes of his saidis subiectis of England, hes bene pleasit to mak chose of thame to be Partinaris with his saidis subiectis of England, in the distribution foirsaid . . .

"4th July 1609. The quhilk day in presence of the lordis of secrite counsale comperit personalie Robert Montgomerie, of Kirktoun, and maid humble sute vnto the saidis lordis That he might be ressaued and inrolled as one of the undertakeris in the intendit plantation. . . ."

It is also agreeable, but not surprising, to find a Montgomery at the head of the long list. That family had no intention of being thrust into the background of the Plantation scheme.

In this first list of Scottish names those of townsmen are more numerous than in the English, which is for the most part composed of knights, squirearchy, and yeomanry; but, in addition to the burgesses of Edinburgh and Glasgow there are also many country lairds. Whether laird or burgess, each brought with him his cautioner, or surety, who gave his bond like a man at the rate of £100 sterling for every 500 acres applied for. And, whereas among the English names there are only a few, such as Archdale, Brownlow, and Butler, which are now familiar, for the most part as belonging to the leading families of Ulster, the Scottish list contains name after name still to be found all over the province, among the great and the little alike, Here are Achieson, Adamson, Alexander, Brown, Colquhoun, Cranston, Crawford, Crichton (or Creighton), Dunbar, Hamilton, Inglis, Irving, Johnstone, Kerr, Lindsay. McCullogh, Meldrum, Muir, Murray, Ramsay, Stewart, Watson, and Weir. Curiously enough, there is as yet no Elliot, one of the commonest of Ulster names to-day, but with that, and with Hanna, Wilson, Hall, and Little added, one could have formed a company bearing the names above from any battalion of the 36th (Ulster) Division in the year 1914.

Another important and interesting adjunct to the great colonization scheme had also been taken in hand, in this case not by the London committee, but directly by King James and his Privy Council. This was the grandiose idea of the settlement of the County of Coleraine by the City of London.

When disputes afterwards arose there was some dis-agreement as to who had fathered this scheme, the Londoners alleging that it had been virtually forced upon them by the King to get him out of a difficulty regarding a county of which other settlers fought shy. The Government's retort was that the grant had been made for the City's present honour and future profit. Perhaps both sides were right. It must be remembered that there appeared at this time a possibility that Sir Donnell O'Cahan would be restored to his ancestral territories, so that the undertakers with their wits about them would be inclined to avoid O'Cahan's Country when they put in their applications. Even if the King could be trusted to see to it that Sir Donnell walked no more abroad, the fact had to be reckoned with that his clansmen were the most warlike in Ulster. There was therefore every advantage in the plantation of Coleraine being undertaken by some powerful public body which would bind together and support the colonists in the same manner as the Chartered Companies were to do elsewhere in later times. There was none such in all England with the wealth, solidity, and prestige of the City of London. The first suggestion came from the King and his Privy Council—that is not disputed and was, indeed, only natural. The seed struck at once, and on the 1st July 1609 the Lord Mayor issued to the Masters and Wardens of the twelve principal London Companies a precept, enjoining them first to discuss the matter within their companies and then to form a committee of four men from each to draw up terms. With this precept was issued the proclamation of the " Orders and Conditions " already mentioned, and also a document which may be described as a prospectus and was certainly calculated to make the mouths of the citizens water.

It was stated that Derry, now more or less a ruin, and a site near the castle of Coleraine were most suitable for the City itself to colonize and for the foundation of corporate towns. All the land between the Bann and the Foyle

would be planted by undertakers chosen by the City—
that is, as seems to have been intended from the first, by
the City Companies. There followed a glowing account
of the wealth and possibilities of the district. It would not
only sustain numerous colonists but would export for
the use of London beef, pork, fish, rye, peas, and beans.
Hemp and flax grew better there than anywhere else, to
furnish cables, cordage, and canvas for the City's fleets, as
well as thread and linen cloth. The soil was suitable for
the breeding of English sheep. The pelts of red deer,
foxes, conies, martens, and squirrels would form another
source of wealth—perhaps those of wolves might have
been added, but this would have led to reflection on a less
pleasant side of the picture, and would not have looked
well in juxtaposition to the sheep. Timber, stone, lime,
and slate were available for building; and there was earth
of the type needed for the manufacture of bricks and tiles.
Copper and iron ore had been found. The harbour of
Derry was excellent, and the Bann was navigable for some
distance from the mouth. The scheme would effect more :
it would be, in fact, a sort of universal provider, and would
even improve the sanitary state of London by removing
some of the surplus population, at a time when the City
was so overcrowded that " one tradesman was scarce able
to live by another."

The City itself, the Courts of Aldermen and Common
Council, and the Companies, were gratified but cautious.
They were not going to buy a pig in a poke. After some
further negotiations and a conference with the Privy
Council it was decided to send to Ireland at the City's
charges a small deputation to spy out the land. John Broad,
John Monroe, Robert Tresswell, and John Rowley must
have set forth without undue delay; for they reached
Limavady, the site of O'Cahan's principal castle, on the

28th August, the day after the arrival at that point of Chichester and his fellow commissioners.

Good staff work, it may be said, but the Londoners did not know just how good. The City might be wily, but a Privy Council with my Lord of Salisbury at the table had nothing to learn from it. First of all, the Privy Council had appointed as bear-leader to the party Sir Thomas Phillips, Governor of Coleraine; and Phillips would be as careful that the worthy citizens saw what they ought to see and no more, as are the guides who look after ingenuous tourists in Moscow and Leningrad. Had they foreseen the relations between Phillips and their mother City for nearly thirty years, it is possible that John Broad and his fellows would have pushed their cicerone into the Irish Sea in the course of the passage to Carrickfergus.

Thomas Phillips, like the gallant Thomas Williams and a good many other officers of the Irish Wars, was a Welshman. He had a fine fighting record, both in France and Ireland. Before the end of Tyrone's rebellion he had forced his way up to Coleraine with only two hundred men, had held the place during the remainder of the rebellion and that of O'Dogherty, and had built a number of houses in the Irish fashion. He had naturally expected a grant in that neighbourhood, but was apparently prepared to content himself with compensations elsewhere. If, however, the Londoners undertook to plant Coleraine and in any way fell short of their undertaking, they might expect to find in him a severe critic.

However, that was all in the future. For the moment the first need was to make a good impression on the London agents. One of them unfortunately fell sick at Limavady and began to talk of going home, but Chichester persuaded him not to. It would not do for him to return prematurely and depress his fellow-citizens. The party had seen Coleraine and the banks of the Bann; Chichester took them on with him to see Derry, Lifford, and the banks of the Foyle. They were delighted with everything, and declared confidently that on receiving their report the City would embark upon the great venture.

Chichester informed Salisbury that he and his Council had done all they could for their visitors, and we may be sure that he spoke the truth. He had advised them to send the Lord Mayor samples of the local produce; and had obtained for them hides, tallow, beef, salmon, herrings, pipe-staves, and the like at easy prices. The sellers, we may suppose, did not haggle with the Lord Deputy on this occasion. He also pointed out to Salisbury that this was a favourable moment for the tour of inspection, when the natives were more submissive and docile than he had ever seen them. Finally, in mid-September, before the Deputy moved on to Fermanagh, the faithful Phillips, who had been " a host, a guide, and a watchman " to the Londoners, took them back to study more closely the River Bann above the Salmon-Leap and the woods of Glenconkeine. Doubtless they really wanted to revisit these scenes, but one suspects that their departure from Lough Foyle was not unconnected with the fact that there was business in hand which it was desirable they should not see.

At Limavady they must already have witnessed the stormy discomfiture of the Bishop of Derry regarding the Church lands. It was the same story as in Armagh. The jury of fifteen Irishmen, who all spoke Latin and were probably all Brehons, found that the *termon* lands were not the possession of the Church, but only paid it a rent. " The lord bushopp of Derry doth sett [1] and dispose atte his pleasure " the lands of Grangemore, said the jurors, but

---

[1] " Set ", for " let " is a Jacobean term still universal, at least in western Ulster. Even in Londonderry to-day you do not " let " a flat, but " set " it.

added that his (Catholic) predecessors had never more than a rent from them. The lord bushopp [1] harangued the jurymen, but could not move them, though they were, as Chichester shrewdly observed, poor men who would have to live under his eye in the future. Here again it was found that the whole county, with some unimportant exceptions and one important one, was at the disposal of the Crown. The important exception was the rich Bann fishery between Lough Neagh and the Salmon-Leap, which had been conveyed by its grantee to Chichester himself. Regarding the City of Derry, which included some land in Inishowen formerly belonging to Sir Cahir O'Dogherty, the same verdict was given.

This, however, was not the business which, as has been suggested, might have been expected to alarm the tourists. Chichester had been instructed to ship off to the armies of Sweden such Irish subjects as liked to go. The phrase was, as may be supposed, a euphemism for " it was desirable should go ". The type of man in the mind of King James was the survivor of O'Dogherty's revolt, the wood-kerne, the " swordsman " or landless kinsman—legitimate and bastard—and retainer of the former lords of the soil. This last was a class which had always puzzled and distracted English officials in Ireland. The swordsmen were too proud to work themselves, and would not leave others in peace to work. Their design for living was to fight, to hunt, to do their lord's bidding, to exist on his leavings, and when those leavings failed to kill and eat the nearest sheep. To turn a pastoral community into an agricultural one while they lurked in the woods and bogs would be very difficult.

On hearing of the scheme, Chichester had accepted the submission of the last prominent outlaws in Ulster, Oghie

[1] Once again, a bishop is still a " bushop " in the speech of Ulster.

Oge O'Hanlon and Art Oge MacBryan O'Neill, on condition that they went as officers. He had gathered up thirty tall fellows that had been out with O'Dogherty, and had had sent up from Leinster some Kavanaghs and Byrnes, ex-soldiers who had forcibly billeted themselves on the inhabitants down there. He had in some cases, it is probable, used the methods of the press gang. Now he had a thousand men ready for embarkation, and the first ship had reached the Foyle. If we may judge by some of their officers, these recruits were likely to be as terrible to the army in which they were to serve as to its foes. Of a lieutenant and an ensign it was noted that they were brothers who, in peace, "ever lived as thieves and murderers, and in war, notorious rebels." "They must be well looked unto," continued the report, "for there are not two such villains in all the regiment." Well might the Swedes have asked: *Quis custodiet istos custodes?*

Chichester's foresight in removing the Londoners from the scene while the swordsmen were embarked was ludicrously unavailing. Three ships were duly sent away from Lough Foyle with 800 men aboard, but a fourth was compelled by bad weather to put into Carlingford and take up its complement there. As ill-luck would have it, the Londoners, having finished their tour, arrived on their way home at this very moment, and in their presence there occurred an incident revelatory of the wilder side of Ulster. The recruits mutinied, broke the compasses, ran the ship ashore, and tried to escape. Eventually they were for the most part rounded up, re-embarked, and despatched to their destination. Another party nearly as strong was sent the following year, and towards the end of his viceroyalty, in 1614, Chichester stated that he had embarked 6000 men of this type for the Swedish service. A number of them appear to have deserted and drifted to Flanders, preferring a Catholic to a Protestant army.

Meanwhile the commissioners had gone on to Lifford, where the jury found that the whole of the County Donegal, but for some Church lands, was at the disposal of the Crown. It pointed out, however, that certain of the O'Boyles, the O'Gallaghers, and the three septs of the MacSwineys showed letters patent for considerable estates in the county, though the jurors did not profess to know whether their claims were good in law.

There was one other very big exception. In the previous April the King had granted the whole barony of Inishowen, known as O'Dogherty's Country, to the Lord Deputy and his heirs, in the same manner as it had been held by Sir Cahir. Chichester was to pay rent on a scale similar to that of the undertakers, and to plant at least one freeholder for every thousand acres of profitable land. While the Assizes for Donegal were being held at Lifford, he rode to look upon his noble estate.

He has been bitterly criticized over this matter, yet it is hard to see why it should be an offence in one of the King's foremost, ablest, most devoted, and most successful servants to ask for a reward and accept it when given. The King knew what he was doing. He was not a sentimentalist except when his suitor was a youth with a pretty face. We might say to-day that it was not " delicate " in Chichester to receive Inishowen while he was Viceroy in Ireland, but delicacy of that particular type was hardly known in those days. The peninsula was going a-begging, and it was owing to the energy of the Lord Deputy that the revolt of its chieftain had been so quickly extinguished and had done so little damage. One other barony, that of Tirhugh, was not available for plantation, having been in large part granted to Trinity College.

The business for Donegal was done by the 13th September, the diligent commissioners working so late that day that they had to ride in the dark to the camp, which had been pitched ten miles along the road to Enniskillen. Here Maguire's castle was in the hands of Captain William Cole, who was to have a servitor's portion in Fermanagh. There was work for a week in Fermanagh, where it was found that there were 48,000 acres of profitable land available for plantation. Once again Bishop Montgomery (in his capacity of Bishop of Clogher) was disappointed regarding the *termon* lands. In this case he came up against a formidable opponent, the veteran Archbishop of Cashel. Mulmorie, or Miller, Magrath was an extraordinary character. He had begun life as a Franciscan friar and had been appointed by the Pope to the see of Down. Then, having become a Protestant, he had been appointed Bishop of Clogher by Elizabeth, as far back as 1570. He had exchanged that see for another, in fact, for several others, and had reared a large and hungry progeny. But he had clung to his letters patent from the Queen for all the lands of Termon-Magrath in Fermanagh, which his father had held as *herenagh*,[1] and could not be shifted. In 1610 the *termon* was, in fact, formally granted to his son, James Magrath. Miller himself, drunken reprobate that he was, lived to a great age. He was alive in 1617 and apparently contemplating a return to his original Church; but neither Catholic nor Reformed is entitled to boast of him.

Sir John Davies had seen Fermanagh before, but its charm made a fresh appeal to him, as it does to all, the county's own sons or strangers, whenever they revisit its

---

[1] " Church lands, being in the possession of certain scholars called *Herenaghes*, and whereof they were in ancient times true and lawful proprietors." These lands had been in the first instance given by the chiefs to the founders of churches and religious houses ; the founders passed them on to certain septs, who paid rents and dues to the bishops for the maintenance of the parish churches and for the purpose of hospitality.

scenes. It was, he said, so pleasant and fruitful a county that, if he should make a full description thereof, it would be rather taken for a poetical fiction than for a true and serious narrative. He loved the " fresh lake called Lough Erne," more than forty miles long, abounding with fish, which divided the county into two. His eye dwelt upon the countless islands, upon the land on either side of the lough rising in little hills of eighty or a hundred acres apiece, the fattest and richest soil in all Ulster. He had already determined to make his habitation there.

We need not delay over Cavan. As for Monaghan, that was settled already, and the commissioners did not even visit it, Winch going on alone to hold the Assizes for the county. The last camp, in a lovely setting near where the town of Virginia now stands, was broken up on the 30th September, and the column rumbled back once more to Dublin. On the criminal side, the circuit had been marked by two executions only, though the shipment to Sweden of many men who might otherwise have found halters round their necks accounted for this clemency.

There was a vast amount of work still to be done, and most of the commissioners probably found that arrears had accumulated in their own offices. The maps had to be finished, and the portions allotted to the three types of tenants in chief, the Church lands, and those assigned to forts, corporate towns, and schools marked on them and distinguished by colours. These maps, by the way, had a curious history. They were by baronies, the sets for each county being bound up into a volume. After having been forgotten for 250 years, they were all, with the exception of the Donegal volume, discovered in 1860 in the State Paper Office, and reproduced by the Ordnance Survey at Southampton.

Next an abstract had to be made of the King's and of his

subjects' titles to the lands of the escheated counties. This labour must have been carried out mainly by Davies himself; for a rough draft in the crabbed handwriting of that indefatigable man exists among the Carte Papers. Then the inquisitions were drawn up in form of law, examined by the bishops—because of the question of the *termon* lands—and exemplified under the Great Seal of England. In these circumstances Chichester found himself unable to obey his instructions, which were to make his return by the 1st November 1609. It was not, in fact, until February 1610 that Davies and Ridgeway set forth with the fateful documents to England. Even then there was a delay, as it was thought necessary to bind the maps in London and emboss coats of arms upon the vellum. On the 15th March, from his lodging in the Strand, Ridgeway sent them on to Salisbury.

Meanwhile the business of the London plantation had gone forward likewise. In the early winter of 1609 the four agents had returned full of enthusiasm, and had presented a report as glowing as the original prospectus which had induced the City to send them over. On the 15th December it was decided to form a company to manage the City's estates when handed over, and the date may be said to mark the birth of that famous association, existing to this day and known by the shortened title of " the Irish Society ". In January 1610 the Commissioners for Irish Causes met the representatives of the City in the Recorder's chambers in the Temple, where the citizens put forward their demands at three successive conferences. Finally, " Articles agreed upon 28 Jan. 1609 [1] between the Lords of Privy Council on the King's Majesty's behalf on the one part, and the Committees appointed by Act of

[1] This means, of course, 1609–10. In the Irish State Papers it is calendared in error under January 1609.

Common Council on the behalf of the Lord Mayor and Commonalty of the City of London on the other part concerning a Plantation in part of the Provinces in Ulster ", were drawn up and signed.

The City was to levy £20,000, £15,000 for the Plantation itself, and £5000 for buying out interests involved. Two hundred houses were to be built at Derry with room left within the fortifications for 300 more; 100 at Coleraine with room left for 200 more. Four thousand acres were to be allotted to the city of Derry and 3000 to the town of Coleraine as their " liberties ". The whole of the rest of the county was to be handed over to the City, but, as was then understood and shortly afterwards put in writing, to be colonized not by the City itself as an entity, but by its twelve principal companies. The woods of Glenconkeine and Killeightra were to be handed over to the City in perpetuity. This meant that the Barony of Loughinsholin was cut out of Tyrone and incorporated in Coleraine, which shortly afterwards began to be generally known as the County Londonderry.[1] Customs duties were to be at the disposal of the City for the term of ninety-nine years. The salmon and eel fisheries in the Foyle and the Bann were to be handed over, present proprietors being compensated where necessary. The King agreed to maintain in the north sufficient forces for the protection of the colonists. Lastly, the City was to have the right to make within the next seven years any reasonable demands such as had been shown by time to be expedient, but could not have been foreseen. The machine was thus set in motion; for, although the Londoners did not at once receive their actual Charter, these articles were held to be sufficient to

[1] The greater part of the liberties of the City of Derry and town of Coleraine already mentioned, were in Donegal and Antrim respectively, and these strips of land beyond the Foyle and the Bann were both added likewise to the new County Londonderry. The map shows the old boundaries as well as the new.

work upon. Phillips received grants of 3000 acres at Limavady and 500 acres at Toome in compensation for what he had lost in and about the town of Coleraine. He and Sir Thomas Staples at Moneymore, both servitors, were the only grantees of any importance in the whole county, apart from the Londoners.

The process of making out the grants in the other five escheated counties to undertakers, servitors, and natives began about December 1609, among the earliest to receive his patent being one of the most distinguished officials, Sir Oliver St. John, Master of the Ordnance, and destined to be Chichester's successor in the office of Lord Deputy. The grants in themselves are uninteresting except to those who know the townlands mentioned, and a single one will suffice as a specimen. We may for this purpose choose one in the Barony of Clankelly, County Fermanagh, to a man of a name that still endures, and is still outstanding in the annals of Ulster.

> Grant to *John Archdale, Esq.* The small portion of *Tallanagh*, containing the lands of Coilenure, ½ quarter or 2 tates, viz., Coilenure and Knockakosy; the ½ quarter of Tallanagh, being 2 tates, viz., Tallanagh and Carrauny; the ½ quarter of Coulcoppocky, being 2 tates, viz., Coulcoppocky and Drumscoole; the ½ quarter of Drommadderdanagh, 2 tates, viz., Drommadderdanagh and Dromdonyne; the quarter of Coylaghmore, being 4 tates, viz., Coylaghmore, 2 tates, and Dollypatrick, 2 tates; the ½ quarter of Coylaghbegg, 2 tates, viz., Coylaghbegg and Lisharra; Etadd, one tate; the island of Crewinshaghy in Lougherne, being one tate; total 1000 acres. Part of the tate of Derryvine, being one part of Etadd, and containing 60 acres, is excepted from this grant, for glebe lands. Free fishing in Lougherne. The premises are created of the manor of Archdale, with 300 acres in demesne; power to create tenures;

and to hold a court baron. Rent 5*l*. 6*s*. 8*d*. English. To hold forever, as of the castle of Dublin, in common soccage, subject to the conditions of the plantation of Ulster. 13 July, 10th.[1]

But the summer was drawing on; no undertakers had come, nor any orders. Once more Chichester was chafing at the delay, and, as he unburdens himself to Salisbury, we detect another note in his rather querulous letter. This man, hard and at times almost ferocious as he was, had a sensibility of which no trace is to be found in the bustling, buoyant, jocular Davies. The next step would include the removal of natives from the land of the undertakers, and, visibly, he shrank from it. There had been no news from England for some time, he wrote on the 27th June; the season was advanced; preparations, though partly made, would occupy at least a fortnight after the word had come, and he did not want to be caught by autumn weather. He scarcely dared hope that the removals would be effected without some disturbance, and had therefore mustered his small army, and laid in a store of provisions for the expedition. That which he perhaps dared not write himself, he forwarded in the words of Sir Toby Caulfeild, who informed him that the natives hoped, the summer being nearly spent, that " so great cruelty will not be offered as to remove them from their houses upon the edge of winter, and in the very season when they are to supply themselves in making their harvest."

As a matter of fact, the King had already issued a warrant for a new commission, or a renewal of the old one. This was that third commission of which we have spoken, and was for the purpose of putting the colonists in possession

---

[1] That is, the tenth year of King James, which is 1612. This is one of the later grants. The spelling is given unaltered. The whole list, extracted mainly from the Patent Rolls, fills nearly ninety of Hill's large pages.

of their portions. It was drawn up on the 9th June, but not received until the 4th July. The explanation of this long delay is that the document was brought over by Ridgeway, who returned to Ireland on the latter date. Davies was detained a little longer, but arrived in time to take part in the circuit. Chichester, in an unwonted flight of rhetorical loyalty—the loyalty being in his nature but the rhetoric not—announced that by God's permission they would be at Cavan by the 25th, St. James's day, " there to begin that great work on the day of that Blessed Saint in Heaven and great monarch upon earth." If James liked butter, he should have it, but the times were changing and courtly flattery with them. This was thin stuff by comparison with what Mountjoy had been wont to offer to Elizabeth.

The first of the undertakers had already landed. The Plantation of Ulster had begun.

## III

## THE COMING OF THE COLONISTS

THE history of the settlement of Ulster is, as has been pointed out, that of the progress of three successive commissions. There is no other way, or only a very abridged and cursory one, of recording it than by following the commissioners once again. Despite his zeal, Chichester set out in a mood of some depression. Let us not misunderstand his attitude. He was an advocate of the Plantation, and in fact its originator, but the scheme had gone further than he held to be prudent. He had begun to think that he would not live to see it carried out in accordance with the instructions he had received. It is possible that his health was already suffering, and that the dropsy which afflicted him in the last years of his viceroyalty had already made its appearance. He pitied the natives who would have to be removed, many of whom had taken to wearing English clothes, and had promised to live in townships and abandon their *creaghting*. He felt that in Tyrone, Armagh, and Londonderry too little provision had been made for the Irish, and for the servitors who could have Irish tenants. He was not on good terms with certain of the commissioners—we do not know which—and they had begun to look upon him as a wet blanket and a marplot. However, there could be no going back now, and if he thought that the plan had become too sweeping and theoretical, he had yet no desire to go back. But for the moment it was duty rather than enthusiasm that drove him forward.

The circuit of 1610 was the reverse of that generally followed, beginning at Cavan, where it was usual to end, and boldly tackling the most difficult situation first. For Cavan bounded Meath, and its inhabitants had alliances with the Pale which made them cunning in their procedure. When the proclamation for the removal of the natives from lands allotted to undertakers had been read, the Irish put up a lawyer from the Pale to argue that they had estates of inheritance. Chichester answered the light artillery with heavy. He called on Davies, who on this circuit was acting not as a commissioner but as the King's Advocate, to refute this argument, which he had no difficulty in doing from the point of view of English law. After some discussion the natives agreed to give way to the undertakers, if the Sheriff, by warrant from the commissioners, put them in possession. That accomplished, an undertaker who had already arrived in the camp was given seizin of his holding. John Taylor, a Cambridgeshire man, was thus the first undertaker to be " planted " in Ulster, at Ballyhaise.

The dispossessed natives then accepted, according to Davies not unwillingly, tickets allotting to them portions of land in other baronies. There was, as has been stated, no trouble in accommodating them in this case, as only a few proportions were reserved for undertakers, and there was little transplantation except in this one northern part of the county, about Ballyhaise and Belturbet. In any case, a further proclamation was issued, giving permission to the natives on the undertakers' estates throughout Ulster to remain until the following spring. We shall find that in many cases they were never actually removed.

In Cavan there were, according to the official statement, 40,000 acres available for plantation. Endless misunderstanding has been caused by this figure and those for the other escheated counties : 98,000 for Tyrone, 34,000 for

Coleraine or Londonderry, 110,000 for Donegal, 33,000 for Fermanagh,[1] and 77,000 for Armagh. Some writers have even suggested that these figures represent a piece of trickery pure and simple on the part of the commissioners, who induced the King and his Privy Council to believe that the counties contained no more land than this. That, it need hardly be said, is ridiculous. The crudest map would show at a glance that, for example, Armagh measured roughly 30 miles by 16, or 480 square miles, or over 300,000 acres. Walter Harris, writing nearly two hundred years ago, but considerably over a hundred years after the Plantation, put the matter so clearly that there is not the slightest room for misunderstanding:

"Where in the Project a County is said to contain a determinate Number of Acres, *Tyrone* for Example, 98187 *English* Acres, it must not be understood, that the County of *Tyrone* has no more *English* Acres (and so of others). For it is well known, that the County of *Tyrone* contains . . . 626959 *English* Acres. But the meaning is, that the County contained so many Acres of escheated profitable land, exclusive of unforfeited, and Church Lands, and also of Boggs, Mountains, Lakes, Woods, and other unprofitable Scopes."

The bogs of Ulster are fairly numerous and extensive still, but far less so than in the early seventeenth century. The mountains have kept their shape, but good pasture and even agricultural land is found on their slopes where it would have then been thought madness to attempt serious farming. The lakes still cover immense areas, though some have shrunk, and a few small ones have disappeared. The woods, alas! are now far too small, and not a fraction of what they were. Bogs and woods were "unprofitable" in that they

[1] That the estimates were rough is proved by the fact that 48,000 was the previous commission's figure for this county.

were unsuited to agriculture, but very valuable none the less. The new settlers were always anxious to have them within easy reach of their holdings so that they should be provided with fuel and timber. Even to-day turbary rights, as opposed to ownership, provide frequent legal problems.

Yet this system of scheduling only the " profitable " lands created uncertainty and lent itself, as may well be supposed, to dishonesty and to differences in the treatment of the various counties. In some cases the " profitable " lands actually covered a very much larger acreage than had been stated; the surplus was sometimes left untouched, but was often quietly annexed. This led to the subsequent discovery of what were described as " concealed " portions, which were disposed of in various ways, or for which compensation was demanded. In Londonderry the whole county, good and bad lands, bogs and forests, was taken over by the London colonists, to their discomfiture in the next reign. Here, however, from the Irish point of view, there were large compensations. Though not a square foot of land was left in the hands of the Irish as owners, yet, contrary to the spirit if not to the letter of the agreement, the Londoners allowed the Irish to remain as their tenants.

We have lists of all the three classes of tenants in chief—one may, in fact, say four classes, as newcomers from England and Scotland were placed as a rule in different baronies—that is, undertakers, servitors, and Irish, for each county, with the size and situation of their holdings. To give them in full would not be in accordance with the scheme of this book, and would not be very valuable for the purpose of throwing light upon present-day conditions. Portions began to change hands almost at once. Some of the undertakers were unable to shoulder the responsibilities of their tasks; others changed their portions, even moving from one county to another. The consequence is that when we are given a new picture of Ulster by Nicholas Pynnar we find a very great change. It may, however, be of interest, as showing the extent of the colonization scheme, to give very brief particulars for each county, including the number of settlers of each class and a few of the more prominent and enduring names.

In Cavan there were six English undertakers, including Sir Stephen Butler, unrelated to the great Irish house of that name but the ancestor of the Earls of Lanesborough, and nine Scottish. There were twenty-two servitors, among whom were Sir Oliver Lambart, from whom descends the earldom of Cavan, John Ridgeway, the Treasurer's brother, and Sir William Taafe of Kinsale fame. The natives numbered fifty-five, for the most part O'Reillys. They had one grant of 3000 acres, to young Mulmore O'Reilly, son of the gallant loyalist who had fallen at the Battle of the Yellow Ford,[1] one of 2000, and two of 1000 acres, the majority of the rest being comparatively small.

Among the eleven English undertakers in Fermanagh we find the names of Wyrrall (or Worrall), Archdale, and Barton, good Fermanagh names all. Of the thirteen Scottish names those of Hume and Dunbar made their mark in the county's annals. The servitors are particularly interesting. At the head we may set the Governor of Enniskillen, Sir William Cole, ancestor of the Earls of Enniskillen, and Sir John Davies himself, the only civilian who was admitted as a servitor throughout Ulster. Another was Sir Henry Folliott, the Governor of Ballyshannon, but he and his well-known family are more closely associated with Donegal, where he afterwards made large purchases

---

[1] These 3000 acres granted to the head of the clan appear to have constituted all the " profitable " lands of a whole barony, so that this method of distribution cut both ways.

to add to his servitor's grant. There were fifty-four natives, again for the most part with small portions. Connor Roe Maguire, who had been provisionally granted half the county, was bitterly disappointed when he learnt that he was now to have but one barony, that of Magherastephana, though he was accorded in compensation of his loss £200 a year for life, with £50 a year to his son Bryan after his death. Connor Roe's young half-brother, also named Bryan, received a grant of 2000 acres, and Con MacShane O'Neill, son of the great Shane, 1500. It is to be noted that it was the son of the first of these two Bryan Maguires who was to become the inhuman fiend of the Rebellion of 1641.

In Donegal there were nine English and seventeen Scottish undertakers. Among the servitors were the Deputy's brother Edward, from whom descend two peerages, Donegall and O'Neill. Henry Hart, who had been in trouble with the authorities owing to the capture of Culmore by Sir Cahir O'Dogherty but had been forgiven, was also of the number. The heads of the three branches of the sept of MacSwiney—MacSwiney Dogh, Fanad, and Donogh —received 2000 acres apiece.

In Tyrone there were fourteen English and thirteen Scottish undertakers, among the latter being the Earl of Abercorn, an earldom which has since been raised to a dukedom. The servitors numbered only five, but they made up in quality what they lacked in quantity. They were the Lord Deputy himself, Sir Thomas Ridgeway, Sir Richard Wingfield, ancestor of the Earls of Powerscourt, Sir Toby Caulfeild, shortly afterwards created Lord Charlemont, and Sir Francis Roe. There were sixty native grantees, headed by Sir Tirlagh MacArt, grandson of Tirlagh Luineach, with 2300, and Bryan Crossagh, son of Cormac MacBaron O'Neill, with 1000 acres.

In Armagh there were ten English and five Scottish undertakers, nine servitors, and thirty-nine natives. The most notable English names here are Powell and Brownlow, while a Sir James Craig—may there never fail to be one!—appears among the Scots. Among the servitors is a name equally welcome, that of the hard-fighting Sir Thomas Williams, the defender of the Blackwater Fort, who, broken in health and fortune, now had some reward for his long and honourable service. Of the Irish, Sir Tirlagh MacHenry received in the Fews the biggest grant in all the escheated counties except the Deputy's at Inishowen, 9900 profitable acres, for which he was to pay the King £40 per annum and a hawk. Art MacBaron, half-brother to the Earl of Tyrone, received 2000 acres, and Henry MacShane O'Neill, 1500. The other native portions were small.

As they passed from county to county, the commissioners met the English and Scottish undertakers, who had nearly all arrived, or had sent representatives when they were unable to come themselves. They were given seisin and possession of their portions, but then for the most part returned home to equip themselves and collect labour for the great work ahead. A few, indeed, especially the enterprising Scots, were ready to start at once. The energetic Ridgeway had brought over with him twelve labourers and their families, and at once began cutting stone, preparing boards, and setting up a water-mill at Clogher. Chichester, still in his despondent mood, was not altogether favourably impressed by the colonists. The English, he found, were for the most part plain country gentlemen, who did not give the impression that they had sufficient enterprise or resources for their task. If they had money in their purses they kept it there, and, by the look of them, were likely to be scared away if trouble arose. The Scots had an air

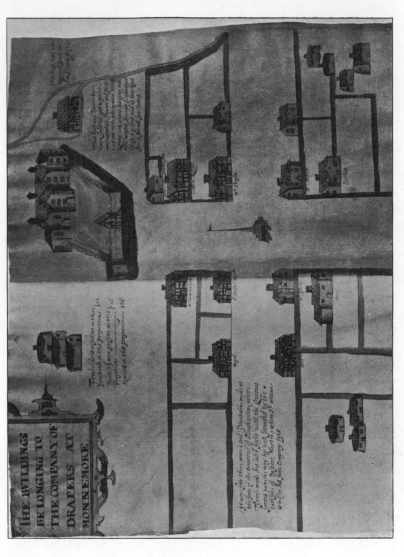

THE DRAPERS' BUILDINGS AT MONEYMORE

*From the 17th century MS. at Lambeth Palace, London*

(For Letterpress see Appendix II.)

of greater assurance and had brought more adherents with them; but they were already bargaining with the natives to supply their wants and promising in return to obtain licence from the King to keep them on their lands as tenants, despite the terms of the grants.

County Londonderry we have left until the last. Here there were no grants to natives. The city of Londonderry and the town of Coleraine were, as has been stated, undertaken directly by the City of London itself. The rest of the county, with the exception of the grants to Phillips and Staples, was parcelled out among the twelve principal London Companies: Goldsmiths, Grocers, Fishmongers, Haberdashers, Clothworkers, Merchant Taylors, Ironmongers, Mercers, Vintners, Salters, Drapers, and Skinners, with some of which lesser Companies were associated. The Londoners were concentrating first upon Coleraine, having decided merely to build a wall round Derry and leave the construction of the city until later. Sir Thomas Phillips had cut 10,000 trees for them; they had brought over a large number of workmen and hired others locally; and the whole scene was one of extraordinary bustle and excitement. It went to the head of Davies. Here, before his eyes, his plans were taking shape, and all he had worked for was becoming a reality. As he watched all those busy hands at work the dormant poet in his enthusiastic nature was re-awakened.

"We found there such a store of timber and other materials brought in place, and such a number of workmen so busy, in several places, about their several tasks, as methought I saw Didoe's colony erecting of Carthage, in Virgil.

> Instant ardentes Tyrii ; pars ducere muros
> Molirique arcem, et manibus subsolvere saxa ;
> Pars aptare locum tecto et concludere sulco, etc.
> Fervet opus.

So as we returned with an assured hope that the plantation will go on roundly and prosperably, and that God will bless it."

Back in Dublin, Chichester addressed to his sovereign a letter which does credit to the recipient whom the writer had never yet seen, as well as to the writer himself. It is, indeed, one of the finest documents in the whole correspondence of the reign, and infused with a spirit of much more than conventional loyalty. Perhaps it was as well that the Lord Deputy had not yet seen the King, who was an unimpressive figure at close quarters, whereas from a distance it was easy for his Viceroy in Ireland to respect him. James had, of course, Salisbury by his side, and while that great man lived the traditions of Elizabethan statesmanship were maintained, to lapse sadly after his death. Yet it is always apparent that the King counted in matters of Irish policy, and especially in that of the settlement of Ulster, a scheme very near to his heart. He knew his own mind, but was ever willing to take the advice of the man on the spot; he was critical but never captious; when he considered that mistakes had been made he did not grumble, but pointed out firmly what was amiss and what steps were to be taken to mend it; he persevered steadily and patiently with the task to which he had set his hand, and he saw it through. At the foot of one of his letters, insisting that all undertakers should be forced to fulfil the letter of their contracts, he wrote with his own hand: " My Lord, in this service I expect that zeal and uprightness from you, that you will spare no flesh, English or Scottish, for no private man's worth is able to counterbalance the perpetual safety of a Kingdom which this Plantation being well accomplished will procure." That was typical of his attitude.

It was now, wrote Chichester, nearly six years since

James had advanced him to the government of the Kingdom of Ireland, during which time he had laboured for the royal service, and had never lacked his master's support. He went on to speak of the Plantation with his usual frankness and his now habitual plea for the natives.

" And for this great work of the plantation of the escheated lands of the province of Ulster now in hand, though it be a matter of difficulty and will be infinitely opposed by the natives, who are many in number, and not sufficiently provided for by the distribution of the precincts made there, yet am I confident of the success in some good measure if the purses and resolution of the British undertakers be answerable to the work they have in hand. . . ."

Again he expresses his doubts regarding certain of these undertakers. Some, indeed, were " noblemen and gentlemen of good spirits and sufficiency ", but others seemed scarcely of a calibre suitable to their task. And then, again, he looks forward to the future with more assurance.

" Great things move slowly, and if this be not brought to pass within two or three years, yet if it be fully effected in your Majesty's time it will be a great happiness to all your dominions and memorable to all posterity.

" If my poor endeavours may give any help and furtherance to so glorious and worthy a design, besides my obedience and duty to your Majesty, my heart is so well affected unto it, that I had rather labour with my hands in the plantation of Ulster, than dance or play in that of Virginia."

If Chichester was not wholly satisfied with the colonists, it cannot be said that in the majority they lacked energy or zeal. During the winter of 1610–11 they came over by every passage, accompanied by servants, carpenters, masons, and future tenants, so that by the spring they should have ready timber and stone to build their houses. Let us strive to picture the advent of one of these little communities, say, a squire and half a score of retainers of one sort or another. He had left behind a little manor-house, perhaps sold it; for many of the undertakers were cutting loose from their old homes, attracted by the prospect of a considerable estate at a low rent, and probably also by the prospect of being able to buy more land cheaply. He had left behind an easy, ordered life, in essentials not so very different from that in small country manor-houses to-day, with all reasonable comforts and no anxieties. He arrived in Dublin, in the midst of the wet though generally mild Irish winter. There he had to buy carts and teams, unless, perchance, he had brought them over with him. After long and anxious preparations, questionings as to whether he had all he needed, the day came when he fared forth into the unknown north, probably with one or two others bound for neighbouring destinations.

The American frontiersmen following the setting sun in his covered wagon embarked on no greater adventure, though he and his family must have been harder and more experienced. One can picture the wagons stuck in fords or defiles, till, with doubled teams, they had been hauled out one by one. One can imagine the wayside camp in the rain and mud, watched over by a weary sentinel; for that woodland on the hillside might well hold a swordsman or two; and if there were no swordsmen in it there were surely wolves. Welcome at evening must have been the lights of fort or little town such as Monaghan or Omagh.

Then, upon the new holding, pleasant country at worst— it were hard to find any in Ulster not good to look upon— and for a few, as those whose lot was cast in Fermanagh or southern Donegal, a fairyland of beauty, even in winter;

cattle, sheep, swine, and flour to be had cheap; perhaps some clumsy labour to be hired; but naught else. Contemplating the virgin fields, the settler might say: " Here I will build my house; my garden and stables and cowsheds will be there; over there, I hope, by my son's time if not in mine, there will be a village."

The materials for house and village were not lacking, but they were in the uncut trunk and the unopened quarry. First, then, there must be built " Irish houses " for the shelter of master and man, and an enclosure into which to drive the live stock at night. This was the most important work of all in the early stages. True, there was now in all Ulster hardly a single rebel of note " standing upon his keeping", and not a robber band of any size. Yet in little nests of about half a dozen the shaggy, trousered outlaws still haunted the woodlands, and woe betide the colonist who let his cattle stray after dark. Sir Toby Caulfeild at Charlemont was one of the most powerful, experienced, and popular Englishmen in Ulster, yet within caliver-shot of his fortress the wood-kerne often shared with the wolf the spoils of his pastures. If such was the fate of a formidable servitor, with a fort behind him and soldiers at his bidding to avenge robbery or arson, what must have been that of the undertaker, set down in the open and almost as defenceless as a hermit-crab outside its shell? When he had protected himself, cut and shaped his timber, quarried and squared his stone, there was ahead of him the long drudgery of building houses, barns, stables, byres, and flour-mills, while simultaneously the land had to be prepared for harvest. According to tradition, almost the only one of the Plantation period still alive in Ulster, the caliver, snapchaunce, pike, or sword lay always in the furrow last turned, while the ploughman and his team turned the next.

It is obviously not to be supposed that the great or even

the well-to-do went through this initiation to Ulster. There was, for example, among the Donegal undertakers a Scottish duke, Ludovic Stuart, second Duke of Lennox and afterwards first Duke of Richmond, who had been Scottish Ambassador to France and was now Master of the Household in England. He, with his vast estates and his duties at Court, can hardly have been expected to put in an appearance—and he did not. He did, however, send over an agent and some Scottish tenants. Many undertakers of means looked upon their portions as colonial estates, which they would visit and perhaps reside upon for half the year when the work was done and they were assured that the country was quiet. Yet there were many others who embarked all their fortune in this new venture. On the whole it was the English who were most forward in building and the Scots who were busiest with cultivation.

As Chichester had remarked, " great things move slowly ". Hearing that this was not moving as fast as he had expected, James decided to send over on a tour of inspection the most experienced adviser on whom he could lay his hands, George Carew, the former President of Munster, now Lord Carew. He was careful to point out to Chichester that this visit was not to be taken as reflecting adversely upon him, and that he had in no way lost confidence in his Viceroy. What he wanted was a personal report. It was, in fact, too early for a report, and that of Carew's is of no great interest. He had only to record that such-and-such an undertaker had built an English house, with three rooms on the ground floor, an oven and a chimney, a loft overhead, and a roof already partly thatched; that another was burning lime and had a boat on Lough Erne; that a third had fifteen well-armed tenants and two ploughs, and was sowing wheat; and that many another had done little or nothing. At Coleraine, indeed, he was able to add a little to Davies's enthusiastic and poetical picture, informing us that there were 379 workmen in the town or in the woods, including carpenters, sawyers, wheelwrights, bricklayers, tile - makers, lime burners, quarrymen, and carters. We have to wait another eight years for a picture of the Ulster Plantation after it had really taken root.

Before we turn to that, there are one or two events to record, the chief of which is the calling of the Irish Parliament of 1613. Parliament is a word that has scarcely appeared in these pages, and with good reason. Irish Parliaments had been infrequent since the passing of Poyning's Act. There had been five in the first half of Elizabeth's reign; but since that of 1587, called by Perrot to pass the attainder of Desmond, there had been none. That called twenty-six years later was also largely for the purpose of passing attainders. It was to differ from its predecessors in that not only were all the shires of Ulster to send knights, as even the least remote had done only for the first time in Perrot's Parliament, but Ulster boroughs were to be represented in it by burgesses. For this purpose a number of corporate towns were created in the winter of 1612 and the first months of 1613, Enniskillen having the honour of heading the list, and being followed by Lifford, Donegal, Belturbet, Coleraine, Limavady, Killyleagh, Rathmullan, Strabane, Bangor, Newcastle, Clogher, Newtownards, Augher, and Charlemont. Certain towns outside Ulster were also added to the list.

This action aroused a storm among the Roman Catholic nobility and gentry, who realized at once that the Parliament would contain a Protestant majority. They suspected anti-Catholic legislation and the imposition of the Oath of Supremacy, which was in its terms almost impossible for a Catholic to take. James had, in fact, no such intentions, and was prepared to let recusants sit in his Irish Parliament, though they were, of course, disqualified in England; but the feeling that the constituencies were being rigged created a bitter feeling and a bad prospect for the Parliament. There were angry protests against the creation of the new boroughs, some of which were as yet no more than villages, though almost all were expanding rapidly, and against various actions taken by the Sheriffs. There was a renewed and rather amusing protest when it was learnt that both Houses were to sit in the Castle. Was there not a great store of gunpowder there? Gunpowder Plot, said the Catholics nervously, was too near for them to sit in comfort over a magazine. Chichester soothed them by remarking that his intention to sit among them in the Upper House was their best protection; and, his grim sense of humour getting the better of him, went on to remind them " of what religion they were that placed the powder in England and gave allowance to that damnable plot ".

That Chichester was to sit in the House of Lords was due to the fact that he had been, on the 24th February 1613, created Lord Chichester, Baron of Belfast. The King, with his genuine but rather pompous kindliness, wrote to inform him that the peerage had been bestowed without mediation on his behalf from any man, adding that the Lord Deputy would find that he served " a master with a liberal hand " and might expect further honours.

According to the final arrangements, the Upper House was to consist of twenty spiritual and twenty temporal peers, and the Lower of 226 members. Among the peers it is of interest to note that Lord Buttevant was called, though he had an elder brother living. The latter, being blind and dumb, was passed over, a very ancient English tradition being thus revived in Ireland.

There were delays and doubts whether some of the defeated candidates would not present themselves and demand to take their seats, even some fears of riotous behaviour. However, on the 18th May, Parliament assembled quietly enough, and all the members of the Lower House were admitted to the House of Lords to hear the Lord Chancellor's address. Chichester then bade the Commons adjourn to their own House for the election of a Speaker, adding that certain of their number who were of the Privy Council knew the King's pleasure in that respect. After they had taken their places, Sir Thomas Ridgeway named Sir John Davies, explaining that it was he to whom the Lord Deputy had alluded as the person recommended by the King for the office of Speaker. Immediately Sir James Gough rose and began a speech, alleging that those returned for the new boroughs and others not resident in the boroughs for which they were returned were not members of the House, and demanding that that matter should at once be examined and decided. He was interrupted and asked to whom he gave his voice as Speaker, whereupon he named Sir John Everard, an able lawyer, but one of the most notable recusants in the kingdom, who had been removed from the King's Bench for refusal to take the Oath of Supremacy.

His proposal was seconded, but Sir Oliver St. John then intervened to inform the House, from his experience in English Parliaments, that the proper course was, first, to choose a Speaker, and then to nominate committees to examine alleged abuses. He next summoned all who were in favour of Sir John Davies to accompany him outside the Chamber to be numbered, and went out, followed by the whole governmental (and Protestant) majority. The division having thus been made, Ridgeway and Sir Richard Wingfield returned to the Chamber and requested the Opposition to appoint tellers and assist them in making the count. This they flatly refused to do, and when the

" tellers for the Ayes " made an attempt to number them in the Chamber they rose from their places and gathered together " in a plumpe ", so that it was impossible to count them.

There followed what must be one of the most curious scenes in the history of parliamentary procedure. Ridgeway and Wingfield went out to count their own party. The Catholics slammed the door behind them and, with excited shouts of " An Everard! An Everard! " installed their own candidate in the Speaker's chair. Ridgeway and Wingfield were, however, quick-thinking men, who had encountered more serious emergencies than this, the one in Glenveagh, the other at Kinsale, without losing their heads. They retorted by bringing their supporters back into the Chamber and counting them as they passed in. The tally was 127, considerably more than half the House. Ridgeway then declared that the intrusion of Everard into the chair was contemptuous and disorderly, and requested him to leave it. On his refusal, the two tellers took Sir John Davies by the arms, lifted him off the ground, and deposited him in Sir John Everard's lap. Davies, it may be added, was no light-weight. That not sufficing, they laid hands— gently, according to the Protestant account, violently, according to that of the Catholics—upon Everard, removed him from the chair, and placed Davies in it. Everard and his supporters then walked indignantly out of the Chamber and refused to return.

Next day, as they still absented themselves, Sir John Davies was presented to the Lord Deputy in the Upper House by his own supporters only.

We have dwelt upon this scene because it is so closely connected with the first appearance in an Irish Parliament of the representatives of the Ulster boroughs. The long and difficult negotiations which followed may be sketched rather more briefly. The business of Parliament was completely suspended; Chichester had to send over representatives to London to obtain the King's instructions as to how he was to proceed; and at the same time the recusants were permitted to send a delegation, headed by the inevitable Lord Gormanston, to put their case before the King. Parliament was then prorogued, and the King granted an inquiry. After all, many of the recusants were loyal subjects enough.

His Majesty of England had made no mistakes in administration, but when politics and religion came in he was not to be trusted. Carried away by his own garrulity, he now proceeded to pile up a peck of trouble for his Lord Deputy. In an audience granted to the recusant delegates at Royston, he used words which they construed, apparently with good reason, as a promise of religious toleration. On his return to Ireland, Sir James Gough broadcast this message in several speeches. Not content with that, on the 20th November he came with a considerable following to the Castle when Chichester was sitting over his wine after dinner, and suddenly began, " in the action and tone of an orator ", to make a set speech to the Deputy. He averred that it was not the King's purpose to " extort upon the consciences of his subjects," and that James himself had charged him " to divulge the same to the rest of the King's subjects in Ireland ". Chichester drew him into another room and begged him to retract his speech. He refused. The Lord Deputy had only one answer to this. He handed Gough over to the Constable. He then wrote to the Privy Council in England, for the King's ear, what was in fact a peremptory demand that James should explain himself and, if necessary, eat his own words.

Once more, let us strive to look at the episode as it appeared to the eyes of the Deputy. Toleration to us is a sacred word, but it was then a term of reproach, as in a large part of Europe it is again to-day. It was not merely the sentiment that offended; the reality was also dangerous. At a moment when James was fighting the second wave of the Counter-Reformation, when he was repressing and fining his Roman Catholic subjects in England, a public admission that he intended to grant toleration to those in Ireland would have been by contemporary standards disastrous. We ourselves may admit that such a sudden and complete reversal of policy would have caused great difficulties.

The King surrendered, as was inevitable. He did not disavow the words attributed to him, but declared that they did not bear the meaning put upon them by Gough. To show his repentance he directed the Lord Deputy to proclaim that he would never grant toleration, and that all Roman Catholic bishops, priests, and friars must quit the kingdom—which he probably did not in the least expect them to do. To show further that he was ready to support Chichester, he committed to the Fleet Prison Thomas Luttrell, one of the recusants who had most bitterly attacked the Viceroy, and kept him there until he had acknowledged his fault in writing. And then, on the 2nd February 1614, so serious did he consider the situation, that he summoned Chichester over to advise him concerning the present state of Ireland.

Chichester, having appointed Jones and Wingfield, the Lord Chancellor and the Marshal, to be Lords Justices in his absence, crossed the Irish Sea for the first time since he had received the Sword of his office. He saw his King at last, and one would very much like to have his considered opinion of him. For, on the 20th April, in the Council Chamber at Whitehall, James made a very odd speech to the recusant delegates. It was resolute, learned, yet witty and good-humoured; but it was also childishly indiscreet, and undignified to the point of buffoonery. One can see Chichester's grim eyes staring at the ceiling in the embarrassment of a schoolboy when the head master is making a sad exhibition of himself in public.

Faults in the returns of the Sheriffs? It might be there were some, but could one hope for perfection before the Kingdom of Ireland became the Kingdom of Heaven. And then this petition to the Deputy, before a Speaker had been chosen! What right had a headless body to protest? One would be afraid to meet such a body in the streets—a very bugbear! Then he varied the metaphor. Having a committee before a Speaker was chosen was putting the plough before the horse, " so that it went untowardly, like your Irish ploughs ". (Loyal and dutiful laughter from all who remembered the disputes about ploughing " by the tail ".) They complained of new boroughs. He had the right, he went on with a flourish, to make four hundred if he chose. The more the merrier; the fewer the better cheer. He concluded:

> " My sentence is that in the matter of Parliament you have carried yourselves tumultuously, and that your proceedings have been rude, disorderly, inexcusable, and worthy of severe punishment, which by reason of your submission I forbear, but do not remit till I see your carriage in this Parliament, where by your obedience and future good behaviour you may redeem your past miscarriage and deserve not only pardon but favour and cherishing."

The King then went very carefully into the question of the returns, and eventually annulled thirteen of them as a matter of royal grace. Strange as it may appear, his curious methods, his mixture of bullying and yielding, of fierce reproof and ill-timed jocosity, were entirely successful. Perhaps the Opposition considered that he was genuinely anxious to see justice done. Perhaps he was none so bad a diplomatist after all. When Parliament was opened on the 11th October there was no more serious trouble. The Catholics even attended daily prayers in the Lower House until prevented by their priests; they then came in immediately afterwards. Both sides talked themselves friends, and the recusant gentlemen and merchants freely accepted the Speaker's invitations to dinner, when they were dined and wined to their hearts' content. John Davies at the head of his own board must have been a pleasant host.

The first measure introduced, the Bill of Recognition, which reaffirmed the King's right to the escheated lands of Ulster, went straight through both Houses. Then came a Bill against piracy—very prevalent at the moment both on the Irish and western English coasts—and another minor measure respecting crimes of violence. Finally, the Bill of Attainder, having passed the Lords, was introduced in the Commons, at his own special request, by—Sir John Everard, the defeated recusant candidate for the Speaker's chair! It was passed without a voice being raised against it.

This was an outstanding triumph for the Government, which has left Nationalist historians without an argument, except abuse of the recusant lords, knights, and burgesses. Tyrone had been attainted by the assembled representatives of all Ireland, Catholic and Protestant. Foreign nations, as Davies reminded the King's favourite and adviser, Robert Carr, Earl of Somerset, the unworthy successor to the power of the dead Salisbury, had declared that it was only the Protestants who desired Tyrone's ruin. Now it had been proved to them that in this matter the Catholics entitled to speak for Ireland stood beside the Protestants.

It was final and decisive. "Besides," concluded Davies, "this attainder settles the plantation of Ulster."

The second event to be recorded is an unsuccessful native plot in 1615 to seize Londonderry, Coleraine, Lifford, and Carrickfergus, massacre the new settlers in Ulster, and recover the lands on which they had been planted. The chief figures in it were Bryan Crossagh O'Neill and Rory Oge O'Cahan, the sons respectively of Sir Cormac MacBaron O'Neill and Sir Donnell O'Cahan, both of whom, it will be recalled, had been committed to the Tower, to end their days there. Bryan Crossagh had nothing to complain of except the locking-up of his wretched old father, a figure contemptible to all parties; he himself had been left in possession of Sir Cormac's castle at Augher and had been well provided for in the Plantation scheme. Rory O'Cahan may well have smarted under what he conceived to be an injustice in the treatment of his father and of his clan. Their plot was discovered, and they were executed with one or two of their principal adherents, the small fry being spared.

The third event is the recall of Chichester in November 1615. The various explanations of its cause: that Somerset was weary of him or, alternately, that the disfavour into which Somerset was falling lost him a protector; that he would not take measures stringent enough against the recusants, seem unnecessary.[1] Eleven years was a long spell for a Viceroy, and dropsy had now affected him severely. The King remarked, with many compliments, that he did not desire to wear out a faithful servant, and there is no reason to disbelieve him. Chichester received few honours, though he could have had the Garter had he desired it, and probably a step in the peerage also, but stated that his means sufficed only to support a barony.

[1] The last is that of Samuel Gardiner, but the evidence produced by him is unconvincing.

The death of Ormonde, however, left open the ancient and honourable office of Lord Treasurer, and to this he was appointed.[1] Later he became a Privy Councillor. He lived for some time at Carrickfergus at his magnificent mansion of Joymount, retained health enough to undertake an embassy to the Palatinate in 1622, and died in London without surviving children in 1625. From his brother Edward descend the present Marquess of Donegall and also Lord O'Neill of Shane's Castle, County Antrim.

If the portrait of this great Viceroy painted in the preceding pages be inadequate, the cause is the artist's lack of skill, which he is unlikely to remedy at this stage; if adequate, there is no need to retouch it now to any great extent. It need only be said in summing up that Arthur Chichester was a savage and ruthless foe, a stern but just ruler, an able soldier, a still more able administrator, high-tempered but cool, resolute but given to self-questioning, a pessimist with a conscience and a sense of humour. No man, not Strafford, nor Cromwell, nor William III, has left his mark deeper on Ireland. He was the " Planter of Ulster "; and the fruits of his Plantation, however they taste in the mouth, are there to-day to bear witness to him.

---

[1] Sir George Carey, Sir Thomas Ridgeway, and Sir Henry Docwra have been spoken of as " Treasurers ". The title of their office was actually " Vice-Treasurer and Treasurer at War ". The office of Lord Treasurer was a far loftier one, but now without duties.

MONEA CASTLE, COUNTY FERMANAGH

IV

## TAKING ROOT

A ND now for the picture of Ulster in the survey of
Captain Nicholas Pynnar, a thorough and painstaking piece of work carried out in the year 1618.
By this time the Plantation had been definitely established;
its results had already reached the stage when they could be
tabulated; and its weaknesses as well as its strength were
apparent.

There had been an interim report in 1615 by our old
acquaintance Sir Josias Bodley, which had been generally
unfavourable and had displeased King James. His displeasure had been an inspiration. Undertakers who had
not come over or had not settled British families had since
done so in haste, for fear of forfeiture. Others had disposed
of their portions to more ardent colonists, and several of
these had already built up large estates. In consequence,
Pynnar found the Plantation not yet, indeed, in the state
which the King had expected it to attain by now, but, on
the whole, active and on the high road to the prosperity
which it was to reach by the eve of the Rebellion of 1641.

The report is on its face a bald and uninspiring document.
Pynnar had been given very definite instructions, with the
headings of the information he was required to supply.
He was first of all to discover whether the conditions had
been fulfilled as regards building, that is, whether the
undertakers of the small grants had built a strong *bawn*, or
walled court; whether those of the middle grants had built
a stone house and a *bawn*; and whether those of the large, or

213

2000-acre grants had built a strong castle with a *bawn* about it. He was to find out if the due proportion of British settlers had arrived—at least ten families of twenty-four men to the thousand acres—and if they had been given leases; if the tenants had been grouped in townships for safety, and sufficiently supplied with arms; and if the natives were practising husbandry according to the methods of the Pale. He confined himself pretty closely to these questions, so that his "survey" makes heavy reading. Nevertheless, one can extract from it a general sketch which is instructive and by no means unattractive.

Starting off in County Cavan, Pynnar found that in Clonkee Lord Aubigny had sold his estate to Sir James Hamilton, the famous County Down colonist, whose activities have already been described. It is evidence of this man's enormous energy that, in addition to the development of his large estates in Down, he had found time within five years to raise his Cavan property to the highest standard of the Plantation. Not only that; he had time also to live there at least part of the year. Pynnar found him in residence, with his wife and family, in a newly-built five-storey castle, 50 feet long and 20 feet in breadth, flanked by four round towers. On the estate there were eight freeholders, with from 120 to 480 acres; three leaseholders for three lives; five for five years; and twenty-five cottagers, with common land for their cattle. In all there were forty-one families, the heads of thirty-six of which had taken the Oath of Supremacy, and eighty men of fighting age. The lands were all well farmed according to English methods.

Not all the Cavan undertakers had done as much, but on the whole there was very little to complain of on their estates. Sir Stephen Butler had settled forty-one families, comprising 139 men, and had arms for 200 within his castle. He had begun the building of the town of Belturbet and had already two corn mills. The servitors, on the other hand, had done little, and few of them had any but natives on their lands. As for the Irish grantees, it was almost always the same story, here and throughout Ulster—a *bawn* of sods, an Irish house inside it, a swarm of native tenants without leases except from year to year, and—" all his tenants do plough by the tail ".

Passing on into Fermanagh, Pynnar found Sir Stephen Butler again represented on two portions which he had bought from the original patentees; Sir Gerald Lowther building his castle at Necarn and the town of Irvinestown, still sometimes called Lowtherstown; John Archdale with twenty tenant families numbering forty-two men; Thomas Blenerhasset who had made the beginning of a village at Ederney; and Thomas Flowerdew, who had as yet done naught and whose lands were inhabited wholly with Irish. In the park now known as Castletown, Malcolm Hamilton, afterwards Archbishop of Cashel, had built Monea Castle, one of the finest and best-preserved of the Plantation fortresses, which, to tell the truth, were generally " slung together " in haste to fulfil the patentee's contract. Fermanagh, at all events, could show one Irishman who had accomplished something, Bryan Maguire having built a good stone house and created five leaseholders, though they and all his other tenants ploughed " after the Irish manner ". Bryan's " good stone house " is still represented in the stables and turf-house of Tempo Manor, set in one of the prettiest of small demesnes, where phloxes and rock-plants seem to grow out of a little lake side by side with white, red, and golden water-lilies, all enclosed by high woodlands as by gigantic green walls.

Donegal was generally less satisfactory. The wildness and inaccessibility of a great part of it repelled the colonists, some of whom, after one terrified glance at their holdings, returned home incontinently, while others made no attempt to bring over English or Scottish tenants. For example, the two baronies of Boylagh and Bannagh, on the western flank of the county and comprising one-third of it, were all by a special arrangement in the hands of John Murray of Cockpool, a Scottish favourite of the King's, as tenant-in-chief. The patentees under him on this vast estate had only a handful of Scottish tenants, virtually none of whom had leases. This district was as Irish as it is to-day. It may, indeed, be said that only on the Londonderry, Tyrone, and Fermanagh borders was Donegal ever really affected by the Plantation. Of estate after estate Pynnar had to record that there was nothing built and not a British tenant. However, Sir George Malbury had built at Letterkenny a market town of forty houses, all inhabited by British; and in the neighbourhood of Lifford Peter Benson had a good house, a water-mill, twenty-four families with sixty-eight armed men who had taken the oath, " and not one Irish family on the lands ". There were a few other estates of this type, but none of them in the more remote districts of the county.

Donegal, however, has a point of interest which distinguishes it from all the other escheated counties. If it was never really colonized, it was held as an outpost. If its undertakers as a whole did not cover themselves with credit, its servitors did. It was essentially a servitors' shire. In some respects, Donegal, with its strong clan spirit, its mountain fastnesses, and its excellent harbours, wherein, if the man on the spot slumbered, continental shipping might lie without the knowledge of the authorities, was the danger spot of the whole Plantation. The servitors, living among the Irish, encouraging the loyal and never taking their eyes off the doubtful, met that danger with a large measure of success. It was the pluck, skill, and tact of hard-bitten, experienced soldiers such as Sir Henry Folliott and Sir Basil Brooke that held Donegal quiet, and so gave protection to the infant colony.

In Tyrone the chief Scottish undertaker was the Earl of Abercorn, who had made large purchases to add to his original grant. He had 1000 acres at Strabane, which town now consisted of eighty houses, for the most part of stone, holding no less than 120 families, with 200 men all armed. At Dunalong, once the home of Tirlagh Luineach O'Neill, he had 2000 acres, with another twenty families, but little building done; about Omagh three more 2000-acre proportions in the area originally allotted to English colonists. His brother, Sir George Hamilton, held two more. Lord Chichester, the ex-Deputy, was building Dungannon, and under his stern eye there were, in addition to numerous British tenants, " thirty-six Irish which come to the Church, and have taken the Oath of Supremacy ", that is to say, who were professing Protestants. Tirlagh MacArt O'Neill, Tirlagh Luineach's grandson, and once described as " a poor young gent of some hope ", had belied his promise. He had been removed from his lands in the barony of Strabane to make room for Lord Abercorn, but, in recognition of the loyalty shown by his good old grandfather, his bibulous father, and himself, had a splendid grant of 4000 acres in that of Dungannon. But Tirlagh was not a man who loved an arduous life or had any desire to improve himself. He had made no leases to his tenants, who continued to plough by the tail. As for his building, he had in a moment of unwonted energy begun to make a *bawn*, but when one side of it had reached a height of five feet had grown weary and abandoned the task. It is perhaps not surprising that the greater part of his lands passed in course of time to the Caulfeilds.

In Armagh, in the barony of Oneilland, on the southern

shore of Lough Neagh, there was in William Brownlow perhaps the most praiseworthy " planter " in the whole of Ulster. His new town of Lurgan had forty-two houses, paved streets, two water-mills, and a wind-mill. On his two estates there were fifty-seven British families as lessees or freeholders, all of whom had taken the Oath. Tanderagee, the town of the Viceroy, Sir Oliver St. John, was growing swiftly also, but on the portion of Michael Obbyns at Ballywarren there was as yet only the promise of the considerable town of Portadown.

Last comes Londonderry. Here the Londoners had surrounded their city of the same name with the " very strong wall, excellently made and neatly wrought ", 24 feet high and 6 feet thick, which was to prove impregnable in two great wars and to win for the place the proud and lofty title of " the Maiden City ". A school had recently been finished, but in other respects building had fallen far short of requirements. Within the walls there were so far only ninety-two houses, holding 102 families, too few for the manning of the defences. At Coleraine, where the Londoners had started off with such a burst of enthusiastic activity, affairs were still worse. The wall, unlike that of Londonderry, was of sods filled in with earth and already showing signs of decay; nor were there nearly enough male inhabitants to man it.

The estates of the City Companies varied, but in general their progress was unsatisfactory. The Goldsmiths southeast of Londonderry City itself, the Grocers at Muff, the Fishmongers at Ballykelly, the Merchant-Taylors at Macosquin, the Haberdashers at Artikelly, the Clothworkers at Articlave, the Skinners at Dungiven, the Vintners at Bellaghy, and the Salters at Magherafelt had all leased their proportions, apparently without incurring displeasure. The Ironmongers at Aghadowey and Agivey, the Mercers at Movanagher, and the Drapers at Moneymore had resident agents. In most cases a castle and a *bawn* had been built or were being finished, but the Grocers and Vintners had no castle, while the Merchant-Taylors and Haberdashers had no *bawn*. The Goldsmiths, who had thirty families, making with the under-tenants ninety armed men, may be taken as typical of the better undertaking Companies. The Grocers, probably owing to the fact that their lessee had recently died, were one of the worst, there being no tenants with freeholds or leases, and few or none of British birth. It may be added that this state of affairs was shortly to be remedied, and that the Grocers' estate was to be one of the best cultivated in the county. The Clothworkers were perhaps the worst of all, Pynnar remarking disgustedly that their only British tenant was the parson of the parish, and that " all this land is inhabited with Irish ". It was certainly not to the credit of London that of the six escheated counties theirs had, exclusive of the two big towns, by far the lowest total of British families, namely, 119, as against 447 in Tyrone, 417 in Donegal, 386 in Cavan, 321 in Fermanagh, and 290 in Armagh.

In all Pynnar found 1974 families, making with cottagers 6215 English- or Scottish-born men of military age, and reported that " on occasion ", that is, when they were not in England, Scotland, Down, Antrim, or the Pale, there might be as many as 8000 men. Judging from the facts that in 1614 there were " above 2000 able Scotsmen " on the lands of Hamilton and Montgomery in Down and South Antrim, and that Randal Macdonnell had large numbers on the Antrim coast, we may perhaps put the fighting strength of the colony at about 12,000. In the six escheated counties there were built 107 castles with *bawns*, 19 castles without *bawns*, 42 *bawns* without castles, and 1897 English houses which Pynnar had actually seen.

There was a black and dangerous side to the picture apart from the sloth of the Londoners. The English tenants were not ploughing, apparently from nervousness as to the state of the country; the Irish who had been left on the undertakers' estates often thought it not worth while to do so, never knowing when they would be turned away; and, had it not been for the Scots, who were vigorous in tilling the ground, there would have been hardly any crops in Ulster. In many districts, and especially in Londonderry, the settlers were in grave danger of extermination in the event of a sudden Irish rising. Here Pynnar was a true prophet, as Carew had been before him, of the terrible Rebellion of 1641, which would have wiped the Plantation off the face of Ulster had it not been tough in itself and supported by the fortifications of Londonderry and Enniskillen, and by castles such as Carrickfergus and Belfast.

Nevertheless, Pynnar's survey marks very considerable progress within a short period. Its effect, too, was to bring a fresh influx of tenants, and to stimulate some of the backward colonists to new efforts. Despite all the shortcomings brought out in the report, it also proves definitely that the Plantation of Ulster was so far a success.

· · · · ·

The Anglo-Scottish colony, "planted" on the initiative of Queen Elizabeth and King James I by the latter's gardeners, Salisbury, Chichester, and Davies, in the northern province of Ireland, had thus struck. It may be described as deep-rooted and strong, but not free-growing or luxuriant. In the latter part of James's reign it acquired fresh stock uprooted from his home gardens—the Presbyterians who crossed the Irish Sea to escape his hostile legislation, and

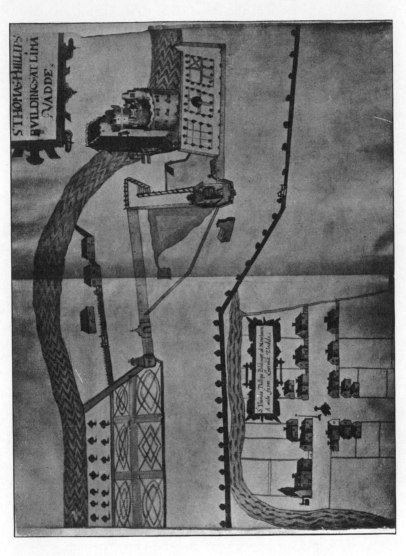

SIR THOMAS PHILLIPS'S BUILDINGS AT LIMAVADY AND NEWTOWN

*From the 17th century MS. at Lambeth Palace, London*

(For Letterpress see Appendix II.)

who contributed so much to its present complexion and character. Yet the native stock was equally hardy and continued to grow beside it.

The question which naturally arises is, how much hardship and suffering to the Ulster Irish was involved by this colonization? The only possible answer is that no such operation could be carried through without serious hardship and suffering, but that few have caused as little, and few have been undertaken with more regard for the native inhabitants.

Adverse critics seize upon the fact that the grants to native Irish undertakers were comparatively small. They speak of the whole province, minus these grants, as being torn away from the Irish and placed in Anglo-Scottish hands. But, if this be proof of hardship, it applies only to the land-holding Irish aristocracy. To the mass of the people the lands granted to the servitors were also open. These holdings were almost always in good, low-lying country, because it was desired that the Irish tenants of the servitors should be under the eyes of their landlords, and that they should be induced to practise agriculture, neither of which ends could have been achieved had the holdings been in mountainous or woodland country. Now, the servitors had, as a rule, few but Irish tenants. Much the same may be said of the extensive Church lands. Then, we have seen that all over the six escheated counties, but especially in that of Londonderry, Irish tenants were maintained on the lands in defiance of the terms under which the Anglo-Scots colonists had received their grants. Despite the efforts of the Government, the Irish remained there in many cases. The counties of Cavan and Donegal, which with Monaghan have now returned to native Ireland and form part of the Irish Free State, have always been predominantly Irish and Roman Catholic. Lastly, the Irish had everywhere the bad or mountainous lands to themselves, for what they were worth.

The lot of the Irish herdsman or cultivator under the chieftain of his own race in the days before the Plantation was not enviable. There are many who wax sentimental over it to-day who would be sorry indeed to find themselves in it. Sir Henry Docwra once remarked to Neill Garve O'Donnell that he would probably have to do without his rents for a while because his people had suffered so heavily in the wars and had lost so many of their cattle. The Donegal princeling was astonished at such a suggestion. Were they not his own people? He would, he said, tax them to the bone, and while there remained one cow in Donegal there would be one cow for him. It would be absurd to pretend that the peasantry liked the change; for a tyrant of one's own race is generally preferable to a mild ruler or land-owner of another, especially when the latter is a heretic. Materially, however, with definite holdings at fixed rents—so that they were no longer liable to be shifted at the whim of their lords—and with complete peace—so that they were no longer liable to be knocked on the head or robbed of all they possessed because their lords were at enmity with others—their position was in some respects improved. So long as their lands were not overcrowded, their sufferings were not unbearable.

Unfortunately, however, there was overcrowding, due to the prolificacy of a people who married in their teens and reared very large families. The checks to the population caused by inter-tribal warfare had almost disappeared, and the country was peaceful from the suppression of O'Dogherty's revolt until the year 1641. The potato, introduced in Cork in 1586, seems to have spread towards the north but slowly, but when it did it hastened the process. One man's planting would keep forty people for some nine months out of the twelve, and no enemy could take or harm the crop save by digging up one by one the clusters of tubers. So the Irish population of Ulster, a considerable proportion of it upon the poorer and higher lands, grew and grew. Soon there was lack of elbow-room, and then the dispossessed began to look down with envy and hatred upon the settlers from over the seas. The barrier of religion, proving far stronger than that of race had in the past, prevented intermarriage. Though between the surviving Irish aristocracy and that of the colonists there were often friendly social relations, these rarely extended to the common people even in the towns, and still less to those who dwelt on isolated farms.

The glimpses that we can obtain of the colonists between Pynnar's report and the Rebellion of 1641 are few, and they are for the most part of the Londoners' Plantation in Londonderry. It is to a long and bitter quarrel between the Londoners and Sir Thomas Phillips that we owe them. Phillips was a man of orderly mind, who preserved his papers carefully during his lifetime and handed them over by his will, with a fee of £30, to a literary executor. This was "one Mr. Withers, a poet", none other than the soldier-poet, George Wither, known to all the world by :

> Shall I, wasting in despair,
> Die, because a woman's fair ?

The manuscript book compiled by him was published a short time ago by the Public Record Office of Northern Ireland.

One thing not revealed in it is the exact cause of the quarrel which gave it birth. Public spirit, says Phillips, repeatedly and with emphasis. Well, perhaps, one may even say, probably, in some degree. That it was the sole cause appears unlikely, public spirit being in those times a tender plant. Jealousy, others have suggested. Perhaps,

again, but it is hard to see why Phillips should have been
jealous. He had shown no sign of annoyance at the loss of
Coleraine, for which he had exchanged Limavady and a fine
estate, and he had undoubtedly been an enthusiastic advocate and supporter of the plantation of County Londonderry by the Londoners. Possibly an insolent letter from
their chief agent, Tristram Beresford, was the grain of grit
which caused a festering hatred between him and his
neighbours.

Phillips commanded the garrison, a company each at
Londonderry City, at Coleraine, and in Loughinsholin, and
had besides a somewhat vague superintendency over the
county. His chief accusations against the Londoners were
that they exploited the country, selling the timber for profit;
that they neglected building and fortification; and that, so
far from encouraging British tenants, they repelled them
and retained or even attracted Irish, who would pay higher
rents. Phillips was challenging powerful adversaries, but
he had the ear of the Government, and had Chichester
remained as Deputy for a few years longer it is probable
that his suggestions would have been put into force. With
less powerful and determined Viceroys, St. John and
Falkland, as his supporters, the Londoners carried on a
running fight for many a long year, now pleading, now
openly defying, now procrastinating.

The first victory gained by the Londoners was on the
29th December 1612, when the Lords of the Council,
sitting at Whitehall, decided several questions generally in
their favour and reserved judgment on their plea to retain
the natives. However, the decree went forth later that the
Irish tenancies were to be ended by May 1615, so Phillips
may be held to have counter-attacked successfully. The
next move of the Londoners was a suit for leave to keep
" conformable " natives, that is, those who took the Oath

of Supremacy, wore English clothes, and practised agriculture after English methods; and of this the Council
took a favourable view. It is not surprising to find that the
London agents made the most of this complaisance and
moved no natives, trousered or breeched. Nor is it hard
to understand their position. The higher rents paid by the
Irish were an attraction. The colonization of Londonderry
was not supposed to be, and probably was not, a commercial
venture, but the agents and lessees were in a position not
unlike that of the resident officials of a chartered company
in modern times, and they naturally wanted to show the
citizens of London that some return was forthcoming for
the money sunk.

So the affair dragged on. In August 1617 Sir Oliver
St. John actually appointed commissioners for the removal
of the natives to the lands of the Church and to those of
Irish patentees and servitors by the 1st May 1618. Still
the order was not obeyed. Phillips decided that it never
would be and that the deficiencies of the colonization would
never be understood in Whitehall until he put them before
the Council in black and white. This indefatigable man
therefore produced in 1622 a survey accompanied by maps
of the holdings of the City Companies, and picture-plans
of towns built in them. For that we owe him a debt of
deepest gratitude. His battle with the Londoners means
little to-day, but the fact that it resulted in the production
of these fascinating and delightful pictures gives us reason
to bless it.

In each case we see the castle and its *bawn*, the church
where one has been built, and the little town of from a
dozen to a score of houses, each standing in its garden plot.
Very often the occupant's name is written below the house.
The buildings are attractive, often in black-and-white.
The Irish Rebellion of 1641 and the succeeding decade of

fierce warfare, and the Williamite War later in the century were to destroy these comely beginnings. " But for this," sadly remarks Mr. D. A. Chart, Deputy Keeper of the Records and editor of Phillips's book in its modern guise, " Ulster, too, might have preserved an ancient town which could be compared with Chester or Warwick." In the picture of Phillips's own castle and town of Limavady we see that he had laid out large and stately formal gardens. There are three beautifully coloured plates : a map of the county and town plans of Londonderry and Coleraine. It is also of interest to note that outside one or two of the towns appear round cottages built after the Irish manner.

The struggle continued, but the detailed evidence brought forward by Phillips had its effect. In September 1624 the Londoners received an order to carry out a series of twenty-three measures of reform, and, what must have been unpleasing to them, Phillips was appointed to see that they did so. The chief of these were the building of a new church in Londonderry; the improvement of the fortifications there, at Culmore, and at Coleraine; the building of a quay at Londonderry; the building of 200 houses at Londonderry and Coleraine within four years; and the granting of six large freeholds by each City Company. The remainder of the lands were permitted to be let for the period of the lessees' lives to native Irishmen professing the Protestant faith, taking the Oath of Allegiance, learning the English tongue, and wearing English clothes. A year later, as it was considered that enough progress towards the fulfilment of the articles had not been made, the Lords of the Council ordered the rents and revenues to be sequestrated and devoted to the purposes which they had in mind.

Now, it will be thought, Phillips had finally triumphed. But no, not at all. By various obscure devices the wily

Londoners avoided payment and involved Phillips in heavy expenses. All that was achieved was that they began to remedy some of the deficiencies in their plantation, never, however, touching the most serious of all, the lack of British colonists. Of these there were still less than a thousand in Londonderry, Coleraine, and the twelve estates, as against nearly 2500 Irish. Regarding the removal of the Irish, indeed, they suddenly ceased to prevaricate, and declared that they were not bound by this condition, which was considered one of the most important in the Plantation scheme. Moreover, a commission of inquiry appointed by Charles I in 1627 made the astonishing discovery that the condition was neither mentioned in the preliminary articles between them and the Privy Council nor included in their Charter. The commission remarked lamely that though it had not been inserted, it " was presupposed and taken for granted as being at first desired and intended on both sides ". This would not do. The Londoners strengthened their strong case by declaring that the fortifications, which by this time were concerning the Privy Council more than were the natives, had been completed, and the sequestration was thereupon removed.

And then it was found that the fortifications were much as they had been, so on the 3rd May 1628 the King ordered Falkland to renew the sequestration. It was a crazy business, and it was not ended yet. The Londoners got up and obtained many signatures to a petition to the effect that Phillips was seeking their ruin, that they were being shamefully treated, and that London was the best of all landlords. Phillips countered with a second petition, his signatories ending with a clever plea that they were in need of protection because of their virtuous refusal to sign the first. The City of London itself put in a third, and—the sequestration was lifted once more.

In Wentworth there came to Ireland a Viceroy as able and determined as Chichester himself, but, unfortunately, without his abstract sense of justice. Wentworth was not only hostile to the Protestant colony in Ulster, because he feared and distrusted the Presbyterian element; he was also eager to strike at his sovereign's opponent, the City of London, through her Londonderry plantation, and in the process to put money into the exhausted Treasury. The affair had become political rather than legal.

In 1635 Wentworth brought the case before the English Privy Council, which found that in twenty-five years the City Corporation had defrauded the revenue of £85,000 by concealing the size of its grants, and with an air of generosity fined it £70,000. The judgment was not only unfair but grotesque; for it had been quite well known since the first that the Corporation and the Companies had virtually the whole county in their hands. In fact, their rents had actually been increased for this reason in the last year of James I. The distracted Londoners compounded with the King by payment of £12,000 and the surrender of their patents; but the lands were in most cases re-let to the original grantees, the Irish at doubled and the colonists at trebled rents. This cash, welcome as it was, was to be dearly paid for by both Viceroy and King. London was largely instrumental in bringing Strafford to the block, and at least one prominent colonist, Sir John Clotworthy, was among the fiercest of the hounds at the death. As for Charles, it was his persecution—for it can be called nothing else—of the colonists, his discovery of legal flaws in their contracts, his swingeing fines exacted for the grant of fresh patents, and, later, his friendship with the men who had barbarously murdered their fellows, that drove so large a proportion of them to take up arms against him. The Irish Society's Charter was not renewed until 1662.

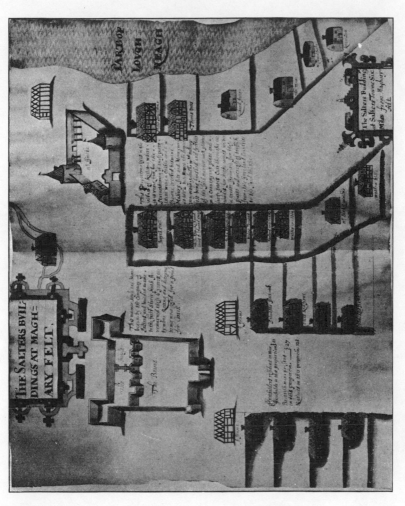

THE SALTERS' BUILDINGS AT MAGHERAFELT (LEFT) AND SALTERSTOWN (RIGHT)

*From the 17th century MS. at Lambeth Palace, London*

(For Letterpress see Appendix II.)

That was the one great question in Ulster between 1613, the year of the Parliament, and 1641, the year of the Rebellion. A few glimpses, again for the most part of the Londoners' lands, reveal some of the growing pains common to all new settlements. There is constant agitation for schools, churches, and bridges; there are many complaints of excessive customs duties and minor administrative abuses. In December 1618 we find the good folk of Draperstown grumbling about the conduct of the agent of the Drapers' Company, Robert Russell. The townsmen, evidently sober Puritans and perhaps rather smug, alleged that he was turning Draperstown into a saturnalia. The enterprising agent desired to create a " Merry Ulster " to his own profit. He had built a brewery, and was converting the town's meagre water-supply into beer. He was buying up houses to turn them into drinking-dens, and actually paying his own workmen partly in beer; with the result that the Sabbath was profaned, drunkenness was rampant, and there were distressing brawls in the streets. Evidently this complaint caused Mr. Russell and his remarkable powers of organization to be transferred from a scene where they were not appreciated by the more powerful citizens, who knew what was good for the others. A couple of years later we find the people of Draperstown better pleased with a new agent. They still had matter for complaint, however. The water-supply was not yet adequate; there was no market; the streets were so foul that they had to don high boots when they walked from one house to another; and— eternal trouble, especially in that wild country of Glenconkeine, Tyrone's last refuge in 1603—the wood-kerne was abroad and at his thieving.

V

# THE FRUITS

SO modern Ulster was born and fairly set upon the
road which she was to tread. Unlike every other
settlement in Ireland, this was never swamped or
assimilated by its surroundings. On the other hand, it
evolved into something rather different from its parent
stock, partly because, though not assimilated, it was in
some degree gradually affected by its new environment,
partly because all colonies, even in virgin lands, undergo
this evolution.

The predominant type, the Ulster Scot, ceased to be a
Scot, and is very far from being one to-day. He is as
energetic and as hard-working, but he is less in a hurry and
takes less account of time. One may say that in Belfast he
approaches the Scot most closely and that in the country
districts he has gone farthest towards a new national type.
In neither does he resemble the native Irish of Ulster, with
whom he dwells side by side.

Racial differences have been preserved through over
three centuries in an astonishing fashion. An experienced
observer walking among the crowds of small farmers on
Fair Day in Omagh or Enniskillen could pick out settler
from native with ease. He would not, of course, use those
terms. He would say, " Protestant face! Catholic face! "
and he would be right nine times out of ten. If, instead,
he were handed a roll of surnames, he could find his way
equally well. Occasionally he would be balked by names
held in common among the two peoples, but his average

230

of accuracy would be even higher than with the faces. Moreover, the gap between races and religions—almost synonomous terms—has in recent times grown wider rather than diminished. Readers of Thackeray's Irish sketches will recall that he found the younger Protestant and Roman Catholic children being educated in the same schools, under the supervision of Church of Ireland parsons. A tourist of to-day would have to travel far to find a single such case. Intermarriage, uncommon as it has always been, has also decreased since the promulgation of the Papal " Ne temere " decree. There are two nations in Northern Ireland, the larger looking across the sea to its motherland of Great Britain, the smaller with its eyes on Dublin, the capital of the Irish Free State.

Everywhere in Ireland there are to be found survivals of the speech introduced by Englishmen in the old days and forgotten or disused among Englishmen to-day. In Ulster, however, especially outside the industrialized and Scotticized north-east and the larger towns, there are more than anywhere else, and they are of the language of the first colonists, the language of Shakespeare, of the Jacobean Privy Council, of Chichester, and of Davies. When James wrote of a " civil Plantation " he used the adjective as it is still used in Ulster ; " civil " is orderly, and " civility " means orderly behaviour more often than courtesy. Chichester's description of Audley as " near to himself " stands for any close-fisted fellow. Davies's " prosperably " is a common version of prosperously—and how much handsomer ! His hope that the Ulster Irish would learn " to love neighbourhood " —to live in communities in neighbourly fashion—also embodies a current phrase. A " cross man " is, not a man in a temper, but a cross-grained man. A schoolboy does not crib but " cogs ", a word which implies foul throwing of dice. A girl who has " great resort " is one very fond of (male) company—a fast minx. If you ask your way in hill country you may be told that your road later becomes " dangersome " for a car. If you visit a lonely farm at night the owner will offer you a wee drop from " the bottle in the press ". He may then volunteer to " convoy " you as far as the main highway. And if it is not raining—perhaps, indeed, if there is only a little rain—he will speed you on your way by observing that it is " a brave night ".

Sometimes the Elizabethan or Jacobean form is one that is still current English but has ceased in England to be the usage of the people. " He'll rue the day he crossed me "; " I'd as lief go without," are anyone's phrases in Ulster. Sometimes a word has disappeared, like the Shakespearean " renage ", for, back out of an undertaking, change one's coat. " I thought he was to be trusted, but he renaged on me."

With these are mingled turns of phrase that are either translations of a Gaelic idiom, or transliterations of the Gaelic itself into English words which are not a translation but yet graphically express the meaning of the original. " It was only yesterday I saw him, and I on my way to the town," is an example of the former, immortalized by Charles Wolfe—a parson in Tyrone—in the lines on the burial of Sir John Moore:

> That the foe and the stranger would tread o'er his head,
> And we far away on the billow.

" Through-other ", meaning feckless, is an example of the other type. It is a transliteration of *tri n-a cheile*, confused, and if it cannot be called a translation because it is not English, at least no one is likely to be in doubt as to the meaning of a through-other way of doing things.

In the back streets of Belfast the dialect is as ugly as any in the British Isles, though even it has its virility; but the talk of the countryman in Londonderry, Tyrone, and Fermanagh has a general effect of strength without harshness, raciness without extravagance, the sweetness of fine old words that have become embedded in the soil. The English talk vaguely of an " Irish brogue ", but the language of Enniskillen differs as much from that of Dublin or Galway or Cork—which, incidentally, differ to an equal degree from each other—as Norfolk from Devonshire. They say that the broadcaster and the film actor are affecting the accent of the younger generation, but this is hardly noticeable as yet. Two old women were listening to the silver tones of the National Broadcasting Station proceeding from the open door of a shop. Said one, tugging at her companion's arm: " Ah, come on away out o' that. Sure ye couldn't tell what the hell he's sayin'! " The colonists have kept their own tongue.

. . . . .

The colony's career will be followed no farther in detail, but we may note the principal milestones on its long and chequered path. They are the Rebellion of 1641 ; the Revolution of 1688 ; the Volunteer Movement of the last quarter of the eighteenth century ; the Rebellion of 1798 and its natural consequence, the Act of Union ; the Home Rule campaigns of the nineteenth century and the first few years of the twentieth ; the Rebellion of Easter Week, 1916 ; and the Partition of 1921.

The Rebellion of 1641 had its birth in Ulster. *Qua* rebellion, indeed, though its plan included the capture of Dublin Castle, it was mainly an Ulster affair. It developed in the course of the next eight years into a ghastly struggle all over Ireland, but that was because it became part of the Civil War in Great Britain. Its main cause was undoubtedly the Plantation itself, or, in the words of Carte, " the mortal

hatred which the Irish in general, and the gentry in particular, who had been dispossessed of their estates by the
Plantation, bore to the English nation." It must, however,
be added that its principal leaders, Lord Maguire and his
infamous brother Rory, the grandsons of Connor Roe,
and Sir Phelim O'Neill, great-great-grandson of Shane,
were men who had been generously treated by the Government, and owed their high position almost entirely to it.
If Tyrone had had his way the descendants of Shane would
have been ground into the earth. If Cuconnaught Maguire
had maintained himself in Fermanagh, Connor Roe and
his seed would have gone to the wall, and his grandson
would certainly not have been a peer. These men were
up to the ears in debt, but that was owing to their own
wanton extravagance. The foolish peasantry who came
out to murder and burn at their bidding had already found
Sir Phelim a notably bad landlord, and would have found
him and his associates harsh task-masters and tax-gatherers
had the revolt succeeded.

Ireland was extremely prosperous, and the easiness of
the times no doubt helped to lull men's minds to a sense
of security. At all events the rebellion, which was, in fact,
an organized attempt to exterminate the whole British
element by massacre, came as a complete surprise.

Within a week the rebels had possession of practically
all Fermanagh, Cavan, Monaghan, Tyrone, and Londonderry; most of Armagh and a large part of Down; and,
outside the borders of Ulster, Leitrim and Longford.
Donegal was relatively quiet, owing to the watchfulness
of the original servitors and their descendants, and the
British families, even in the remoter districts, suffered less
than in many parts which had appeared safe. But almost
everywhere the Protestant inhabitants who could not find
refuge disappeared, having been burnt in their houses,

drowned in streams and bog-holes, or stabbed to death with pikes and skeans, often after ingeniously contrived tortures. Many of the stronger places held out and served as asylums to refugees from the general destruction; but in several places, as at Clones, Glasslough Castle in Monaghan, and Tully Castle in Fermanagh, the colonists surrendered on promise of quarter and were then slaughtered in cold blood. A few Irishmen, foremost among them Bryan Maguire of Tempo, distinguished themselves by their good-heartedness in feeding and protecting the colonists in their districts, who were never molested while in their charge. The Irish had a curious sense of honour, which had some kinship with that of the Arabs. They reproached and reviled their compatriots for sheltering the British, but made no attempt to drag them from their sanctuary, as would probably have been easy. In a few other cases, as where the men of Cavan were under the leadership of O'Reillys—always honourable gentlemen, on whichever side they stood—they fought like soldiers rather than butchers, and kept their word to the garrisons that surrendered to them. Generally speaking, however, no quarter was given. It is certain that the whole Plantation would have been uprooted and thrown to die upon the refuse-heap but for the defence of certain towns and castles, the vigour of the Antrim settlers in aiding their less lucky neighbours, and above all the magnificent rescue work of Sir William Stewart's Laggan Force, based on Newtownstewart.

There followed a period of nightmare. Reprisals almost matched in savagery the crimes that incited them. Blood had perhaps flowed as fast in former times in Ireland, but never was the blood-letting more inconsequent or confused.

There were six, if not more parties in Ireland. On one extreme flank were the Ulster Irish under Tyrone's nephew, the celebrated Spanish commander, Owen Roe O'Neill.

He personally was a moderate man, but his cause was hatred of the English, the " Old English " or Anglo-Irish as much as the recent settlers, and desire to recover the Plantation lands. Next came the Catholic Lords of the Pale, who first joined the rebels and then declared themselves Royalists, under Sir Thomas Preston. They wanted freedom of religion and power for themselves, at which price they were prepared to give a measure of support to the King. There was the party grouped about the Papal Nuncio, Giovanni Battista Rinuccini, which put the Catholic Church first. There was another grouped round the Viceroy, Ormonde, generally Protestant as he himself was but containing some loyal Catholics, which put the King first and was ready to league itself with very distasteful allies for the King's service. There were the Ulster colonists, uniting against Owen Roe, but gradually dividing into two parties, Cavalier and Roundhead. There were the Scots who came over to put down the rebellion, who were Roundhead in the early days and Royalist when their countrymen had changed sides. The cross currents were even more bewildering. Thus, in August 1649, the month of Cromwell's landing, Owen Roe the Nationalist relieved Charles Coote the Parliamentarian besieged in Londonderry City by Scots and Royalist Ulstermen, the allies of Ormonde, and then marched south with the intention of joining hands with Ormonde. It was all ended by Cromwell in a fresh bath of blood.

The Plantation in Ulster had been almost extirpated. How many of British birth had perished is one of the most hotly-disputed problems of history, and one which is never likely to be solved with certainty. There is one grimly humorous aspect of it : Irish writers first of all took pride in exaggerating the numbers to a fantastic degree, to 150,000 or more, and since then, discovering that massacre was not matter for pride, have done their best to diminish them, equally fantastically, to two or three thousand. At all events the root was left, and it was tough. The farmers came back from the towns wherein they had taken refuge to their ruined villages and homesteads. Those who had been escorted to the Foyle by the Laggan Force and had taken ship to England or Scotland returned.

At that moment, as again at the Restoration in 1660, the colonists had their turn of Fortune's wheel. Even the Royalists among them suffered little under the Cromwellian Settlement, because those who had not "joined the rebels," or, in other words, fought for the King, before the Cessation of 1643 escaped the penalties. The Presbyterians of Down and Antrim were threatened with transplantation to the south of Ireland, in order to put them at a greater distance from England, but not a man was actually moved. Then, when the King enjoyed his own again he did not strike at the Roundheads of Ulster, because it was the former Roundhead Army, which contained many of them in its ranks, that had brought about the Restoration in Ireland.

In the prosperous years of the reign of Charles II, when the revenue of Ireland was doubled, Ulster became herself again. There was some trouble with wood-kernes, called "Tories" now, and in particular with one accomplished ruffian named Redmond O'Hanlon. On the whole, however, times were quiet, and Catholic and Protestant, more or less united in loyalty to the Crown, dwelt together in peace. In peace, but hardly in amity; for they neither forgave nor forgot.

The next disturbance came from outside. James II sent over as Lieutenant-General, independent of the Lord Lieutenant in military matters, John Churchill's brother-in-law, Richard Talbot, whom he created Earl of Tyrconnell.

He cashiered Protestant officers, disbanded the Protestant militia, and enlisted Roman Catholic troops by the thousand. In 1687 he came back again as Viceroy himself, to finish the work of preparing Ireland to be a place of refuge for the King's Roman Catholic subjects, and perhaps for the King himself. He now dismissed Protestant judges and other officials, including the sheriffs of every county but Donegal, where a Protestant Hamilton was pricked by mistake instead of a Catholic one.

Again the Protestants were at the mercy of the Irish, or had only themselves to depend upon for their safety; for the ill-disciplined troops were almost as likely to join in their massacre as to defend them. Their attitude varied somewhat according to their social grade and creed. The gentry, with the traditional loyalty of their class, were loth to oppose the King, and were only driven to do so by force of circumstances. The populace, and especially the strong Presbyterian element in it, was hostile to him from the first. There was, however, unanimity that it behoved all Protestants to agree on some methods, " besides those ordinarily appointed by the laws ", for their own defence, and at the beginning of 1688 they banded themselves together for that purpose. That November, William of Orange, favoured by the " Protestant wind " of the famous ditty " Lillibullero ", landed at Torbay. Before the year was out James had slipped away to France.

Then, indeed, the colonists saw the grin of the wolf. The uncertainty of that winter was more trying to the nerves than the direct threat which succeeded it. Strange rumours circulated in whispers, and the air was heavy with coming catastrophe. There was something like a panic, when the more timorous fled across the Irish Sea, and many, by no means timorous, sent away their womenfolk and children. In March 1689 James landed at Kinsale, accompanied by a small Franco-Irish force and by a French Ambassador-Extraordinary, the Comte d'Avaux, with 500,000 *livres* in his baggage. The colonists stood upon their guard. They were still not fully united in purpose. Some waited on events, even hastening to accept " protections " from James. A few of the gentry never could bring themselves to fight against him, the most prominent being the Reverend Charles Leslie of Glasslough, a Protestant rector, who was afterwards to be found at the Court of the Old Pretender, vainly attempting to convert him. But the great majority decided to fight.

Once more the axe was laid to the root of the tree. The three centres of resistance were Down, Londonderry City, and Enniskillen. The first was at once smashed to pieces by the Jacobite Army. It seemed that Londonderry would go the same way. The city was thronged with troops and refugees, who starved together. The inhuman Conrad de Rosen, a Livonian in the French service, collected all the remaining Protestants from the surrounding districts and exposed them in front of the walls, so that either the garrison should be forced to take them in or they should perish under its eyes. This experiment, furiously countermanded by James, lasted a few days only, but great numbers perished in that wet and unusually cold summer.

The fame of the defenders of Derry is world-wide, and will live as long as heroism and self-sacrifice are accounted virtues. The carcasses of dogs, cats, and rats were dainties that fetched high prices; hides, tallow, and starch were the subsistence of many for days on end. "I saw two shillings a quarter given for a little dog, horse blood at 4d. a pint," says one of the besieged. When, on the 28th July 1689, the *Mountjoy* broke the boom across the Foyle and she and the *Phœnix* sailed through with their precious stores, 15,000 had died of fever and famine, as against a few hundreds from the cannon-balls, bombs, and bullets of the besiegers.

The exploits of the Enniskillen men have less renown outside their own province, but were no less valuable to the cause of William of Orange. Their island fortress was a continual threat to the left flank of the besiegers. They gave shelter to the settlers of their own county, of Cavan, of parts of Donegal and Tyrone. They routed the forces sent successively against them, thrashing one at Crom and another at Belleek. They captured Belturbet with 300 prisoners. They raided as far as Kells, 30 miles from Dublin, bringing back 5000 head of cattle, and so terrifying the Jacobites that the capital was thought to be in grave danger from this body of farmers, labourers, and shop-boys. Crowning glory, they overwhelmed MacCarthy, the titular Lord Mountcashel, at Newtownbutler on the 31st July, and drove his fleeing remnant into the waters of Lough Erne. In September, after Schomberg had landed and their best troops had joined his camp, they gained with what were left another brilliant success at Sligo. The part of the Inniskillingers at the Boyne and Aughrim needs not to be emphasized.

But for the defence of Londonderry and the activity of Enniskillen it is reasonably certain that James, leaving behind enough troops to hold Ireland, would have crossed to Scotland with a considerable Irish Army, and would have been in the country by the hour of the Jacobite victory at Killiecrankie.

The colonists were growing used now to rebuilding burnt towns and farms and to starting life anew. They were hindered in their efforts to restore prosperity by anti-Irish legislation which affected their province in common with the rest of the country. The Cattle Acts and Navigation Acts had been the precursors of this campaign.

Under William III the higher duties on broadcloths ruined the Irish woollen industry, so far as it did not subsist by smuggling to the Continent. To some extent in the north this loss was compensated for by encouragement of the manufacture of linen, which became in the eighteenth century the chief Irish textile industry. In the north also there was no rack-renting, the tenant's right being protected by the famous " Ulster Custom ", which obviated the agrarian troubles of the rest of Ireland.

Yet the first half of the century was a black epoch for Ulster. There was a flood of emigration to New England, mainly composed of Presbyterians, who, to add to their economic difficulties, were without legal freedom of worship and were debarred from holding even municipal office. In the place of the emigrants, Irish Catholics from the south drifted in and were violently opposed by the Protestants who had stayed behind. Protestant Peep-of-Day Boys engaged in horrible nocturnal struggles with Catholic Defenders.

Feelings grew more and more bitter, but for a time the opposition of the Presbyterians to the Government made them forget their hostility to the Catholics. The American War of Independence brought affairs to a crisis. The Volunteer Army, first formed in Belfast and predominantly an Ulster organization, had for its purpose the defence of Ireland against invasion. The very fact that its Ulster leader was the quixotic but rigidly loyal Lord Charlemont, descended from a brother of the Sir Toby Caulfeild of the Plantation, is proof enough of that. Yet it gradually developed into a state within a state, which overawed the Government, and into a political engine working for freedom of trade, the independence of the Irish Parliament, and even Catholic Emancipation.

It won some notable successes. The Presbyterians

obtained a Relief Act, and in 1782 the " Act of the 6th of George I ", which gave the King, Lords and Commons of Great Britain power to make laws binding upon the people and Kingdom of Ireland, was repealed. But Pitt's efforts to promote freedom of trade between the two countries were defeated, and his treaty in its sadly diminished shape was rejected by Ireland. Nevertheless, the Irish Parliament had got its independence, which it was to use to such poor effect, and the country was for the moment less dissatisfied.

The French Revolution altered the character of the Volunteer Army, and gradually alienated the Presbyterian extremists from the Roman Catholics. The former had toyed with republican theories, but a republic under French control, which was now obviously the aim of their strange allies, was distasteful to all but the most violent separatists among them. The majority of them saw the abyss into which they were being led and drew back in time. A movement far more important than that of the Volunteers was set on foot. On the 21st September 1795 the Orange Order had its birth in a house in Loughall, near the battlefield of the Yellow Ford. As a hostile modern historian remarks :

" In proportion as the United Irishmen allied themselves with France, in the hope of establishing in Ireland an independent republic, the main body of the Protestant Ulstermen was thrown on the opposite side. . . . The Orange party, making their choice between adherence to England and adherence to France, chose the former, and they have ever since maintained their position as convinced supporters of English rule, while the opposite party became, on the whole, violently anti-British and looked to France as the deliverer of Ireland." [1]

[1] Eleanor Hull, *A History of Ireland and Her People*, ii, p. 254.

The Orange Order could ask for no better testimonial, with the exception that the bulk of its original members were loyalists by conviction, and that it was only a fringe which required to be converted.

In December 1796 a French fleet appeared in Bantry Bay, but a large proportion of the expedition had been driven back by a gale, and the remainder of the force did not land. Munster remained quiet, not having expected the French until the following spring, and, in fact, throughout 1797 Ulster was the most disturbed of the four provinces. The disloyal propaganda was intensified and on very clever lines. The Defenders, who were the extremists, and whose avowed aim was the extermination of all Protestants, were kept out of sight in Protestant counties, where their place was taken by the less bigoted United Irishmen, who sought to unite Roman Catholics and Presbyterians in revolt. As for the Church of Ireland, its followers never wavered in their loyalty, and places like Lurgan, where they were in the majority, were oases of quiet amidst the tumult.

The Irish Rebellion of 1798 left Ulster, outside Antrim and Down, practically untouched. In the month of June the Presbyterian rebels were soundly beaten at Antrim and Ballinahinch, and that was virtually the end of the revolt in Ulster. From that time forward the Presbyterians of the north showed no sign of disaffection, and from the first day to the last not a single Presbyterian Yeoman violated his oath. Ulster's feet, after a moment's wavering, were set upon the path they have steadfastly followed ever since.

How little the province was affected by the Irish Rebellion is shown by the sums afterwards claimed for damages inflicted by it. They amounted to over one million pounds for the whole country. For Antrim they reached the figure of nearly £18,000, and for Down that of £12,000; Cavan put in claims for £61, Londonderry for £7, 19s. 3d.

Armagh, Donegal, Fermanagh, and Monaghan claimed not a penny-piece.

The project of uniting the Parliaments of Great Britain and Ireland had been considered for some years prior to 1798, but not very seriously. After the Rebellion, Pitt and his young lieutenant, Castlereagh, determined that nothing should stand in the way of Union. Pitt, at the head of a Government engaged in a vital struggle with France, had just seen the Irish rebels league themselves with France against the sovereign who was King of Ireland as well as of Great Britain, and welcome upon their soil the troops of France. Certainly, the force which had landed in Killala Bay had been only a handful and had never threatened serious danger. But what if the previous expedition to Bantry Bay had arrived in full strength and had landed? In that case Ireland would probably have been lost. The Irish Parliament had not been in any way disloyal, but it was unreliable and had shown extraordinary indiscretion, to say the least, over the recent question of the Regency. Pitt felt that he could not as this critical hour risk the chance of disagreement between the two Parliaments on some question in which "the general interest of the British Empire" was involved. There is, however, no reason to doubt that he considered he was serving the general interests of Ireland also. The Union seemed to him the sole means of overcoming the commercial jealousy of the English manufacturers. He intended that Catholic Emancipation should follow it. He sincerely hoped that he was bringing about a new era in the relations between the two countries.

Ulster did not ask for the Union. If one of the great Ulster landlords in Castlereagh was its spokesman and engineer, others of her magnates were opposed to it. Among them were Lord Charlemont, of the house of Sir

Toby Caulfeild; Lord Enniskillen, descendant of Sir William Cole; and Lord Downshire, descendant of Sir Moyses Hill. Many of the Protestant gentry were also more or less hostile, from dislike of losing the power placed in their hands by the Protestant ascendancy and fear of Catholic Emancipation. Probably the majority of the Catholics of Ulster welcomed it. The Protestant populace was friendly. The methods by which the Bill was passed through the venial Irish Parliament are not here our concern. The contemporaneous British Bill received the Royal Assent on the 2nd July 1800.

The nineteenth century was marked by the struggle for Catholic Emancipation, which Pitt was prevented from granting by the scruples of George III, and, when that had been won in 1828, for Disestablishment of the Church of Ireland, Repeal of the Union, and, passing through the ill-defined ideals of Home Rule, for complete separation. It was marked also by the unceasing efforts of the Union Parliament to improve the condition of Ireland, to abolish abuses, to atone for the errors of the past. And in Ulster, among the descendants of the colonists, it was marked by the spread of an intense loyalty, which has been the subject of praise and of derision, of comfort to England in time of trouble and of inconvenience to her more compromising statesmen in time of bargaining. On the economic side Ulster developed in the north-east a remarkable capacity for industrialization.

Perhaps, however, the most significant lesson of that century and the first third of the present one has been that, whenever the party which claims to represent the aspirations of Ireland has been placated, or seemed likely to be, a more extreme party has elbowed it aside and asked for more. So Parnell succeeded Butt, Sinn Fein succeeded Redmond, and Mr. de Valera succeeded Mr. Cosgrave.

Doubtless the policy of the party now in power is governed by the fact that it knows its successors are waiting in the background.

The Disestablishment of the Church and the sequestration of six millions of her funds in 1869 was followed by the Home Rule agitation under the most redoubtable of all the Irish Nationalist leaders, Charles Stewart Parnell. His policy was to make government impossible, to keep a constitutional campaign in the foreground while his secret allies developed one of terror in the background, and above all to ensure that the palliatives of the British Government did not weaken the demand for Home Rule. The murder of Lord Frederick Cavendish, the Chief Secretary, and of the Under-Secretary in 1882 appears to have shocked even him into a measure of moderation, which marked the beginning of his fall. Meanwhile the Liberal Party under Gladstone had become committed to the grant of Home Rule in Ireland.

In that long and confused struggle, which lasted until the Great War, the attitude of the colonists was, whatever view be taken of it, simple and consistent. Home Rule for Ireland they considered would be calamitous; they foresaw troubles of which English and Irish supporters of the measure denied the possibility, but which have occurred in the last few years. They were deeply concerned for the fate of their loyal fellow-countrymen in the other three provinces. But, whether or not they could stave off Home Rule for the rest of Ireland, they were absolutely determined not to submit to it themselves. " We'll not have it ! " was their only reply to arguments, reproaches, or proffered bribes. They denied that any nation had the right to cast off children who loved her in order to hand them over to a rule which they abhorred. With seeming intolerance they opposed tooth and nail even moderate schemes, like

Lord Dunraven's "Devolution" of 1905, because they believed them to be only steps on the hated road.

In 1912 the compact and well-disciplined Irish Nationalist Party, which held the balance of power in the House of Commons, forced the Liberal Government to bring in the third Home Rule Bill. The reply of the colonists was the Covenant, similar in character to that of the seventeenth century—to which many of their forefathers had subscribed —pledging themselves to resist Home Rule by every means in their power and never to recognize an Irish Parliament in Dublin. Two hundred thousand signatures followed that of Sir Edward Carson, their new leader, on "Ulster Day", the 28th September. They then proceeded to arm themselves in order to resist force by force.

Before the third Home Rule Bill had been passed the Great War cut across the internal disputes. For a moment it appeared likely that Ireland would achieve a hitherto unparalleled unity in the face of danger. The Ulster Volunteer Force blossomed into the 36th (Ulster) Division. Under the leadership of John Redmond the Irish Volunteers, formed to oppose it, enlisted in the 10th and 16th (Irish) Divisions. But it was a moment of enthusiasm only. The extreme party, which now called itself Sinn Fein, had been undermining the position of the Irish Nationalists. This apparent truckling to England gave it new impetus, and the straits of the British Empire gave it its opportunity. There was a revulsion of feeling which probably no other country could so swiftly have achieved; Redmond and his kindly, sentimental Nationalists were thrown over; and Ireland turned to her new idol, which was to be a very Moloch to her children. On the 24th April 1916, in the midst of the Battle of Verdun and of the preparations for that of the Somme, another rebellion broke out.

This one was put down by the few half-trained troops

which could be spared for the purpose, though at the cost of the destruction of a notable section of Dublin, but from now onwards a state within a state, the Irish Republic, was at war with Great Britain.

It was expected that at the end of the Great War the complete pacification of the country would not be a difficult task, but actually it was not until then that the revolt really flourished. The British Army, demobilized in haste and with the ranks of the regular forces filled up with immature boys, reached its lowest ebb. That gallant and efficient force, the Royal Irish Constabulary, which contained a large proportion of men who were, on the other hand, too old for this rough work, became to some extent demoralized by losses and lack of support. The rebels brought ambushing to a fine art. Sympathy or terror put most of the country on their side, including operators in all the principal telephone exchanges outside Ulster, so that their Intelligence service was superior to the Army's.

Nevertheless, affairs improved gradually from the British point of view. The Army, which, if short of trained men, had first-class officers, pulled itself together and began to make head against this new sort of warfare. It soon became a question whose nerve would hold out the longer: that of the rebel leaders, incessantly harried and " on the run " from hiding-place to hiding-place, or that of the British Ministers, fiercely attacked on the score of brutality in a large section of the Press, and threatened with a terrorist campaign in England itself. Finally, on the eve of what was to have been the decisive campaign, the British Government gave way, out of fear said their enemies ; weariness, according to critics ; and hatred of the abominable slaughter, in the view of their friends. The Treaty, signed in December 1921, virtually gave Ireland her independence, which was celebrated by the assumption of the title of Irish Free State.

From all this Ulster had largely disinterested herself. Throughout the " war " she had relied mainly upon her own resources to deal with the campaign of terror. Even the Auxiliary Police Force raised by the British Government was not strongly represented where she was concerned, her own Special Constabulary doing the work. " They use the police to direct the thraffic, but when things get a bit rough they call us out," declared a " Special " who had fought his way into a pillbox at Messines and turned the tide of a German counter-attack on Welsh Ridge after the Battle of Cambrai. It is comprehensible, but none the less a reproach to the colonists, that some among them became infected with the fierce and ruthless spirit that was abroad, taking the law into their own hands on evidence which could not be substantiated before a Court, and staining their hands with blood that was often probably innocent.

The Treaty itself concerned Ulster little. She had already accepted the Government of Ireland Act, passed a year before and rejected by the rest of the country. This Act set up two separate Governments closely linked to the British Parliament, one of which was for six Ulster counties, omitting Donegal, Cavan, and Monaghan. The jettison of these three counties and of the Unionists in them brought upon the head of Sir Edward Carson, the trusted Ulster leader, the only adverse criticism to which he was ever subjected by his followers. They afterwards admitted almost unanimously that he was right. These counties had all very large Roman Catholic—and at that moment, Sinn Fein—majorities. In the then temper of Sinn Fein it would have been an impossibility to administer their affairs except by force, and in that case their Unionist inhabitants would have had a more unhappy time of it than under the Free State Parliament. On the

22nd June 1921, H.M. King George V opened the first Parliament of Northern Ireland in Belfast.

Once again, as with the Union, Ulster was accepting a gift for which she had not asked and about which she was not particularly enthusiastic. This time, however, she took the gift only on the understanding that it was to be hers for as long as she desired to hold it. She spoke her mind very clearly when it was claimed that the Boundary Commission, set up in accordance with the Treaty, could be used as a knife to lop off two more counties, Fermanagh and Tyrone. The Boundary Commission had been appointed to determine the boundary between Northern Ireland and the Free State, " in accordance with the wishes of the inhabitants ", but the Government of Northern Ireland had received a pledge that it was only for the purpose of making slight adjustments. Eventually it was decided to disregard and keep secret the findings of the commission. The boundary was therefore left unchanged, the Free State being solaced by release from her agreed obligation to undertake her share of the National Debt. This at the time seemed a bad bargain from the British point of view, but it was really shrewd enough; for it is certain that the Free State would in any case sooner or later have repudiated her obligation.

The Treaty was disavowed by nearly half, and the most vigorous half, of the inhabitants of the Irish Free State. The new Government was lavishly equipped with British arms, but it was half-hearted in its opposition to the Republicans. Destruction of railways, public buildings, and country houses was carried on even more fiercely than in the days of the British occupation. The gentry, many of whom would have been willing to take part in public life and do their best for Ireland, were driven across the Irish Sea in great numbers. However, after the death of the two leaders who had been chiefly responsible for acceptance of the Treaty, the Government pulled itself together, aided by the fact that the country was growing weary of ambush, arson, and murder. But the one really strong figure thrown up by the whole movement, Kevin O'Higgins, was shot dead in 1927, and from that moment the Government began to wobble upon its foundations. With the aid of military tribunals it hung on, growing ever more discredited and disliked, till it was driven out by a General Election in 1932.

The new Government was formed from a party which had never accepted the Treaty and had been, nominally at least, responsible for the campaign of outrage which had followed its signature. So far as that party's programme can be divined, it is as follows: a republic comprising all Ireland, acknowledging no allegiance to the King but enjoying whatever benefits arise from participation with the group of nations which forms the British Empire. It has been privately suggested by some of its admirers and advocates that, were Northern Ireland handed over to it, it might go so far as to consider a milder alternative for the Oath of Allegiance, and might even not insist upon the word " republic ". In that case it would probably be removed from power and replaced by a sterner element, as its various predecessors have been.

At midsummer, after the new Government had taken office, the payment of an instalment of the Land Annuities—for sums advanced by the British Government to allow tenants to buy out their landlords on easy terms—fell due and was withheld. The British Parliament retorted by imposing duties on certain imports from the Free State in order to make good this loss. This has not only been a terrible blow to farming interests in the Free State, but has resulted in a flood of cattle-smuggling over the border into

Northern Ireland to avoid the duties on cattle exported to England.

The last political event to be recorded is the abolition of the right of appeal to the Judicial Committee of the Privy Council in 1933. It had been noted in Northern Ireland, though scarcely elsewhere, that the moderate head of the previous Government had already stigmatized this right as an anomaly and an anachronism.

Northern Ireland, after heavy sufferings, after seeing her great cattle trade in ruins, her unsurpassed shipyards idle, her world-renowned linen industry almost moribund, has had some economic profit from her close association with Great Britain, and probably her share in the general partial revival of prosperity.

The gap between the two Irelands, which had narrowed in some degree, though not to the extent that outside observers imagined, between 1924 and 1930, has greatly widened since 1932. It would appear, indeed, that the prospect of reunion by agreement, never immediate, has been put back fifty years. Reunion by force is another matter, but it is difficult to believe that the Free State really desires that, though some of her English supporters profess that they would welcome it.

Another method has been pursued for the last ten years, that of peaceful penetration: the quiet movement of Free State citizens into Northern Ireland. It is openly prophesied that by this means the Unionist party will eventually be placed in a minority in its own Parliament, which will then abolish itself by its own act. This movement has not been wholly deliberate, being, in part, created by a desire to escape from a distracted, impoverished, and badly-administered country to one better governed and more prosperous; but there is evidence that it has been carefully encouraged. It appears to be dangerous and ill-advised;

for there is every likelihood that the colonists would refuse to recognize a mandate for reunion obtained by such means.

Propaganda is another method, which has been used with some effect, especially in Great Britain and in the columns of a section of the British Press. It is quietly but insistently urged that partition on the present pattern is an anachronism; that two Parliaments are wasteful; that customs barriers in a small country are absurd. Northern Ireland can only reply that there is a measure of truth in the first two statements, but that the present situation was unsought by her and that, such as it is, she infinitely prefers it to being torn away from what she holds dearest. As for the third, it was the Free State that erected the barriers—except for those duties just mentioned, imposed after the breach of faith regarding the Land Annuities.

These very barriers, it may be added, have done a good deal to widen the breach. Behind them the Free State has built up a number of industries which the competition of the longer-established and better-organized ones of Northern Ireland would destroy in a few months. The Free State manufacturers and their workpeople are not going to have reunion, coupled with northern competition, if they can help it. Yet how can they have it without?

In a world full of anxiety the Government of Northern Ireland has internal anxieties as grave as any. The normal swing of party representation, bringing an Opposition into power, might in its case result in disaster and extinction. To find a parallel, one might suppose that in Belgium the extreme Flemish party was pledged to hand over all Flemish-speaking Belgium to Holland if it obtained a majority in the Belgian Chamber. At any moment a new campaign may be launched. What form it will take cannot definitely be foreseen, nor whether all old friends will remain true. The future is uncertain, and cannot be called bright. But then, in three hundred years it has seldom been bright. It is those centuries of anxious watchfulness and of struggle that have made the Ulsterman what he is. The colony, planted by James I to hold Ulster for the Crown, has gone through perils innumerable and has been almost miraculously preserved. ' One may say with Virgil:

> O socii, neque enim ignari sumus ante malorum,
> O passi graviora, dabit deus his quoque finem.

One may, indeed, hope that there will be an end of present ills and perils, or at least a respite from them. It would be vain to hope that, even if that happens, they will never return.

If, on the other hand, as some allege, complete ease and security are national perils in themselves, the colony will escape these in the future as it has in the past. Whatever its fate, it will not perish because its defensive virtues of constancy and tenacity have gone to rust.

# DIX I

# O'NEILLS

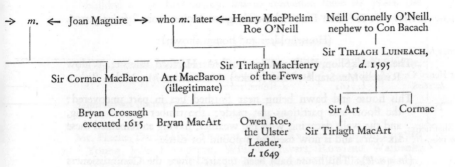

→ *m.* ← Joan Maguire → who *m.* later ← Henry MacPhelim   Neill Connelly O'Neill,
                                    Roe O'Neill          nephew to Con Bacach

                                                         Sir TIRLAGH LUINEACH,
                         Sir Tirlagh MacHenry            *d.* 1595
Sir Cormac MacBaron   Art MacBaron    of the Fews
                      (illegitimate)
                                                         Sir Art        Cormac
    Bryan Crossagh
    executed 1615   Bryan MacArt   Owen Roe,            Sir Tirlagh MacArt
                                   the Ulster
                                   Leader,
                                   *d.* 1649

# THE MAGUIRES

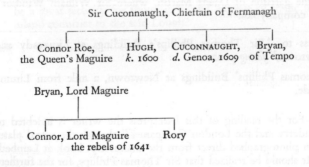

Sir Cuconnaught, Chieftain of Fermanagh

Connor Roe,      HUGH,     CUCONNAUGHT,   Bryan,
the Queen's Maguire  *k.* 1600  *d.* Genoa, 1609  of Tempo

Bryan, Lord Maguire

Connor, Lord Maguire      Rory
the rebels of 1641

# BIBLIOGRAPHY

## Contemporary or nearly Contemporary

Avaux, Comte d': *Négociations de M. le Comte d'A. en Irlande* (1689–90).

Carew, Sir George: *Pacata Hibernae.*

Carew MSS., Calendar of the.

Celtic Society, Miscellany of: Docwra's *Narration of the Services done by the Army Ymployed to Lough-Foyle.*

Davies, Sir John: *Historical Tracts.*

Four Masters, the: *Annals of Ireland.*

Harris, Walter: *Hibernica.*

Maxwell, Constantia (edited by): *Irish History from Contemporary Sources* (1509–1610).

Morley, Henry (edited by): *Ireland under Elizabeth and James I* (Spenser's "View of the State of Ireland," &c.).

Moryson, Fynes: *An Itinerary.*

Ó Cianain, Tadhg (Teig O'Keenan): *The Flight of the Earls.* Edited with translation by the Rev. Paul Walsh.

O'Clery, Ludheidh: *The Life of Hugh Roe O'Donnell.* Edited and translated by the Rev. Denis Murphy.

O'Sullivan Bear, Don Philip: "Ireland under Elizabeth" (being a portion of the *History of Catholic Ireland.* Translated from the Latin by Matthew J. Byrne.)

Phillips, Sir Thomas: *Londonderry and the London Companies, 1609–29, being a Survey and other Documents submitted to King Charles I by Sir T. P.* Edited by D. A. Chart.

State Papers, Ireland, Calendar of the (Elizabeth).

State Papers, Ireland, Calendar of the (James I).

## Modern

Albion, Gordon: *Charles I and the Court of Rome.*

Bagwell, Richard: *Ireland under the Tudors; Ireland under the Stuarts.*

*Dictionary of National Biography.*

# BIBLIOGRAPHY

GARDINER, SAMUEL R.: *History of England, 1603-1642.*

G. E. C.: *Complete Peerage.*

GIBBS, The Hon. VICARY; HOWARD DE WALDEN, LORD; and DOUBLE-DAY, H. A.: *Complete Peerage.*

GILBERT, JOHN T.: *A Contemporary History of Affairs in Ireland from 1641 to 1652.*

HAMILTON, LORD ERNEST: *Elizabethan Ulster; The Irish Rebellion of 1641, with a History of the Events which led up to and succeeded it.*

HICKSON, MARY: *Ireland in the Seventeenth Century.*

HILL, the Rev. GEORGE: *An Historical Account of the Plantation in Ulster; The Macdonnells in Antrim; The Montgomery Manuscripts.*

HULL, ELEANOR: *A History of Ireland and her People.*

JOYCE, P. W.: *A Social History of Ireland.*

MCKENNA, the Rev. J. E.: *Devenish (Lough Erne), its History, Antiquities, and Traditions; Irish Art.*

MEEHAN, the Rev. C. P.: *The Fate and Fortunes of Hugh O'Neill, Earl of Tyrone, and Rory O'Donnell, Earl of Tyrconnell.*

O'BRIEN, GEORGE: *The Economic History of Ireland in the Seventeenth Century.*

Public Records of Northern Ireland, Annual Reports of the Deputy Keeper of the Records.

SHAW, ROSE: *Carleton's Country.*

STEVENSON, JOHN: *Two Centuries of Life in Down (1600-1800).*

STRACHEY, LYTTON: *Elizabeth and Essex.*

TRIMBLE, W. COPELAND: *The History of Enniskillen.*

WEDGWOOD, C. V.: *Strafford.*

YOUNG, ROBERT M.: *Fighters of Derry.*

I have to thank Brig.-General Sir James Edmonds, C.B., C.M.G., for the loan of transcripts of the letters of his ancestor, Sir Thomas Edmonds, Ambassador to the Court of the Spanish Regent in Flanders at the time of the Flight of the Earls. I have also to thank Mr. D. A. Chart, Deputy Keeper of the Records of Northern Ireland, for a typescript of the portions of his last report relevant to the Plantation, unpublished at the time I was engaged upon the work.

# INDEX

# INDEX